sea
bean

sea
bean

A beachcomber's search
for a magical charm

sally
huband

HUTCHINSON
HEINEMANN

1 3 5 7 9 10 8 6 4 2

Hutchinson Heinemann
20 Vauxhall Bridge Road
London SW1V 2SA

Hutchinson Heinemann is part of the Penguin Random House group of
companies whose addresses can be found at global.penguinrandomhouse.com

Penguin
Random House
UK

Please see p. 334, which is an extension of this copyright page,
for quotations permission information.

First published by Hutchinson Heinemann in 2023

www.penguin.co.uk

A CIP catalogue record for this book is available from the British Library.

ISBN 9781529152470

Typeset in 12.69/15 pt Garamond MT Std by Jouve (UK), Milton Keynes
Printed and bound in Great Britain by Clays Ltd, Elcograf S.p.A.

The authorised representative in the EEA is Penguin Random House Ireland,
Morrison Chambers, 32 Nassau Street, Dublin D02 YH68

Penguin Random House is committed to a sustainable future
for our business, our readers and our planet. This book is made
from Forest Stewardship Council® certified paper.

For T, H and D

Contents

CONTENTS

GREENLAND

ICELAND

FAROE

SHETLAND

ATLANTIC
OCEAN

ORKNEY

NORWAY

NORTH
SEA

TEXEL

UNST

YELL

FETLAR

ATLANTIC OCEAN

OUT SKERRIES

VEE SKERRIES

WHALSAY

PAPA STOUR

MAINLAND

FOULA

NOSS

BRESSAY

NORTH SEA

FAIR ISLE

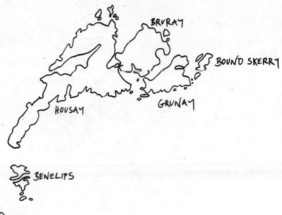

OUT SKERRIES

BRURAY

BOUND SKERRY

HOUSAY

GRUNAY

BENELIPS

FILLA

GILLIA SKERRY

VEE SKERRIES

NORT SKERRY

HELLANS-A-
BLO

ORMAL

RAEVERACKS

SOOTH SKERRY
OR THE
CLUBB

A Note on the Text

Shaetlan is most often described as a dialect of Scots, strongly influenced by the lost language of Norn, a form of Old Norse, but it is also a language in its own right. There is a glossary of Shaetlan terms at the end of this book.

Throughout *Sea Bean*, I use the convention 'in an island' rather than 'on an island'. This is how islanders, in Shetland at least, refer to the places in which they live. To write 'I live on Unst' would sound as strange as 'I live on Edinburgh'. Or as someone once put it, we are not sitting on the backs of whales out here (though I would argue that living in Shetland can feel, at times, like riding through the immensity of an ocean).

Northerly

We moved to Shetland in 2011, on the overnight ferry from Aberdeen – my husband and I, and our baby son. It was late July and we had not given a thought to the weather. Within the harbour walls, the sea was calm. We stood on the deck and waited for the ferry to depart, not knowing that a northerly gale had worked the sea into a heavy swell.

The engine tone deepened, mooring ropes were hauled in and the ferry pulled slowly away from the quay, passing ships that service the oil and gas platforms in the North Sea and a blue-hulled vessel named the *New Venture*. After weeks of packing, it was a relief to be finally heading north. Beyond the harbour breakwaters, the silty water of the River Dee fanned out to meet the bluish grey of the sea. The white trail of the ferry's wake steadily lengthened, and the dull concrete and silvery granite of Aberdeen receded into the distance.

The ferry met the swell when land was still within sight. We made for the cabin and found that it was tiny and windowless and smelt of diesel fumes. My husband and I took it in turns to be sick, unsteadily passing our son between us. Somehow, we fed and changed him, and lay him down in the cot that was tightly wedged between the two lower bunks. He was quick to settle and soon fell asleep, and then we slumped down onto our beds, too nauseous to even think about changing out of our clothes.

The cabin was at the front of the boat, and in a nightmarish semblance of a never-ending fairground ride, the bow would lift high and then drop through the air. Our beds juddered with the impact. The noise was thunderous. I lay awake and watched over the small body of my son and tried to quell a rising sense of terror. We had only just begun a voyage that would last for fourteen hours, and it was already miserable.

I was born in Bristol and spent the first years of my life within sight of the sea. We lived in Portishead, and the muddy Bristol Channel was visible beyond the chimneys of the coal- and oil-fired power station and the chemical works. I learnt about quicksand and fast-rising tides and viewed the sea and the shore with wariness. On one beach there was a derelict tidal swimming pool; its crumbling walls contained a thick gloop of estuarine mud, deep enough to cover the body of a young child. I would falter at the sight of the sea through the gaps in the wooden deck of the Grand Pier in Weston-super-Mare.

We moved inland when I was six and only then did the sea become more inviting. A glass jar of pale-yellow periwinkle shells, gathered from a Cornish beach on a childhood holiday, still sits on my shelf. When I left school, I moved to central Scotland to study environmental science and joined a university mountaineering club. The environment that we studied was only ever terrestrial. Occasionally my hillwalking friends and I would dare each other to swim in the sea in the depths of winter, but I still never really thought of it beyond its surface. The sea remained a place to fear, to admire from a distance.

Part way through the voyage to Shetland, the ferry docked at Kirkwall in the Orkney Islands, and there was a brief respite from all the motion and the noise. I envied the Orcadians and tourists leaving the boat; they would not have to face more hours of a turbulent sea. I had been excited to sail past Fair Isle, a small island that lies between the two archipelagos, but when the moment came, I could not have cared less. The ferry journey seemed like a test, and one that I had already failed.

In the morning, we left the fetid cabin and saw our first view of Shetland through salt-smeared windows. The land looked bleak and so exposed to the wrath of a storm-driven sea. The swell eased as we sailed into Lerwick through the shelter of Bressay Sound. The sky was overcast and, like our faces, the town looked grey and washed of all colour, but the port was crammed with the bright colours of all the fishing boats and ships that had sought shelter from the weather. Sleek-hulled oil-industry vessels loomed over the elegant forms of tall ships with their neat clutter of masts and rigging. Flags and bunting fluttered in the wind. The tall ships were taking part in a race that had begun in Waterford in Ireland and would end in Halmstad, Sweden. The weather had delayed their voyage across the North Sea to Stavanger in Norway.

We drove off the ferry and found our way to the familiarity of a supermarket. I poured milk into my son's bottle and tried to warm it against my skin. We had rented a house and needed to pick up the keys from the solicitor, but it was early in the morning and the office had not yet opened. The wind was still icily cold and we waited in the shelter of the car. Our son played with the steering wheel and my husband and I sat and stared out of the windscreen in stunned silence.

By the time we arrived in Shetland, I had already become unmoored by motherhood. I had resigned from a job in nature conservation. In the department of the research institute in which I had worked, my pregnancy had felt like an admission of a lack of ambition. I had chosen to have children and not a career, it seemed to me, when I had been hoping, like the men that I worked with, to have both.

My husband flies helicopters to and from the oil and gas installations in the North Sea and north-east Atlantic. He works in an industry that makes no allowances for parenting, or for any other caring responsibilities. I knew I would have to take the lead in caring for my son, and this would be to the detriment of a career in which progression is based on a level of productivity achieved through overwork. At times, in those early days of motherhood, it felt as if I were staring at a rainbow through the violence of a squall.

We lived in rural Aberdeenshire, tenants in a poorly maintained cottage that was cold and riddled with damp and mould, but the garden made my heart sing. It was little more than a woodland clearing. A venerable Scots pine guarded the cottage on one side, and a thicket of hazel, downy birch and rowan sheltered us from the north wind. In the summer months, newts swam in a small pond and ringlet butterflies

danced over a meadow. Roe deer left the imprints of their
resting bodies in the long grass. More than once, I removed
a tick from the skin of my legs.

Our son was born in the autumn, when the branches of
the rowans hung heavy with the weight of red berries. The
prospect of caring for a new baby in a damp and mould-
rich cottage all winter was daunting, and so we searched
for another place to rent, one that was warm and dry. Our
budget was limited. My husband had recently qualified as
a pilot and there were training loans to repay, and I was
on statutory maternity pay. We viewed other properties but
each was as poorly maintained as the one in which we lived
and so we stayed put, not wanting to forfeit the garden or
the vole that came through the gap in the back door some
evenings to nibble the crumbs on the kitchen floor.

That first winter of mothering was bitterly cold. Snow
lay deep in the garden for months on end and all the wrens
died. My son and I only ventured outside in short bursts.
The snow was too much of an obstacle for the buggy and
the thick ice on the sloping track was too slippery for the
car. My husband parked his car at the roadside and walked
the track home, and I began to envy his freedom to see the
world beyond the garden. Long icicles hung over the windows and at first they were beautiful but soon they felt like
prison bars. The oil-fired heating system broke down, and
the cold outside and inside the cottage was hard to withstand. It was such an effort to keep us both warm that I
mostly ignored the strange behaviour of my post-partum
body. I carried my son in the crooks of my arms because my
hands were too weak from stiffness and pain to support his

weight. My spine locked almost rigid. Then, just as the snow began to melt away, my body thawed too and I thought little more of this strange episode.

In March, with traces of snow and ice still on the ground, my husband came home from work and announced that his employer wanted some pilots to relocate from Aberdeen to Shetland. The archipelago lies far to the north of the Scottish mainland and is a hub for transporting workers to the oil and gas fields in the northern North Sea.

It didn't take us long to decide that we would move to Shetland. My request to return to work part-time had received a non-committal response. I handed in my notice and hoped that I would be able to find more flexible work in Shetland. On the Internet, I saw an advert for a place to rent that we could afford. In the photographs, it appeared in good condition, somewhere that would be warm and mould free. It had a second bedroom for our son. I looked forward to leaving the ice of Aberdeenshire winters, though my heart sank at the sight of our garden-to-be on the solicitor's website. Low scrappy willows bordered a small patch of lawn that backed onto what appeared to be an expanse of boggy moor. I had never lived in such a wide-open landscape, a place where trees struggle to thrive in all the wind and salt-laden air.

In between packing up the house and caring for my son, I gleaned all that I could about Shetland from the Internet, since we couldn't afford to visit. Shetland was a shiny lure of nature, and at least, in the spaces between motherhood and seeking employment, there would be otters and seabirds to watch, and always the possibility of seeing cetaceans. It was exciting, the thought of living somewhere that is as close to Norway and the Faroe Islands as it is to Scotland, an island place that has its own distinct identity and language and which only became a part of Scotland in the fifteenth century. There would be a new vocabulary of birds to learn, like *shalder*, from the Old Norse *tjaldr*, for oystercatcher.

It was a thrill to zoom in and out on satellite maps and see how unsheltered the archipelago looked – a tight and ragged cluster of islands surrounded by a vast expanse of dark blue. Each day, while packing, I would leave my laptop open and glance at live webcam footage. It all looked so beautiful in the soft light of early summer. The sea shone and the grass was coloured by wildflowers and always moving with the wind. At Sumburgh Head, high cliffs bristled with seabirds. Tight huddles of black and white guillemots jostled on guano-covered rocks, and above them, puffins flew in whirring flight. Though I mostly watched a webcam that looked down onto a street in Lerwick. I studied the people as they walked along between the shops, wanting to know what it might mean to be an islander.

In the weeks before we moved, I'd had a recurring dream of walking in sight of high cliffs formed of black rocks, the light so low that I could barely see where I was going. In the dream, I felt an anxiety akin to the constant vigilance needed to ensure that young children are kept safe from harm when harm is nearby. But the moment that we pulled up at our new home, the power of this dream began to fade. The house was wooden and painted bright red in a Nordic style, and it sat snug at the base of a green valley between heather-clad hills, far from any cliffs. The settlement was close to Lerwick and busy with many dwellings, a community hall and a school. A road followed the shoreline of a brackish loch where a model Viking longship was moored. The grassy shores were mown short, and this, and the two mute swans gliding across the water, gave an impression of genteel suburbia.

We unlocked the door of the red house and set our son free to crawl after the confines of the car seat and ferry cot. My husband and I lay on the carpet of a bare room, too exhausted to boil the kettle for a cup of tea. The floor seemed to roil. It would take three days for our bodies to re-adjust to the stability of land.

Days of sea fog followed our arrival, and Shetland mostly stayed hidden. My husband returned to work. To find my bearings, in the absence of any view, I swaddled my son in a blanket and walked him along the narrow roads in his pushchair. The pale forms of gulls and terns flew ghostlike through the deadening grey of the haar, and meadow pipits and wheatears flitted along the road ahead as if beckoning us on.

The fog formed a blank space, which my mind filled with doubts. I worried that it had been a rash decision to move so far away from the help of family and friends. We knew no one in Shetland and I was conscious of being an incomer to a tight-knit island community. I wasn't sure how easy it would be to find paid work that would cover the cost of childcare. And although I no longer dreamt of terrifying cliffs, I was still troubled by the ferry journey to Shetland. I vowed always to take the plane to Aberdeen, a much shorter journey of just over an hour. But I had read that flights were often disrupted by fog and that landing in Shetland could be a fraught experience in strong winds. The ferry journey had strengthened in my mind the idea of the sea as a hostile place. I questioned whether I would begin to feel trapped, wondered if I did already.

But on the first day of sun, these fears evaporated along with the haar. It did not seem so precarious to be so tightly bound by the sea: it sat calm, its surface strung with light. I clipped my son into his car seat and drove to a beach of pale shell sand that coloured the sea turquoise. A single red-throated diver, head held high and beak pointing skywards, sat on the surface just beyond the breaking waves; closer in, Arctic terns rose and fell in lithe fishing flight. My son was quiet and stared at the waves. The beach looked pristine. I did not know then that the ragged coastline of Shetland accumulates vast quantities of marine litter in the storms of winter. When I returned to the same stretch of sand after the first gales of the autumn, it was a shock to see a strand-line, the line of seaweed and marine litter left by each tide, thick with plastic – for on the sunny August day of this first visit, the tide had left only a slim and wavering ribbon of tiny shells and their fragments. Walking the reach of the sea with my son in my arms, I experienced a sudden and over-whelming certainty that Shetland would come to feel like home.

Autumn arrived, and with the first of the equinoctial gales I began to learn lessons of physical humility in the face of wind. The door of the red house opened outwards, and a gust would snatch the handle from my hands. I'd watch the door swing back and forth with injurious force, wait for a lull to try to catch hold of the handle again. I used my body to shield my son when we left the house on these windy days when car doors similarly transformed into weapons. Out walking, I would lash my son's pushchair to my wrist, but still the wind would try to wrest it from me.

At Christmas, our first in Shetland, we were invited to lunch at the house of one of my husband's colleagues. He and his wife were very welcoming and their good company made me realise how lonely I had felt since the birth of my son. But it was impossible to relax. A storm of the most powerful kind was forecast, and part way through the meal the wind slammed hail against the windows of the house with alarming force. When the meal finished, we didn't linger but thanked our hosts and made our way home. At the point where the road met the shore, waves reached up and over the tarmac. Crossing the higher ground, gusts of wind repeatedly shunted the car into the oncoming lane. Dried stalks of grass, torn from the sward, flew through the air with furious speed.

Back at the red house, we flicked the switch for light but none came. In the absence of electricity, the oil-fired heating could not work and the house was cold. The sun had set at three and so we sat in coats and played with our son by torchlight, trying to ignore the roar of the wind. We all went to bed early but the noise kept me and my husband awake. I lay in our bed, my body tense as if braced for impact. At daybreak, I stood on a stool in the bathroom and looked out of the skylight towards the sea. It had disappeared under a layer of white spindrift that looked dense enough to drown in. There was a deep gouge in the lawn and the soil gaped open like a wound, but whatever had caused the gash had been carried onwards by the wind. It was a relief when the power was restored.

Slowly, we began to learn the ways of the storms. The house would vibrate in sustained high winds and shudder with each gust – enough to jolt the bed in which we tried to sleep. Our young son slept soundly, undisturbed. He still does, but our daughter, who was born in Shetland, comes to our room in fear. I try to show her that I am not scared. I used to think that as incomers we would never become accustomed to the worst of the storms, but slowly I realised that people who have always lived here dread them too.

I learnt to look forward to the calm days – *days atween wadders* – that punctuate a run of violent weather, when the air is so still that it can be hard to believe there is such a thing as wind. After all the noise of a storm, it is a relief to stand in the depths of silence, weak sunlight on skin and with a body more at ease. The surface of the sea stretches taut and mirror-like, broken only in places by seabirds diving for fish or sea mammals surfacing for air.

In the year following our move to Shetland, I failed to secure paid work and had two miscarriages. My gaze turned mostly inward. It was a matter of getting through each day. I've watched birds intently all my life but found that they no longer held my attention to the same degree.

Then I became pregnant again, and this pregnancy held and our daughter was born. It was a happy time. I did not begrudge waking at night to tend to her needs in the magic of the *simmer dim*, the twilight of a northern midsummer's night. I would sit at the window to nurse her, and watch snipe circling through a sky that never quite got dark. The sun would rise before 4 a.m. and suffuse the day with a sense of possibility, however tired I felt.

Soon after the move, I had started to collect all seven volumes of the late Peter Guy's *Walking the Coastline of Shetland* series. Shetland is a place of relatively low hills; the highest, called Ronas, rises to a height of 450 metres. But the coastline of the archipelago is 1,679 miles long and challenging to walk. It folds back in on itself to form long fingers of inland *voes* – sheltered sea lochs – or thrusts outwards to form headlands that bear the brunt of the North Sea to the east and the vast expanse of the Atlantic Ocean to the west. Along the cliffs there are many geos to circumnavigate – deep inland clefts where the land suddenly falls away.

By the time my daughter was a few months old, my collection of guidebooks was complete, a mix of tatty charity-shop finds and shiny new editions with unbroken spines. Shetland is an archipelago of more than one hundred islands, sixteen of which are inhabited still. I pored over maps, lingered in the outer islands. I was ready to reclaim a sense of myself beyond motherhood and I decided to walk the coastline of Shetland, bit by bit. I planned to start my walks in the inhabited islands because these are easier to reach, thinking I could later beg lifts in boats to the islands where people no longer live and seldom visit.

I tended to my newborn daughter and toddler son, and all the while I planned these walks. I had no reason to doubt that I would soon be lacing up my boots. I longed for the lightness of spirit that comes at the outset of a long walk and the welcome fatigue of muscles at the end, all the memories gathered between. This is how I planned to stay afloat during the arduous years of caring for two very young children. I could not wait. I did not know that I would soon be unable to walk long distances. That I would need to find another way to stay afloat, one that would carry me through difficult times.

During my pregnancy with my daughter, I had not been able to walk far. If I did, an immobilising pain would appear in the joints between my pelvis and my spine. I assumed that this was caused by nothing more than the relaxation of ligaments in preparation for birth. I also assumed that the same ligaments would tighten again as my body recovered. Instead, in the months after the birth, this pain and immobility grew worse.

Over a period of several months, a physiotherapist sought to stabilise these troubled joints, and when they did not respond to treatment she sent me for an x-ray. Shortly after my daughter's first birthday, she phoned with the results. The joints were irreparably damaged. It was a shock to realise that I would no longer be able to walk far, or cycle long distances.

Swimming was recommended. I left my daughter and son in the crèche at the leisure centre and pulled my lower body through the pool with my hands, trailing my legs gently behind me. But even this was becoming difficult. My hands were unusually weak and this weakness felt familiar. It reminded me of the bitterly cold winter when my son was a baby and I had carried him in the crooks of my arms for fear of him falling from my weakened hands. I waited for my hands to recover, but by the time my daughter was eighteen months old they had worsened and become tender. I did not know it then, but both pregnancies had triggered the onset of inflammatory arthritis; my autoimmune system had begun to attack my joints.

It was hard to find a way through all this. Motherhood, constrained as it is in a steadfastly patriarchal society, had already cost me the part of my identity connected to my work. Now my body changed my identity again. My guide-books to the coastline of Shetland gathered dust on the shelf, and my beloved road bike slowly corroded in the damp air of the garden shed. Some days I stubbornly refused to accept the new limits of my body and tried to walk beyond them, but this would only increase the pain and reduce my mobility further. I grieved for the days when I could set out on a long hill walk or challenge myself to cycle over dis-tance. It was a struggle to care for two young children when my husband was at work. I wondered how I would be able to cope, physically, if I did find a paid job. I was no longer sure of who I was.

The story of how I found my way forward begins with dead seabirds. My daughter was nine months old and it was our third winter in Shetland. When my husband was not working, we would drive to a beach for a short walk, and among all the plastic debris in the strandline I would notice the bedraggled bodies of seabirds – guillemots and fulmars mostly. They caught my attention. I had never had the opportunity to study the bodies of wild birds so closely before, let alone birds that spend most of their lives at sea. And I was curious to know why the birds might have died. Had they been caught by a storm? Or been compromised by pollution? Perhaps it is no coincidence that I sought to understand what had happened to these birds at a time when I was struggling to understand the changes to my own body.

When I learnt that selected beaches in Shetland are monitored each month for dead seabirds and that most of this monitoring is undertaken by volunteers, I knew that this was something I wanted to do. Not knowing who to ask, I sent an email to Helen Moncrieff of RSPB Shetland, and she kindly put me in touch with the seabird ecologist Martin Heubeck, then the coordinator of the islands' beached bird survey. On a cold February morning in 2014, I met Martin on a nearby beach and he talked me through the process. We walked the strandline and stopped at each dead seabird. Martin showed me how to examine feathers for signs of oil pollution and to check legs for the coded rings fastened by ornithologists who study the movements of birds. Once everything had been noted, we would move on. Martin is tall and I struggled to match his pace as we walked along the beach. He strode swiftly over unstable pebbles and slippery seaweed; I followed in the wake of his tatty jeans and scruffy hi-vis jacket.

At that time, I found it hard to tell different kinds of gull apart and did not know how to identify types of auk – guillemot, black guillemot, puffin and razorbill – from their headless remains. Martin told me not to worry, I could always send him a photo of any puzzling corpses, with my size-five, rubber-booted foot included for scale when I walked the beaches on my own.

The bodies of guillemots and a few razorbills littered the strandline. Many had been heavily scavenged by corvids and gulls. I was surprised to learn that sheep sometimes chew on the legs of dead seabirds too, and will even eat seabird chicks.

Earlier in the month, Martin had been out in a boat counting seabirds and had seen many auks that looked to be near death. South-easterly gales had raged in the weeks before and the birds had been unable to feed. Martin explained that a mass death of seabirds is called a wreck and that the beached bird survey can be useful in identifying wrecking events.

One end of the beach was swathed in a thick layer of plastic that had washed ashore. It repulsed me. But Martin made straight for the mess and bent down to pick up a curved strip imprinted with a code – a lobster trap tag from Newfoundland or Labrador, he explained. He also reminded me to watch for the corpses of fulmars, a seabird that looks a little like a gull and which ingests more plastic than any other in the North Atlantic. If the fulmar's body is intact, I was to keep it, he instructed me. It will be frozen and taken to the Netherlands, where the plastic content of its stomach will be examined. I returned home feeling like a door had opened; I had found a way in to knowing Shetland, by searching for dead seabirds in the strandlines of beaches.

From then on, I checked two beaches each month and recorded any dead seabirds that had washed up. I could park close to the shore and walk slowly along. I enjoyed the challenge of trying to identify seabirds from their remains. Each beached bird survey was a guaranteed escape from the intensity of looking after two young children, in a body in which pain had become a quotidian reality.

Searching for dead seabirds was the beginning of my becoming a beachcomber – someone who searches for curious or useful things that have washed ashore. By the time I would learn that my body would not necessarily recover, I was already obsessed enough with beachcombing for it to carry me forward. I quizzed Shetlanders who *waander aroond da banks* or *hock trow da ebb stanes* looking for *scran*, and bit by bit I became consumed with finding long-drifted objects. It excited me, the thought that each tide refreshes this possibility. Instead of fearing storms I began to watch for them, and when they came I would lie awake at night and listen to the wind, really listen to the wind, and the wind would tell me which beach to visit the next morning. The pocket of my jacket soon became a portable beach. Now, years later, I become tense if it has been a while since I last searched the strandline of a beach. Beachcombing is not a necessity in the sense that I need to search the shore for things to eat or to sell on, but it is more than a hobby. It is a compulsion, and I admit that it involves the emotion of cupidity, the greed to possess.

After four winters in the red house, we had saved up enough for a mortgage deposit and moved to the west of Shetland's Mainland. We now live in a small settlement that strings out along a gentle inland shore. I worried that I might find the intimacy of life in such a community, of knowing so much about others and of being so known, uncomfortable. But we have been warmly welcomed.

Our community is alert to the seasonal movements of birds. News that the first *shalders* have arrived in mid-February soon spreads, because these birds signal the weakening of winter's grasp. We compete with our nearest neighbours to see who will be the first in May to sight a *tirrick*, the Arctic tern that flies all the way here from its wintering grounds in the Southern Ocean. In the dark months of winter, sometimes a message will arrive from a neighbour urging us to step outside because an aurora is blazing overhead. All through the year, the sound of the phone ringing might be someone calling to tell us that cetaceans have swum into the *voe*, and then it is a race to locate their fins through the windows of the kitchen.

I worried that when we moved to this settlement I would be encroaching on another beachcomber's patch. Tex, a retired Merchant Navy man, has beachcombed this stretch of shore since he was a child. I sometimes catch sight of him returning home very early in the morning, dressed in a boiler suit, a weathered baseball cap snug on his head. If it is raining, he wears yellow oilskins. His welcome has been generous. I sometimes find that he has left me fishing floats, of the kind that I seek, heaped by the garage. In return, I leave creel marker buoys on his doorstep.

After several winters in this settlement, it feels as if I have a tacit agreement with the beaches closest to our house. If I clean them of plastic, I will be rewarded with smooth sea glass; if I don't, the sea glass will stay sharp enough to cut, and each walk of the strandline will leave me with only swathes of plastic to choose from: bottle tops, bottles and containers, polystyrene spherules, cigarette lighters, tampon applicators and mussel rope pegs. This list of plastic is boundless and, of course, bound to us. The sea is always giving, but the nature of the sea's gifts changes and there are times when I leave the shore more diminished than when I arrived.

Beachcombing has helped me to place my imagination in the sea and has encouraged me to seek an understanding of its workings; to notice the way the tides respond to the phases of the moon. I have begun to learn the language of the sea and shore, dialect words like *shoormal*, the high-water mark, and *mareel*, the bioluminescent plankton that light the sea like many tiny lanterns on autumn nights. And as I have started to learn the ways of the moon, I have learnt some of the old names for the moon. Some, like *globeren*, which means 'the glaring, staring one', are the taboo names once used by the deep-sea *haaf* fishermen, who dared not use certain 'land' words for fear of invoking bad luck. Other terms, like *mønadrag*, have more than one meaning:

> weakness in the spine; a curvature in the spine of
>   a mammal;
> crossing of clouds coming from opposite
>   directions, driven by winds in the higher and
>   lower strata of air;
> semi-circular piece of rainbow, a kind of mock-
>   sun, to be seen near the moon, esp. behind the
>   moon.

It is said that a *mön-broch* foretells of windy weather. *Mön-broch* (moonbow), *möni* (spinal cord) and *mös* (to be bewitched, benumbed) sit close in a dictionary of Shaetlan words, and in these islands it is not unusual for the weather, the body and magic, of some kind or another, to coalesce.

I have come to picture, in my mind, the sensations of inflammation as behaving like the aurora borealis. Sometimes the aurora is nothing more than a faint green glow in the distance. I sense that it is there but only just, and then there is a wait to see if it emerges in a blaze or if it will fade, flickering, without ever having been fully present. Other times the night sky is full of shapeshifting light. Then it is hard to keep track of any one stream as it morphs and changes, moves, fades and then flares again, and this is exactly how pain can appear and move around my body.

My body is, now, rarely disconnected from my mind, and this has its own strange kind of assurance. Each beachcomb is felt. A heightened awareness of my internal micro-environments sharpens my perception of each shore that I walk. I anticipate the twisting sensations of pebbled beaches and the stretching of stiff joints in the give of sand. I feel storm-force winds in the resistant torsion of my ribcage; I feel a gust in a sear of pain. I find the bone of a seal, cetacean or seabird on the shore and see it for the function that it once had. Damaged joints and chronic illness have, in a way, helped me to close the distance between my body and my mind, and my body and the bodies of other creatures.

By the time my daughter reached the age of three, I had accumulated a lengthy list of things that I dreamt of finding: a message in a bottle, an octopus trap from the coastline of north-west Africa, a tree from Canada marked by the teeth of a beaver, a rubber duck from a North Pacific container ship spill, the mermaid's purse of a giant flapper skate, a piece of plastic litter that could be traced by its label to Greenland, a lump of valuable ambergris from the stomach of a sperm whale, and a sea bean, a type of drift-seed that sometimes washes ashore in a cold northern climate where they cannot naturally grow.

At first, I did not place great importance on finding a sea bean. It was on my wish list because it seemed remarkable that a tropical seed could withstand such a long ocean journey to reach these northern islands. Several types of drift-seeds have been found on Shetland's beaches, from tiny nickar nuts to hefty coconuts. As far as I could glean from my Shetland beachcombing friends, it is the sea bean kind, the seed of a monkey ladder vine, that is most commonly found here. I thought it realistic to hope for such a sea bean, though I've met Shetlanders who have beachcombed for many years and who have never found a drift-seed of any type. Meanwhile, I was told of a family who visited the islands on holiday and found one straight away.

I searched for drift-seeds in Shetland's museums, and the first time that I saw one, my heart contracted. It looked carved from dark wood and lightly polished – a plump and smooth-edged disc that would fit neatly in the palm of my hand. A small notch interrupted the sea bean's neat circumference, and this is why they are also known by the names 'sea kidney' and 'sea heart'. I wished to touch it but it was locked away behind glass.

I ordered a field guide to tropical drift-seeds so that I could familiarise myself with their variety, train my brain to pick out their shapes in a mass of seaweed and plastic litter. The book soon arrived in the post and I opened it to find a lengthy section on folklore. When I read that drift-seeds had been used as protective charms all along the shores of the north-east Atlantic, perhaps for a millennium or more, I became consumed by the need to find a sea bean of my own. The idea of a drift-seed charm took hold when I was most adrift, and I held on to it tightly.

I did not think, exactly, that a sea bean would keep me safe from harm or heal me, but I did feel certain that it might help me in some way. I did not know then that my obsession with beachcombing would bring an unimagined intimacy with these islands of Shetland, or that a small seabird would take me north to the Faroese archipelago, that a fish would take me south to the Orkney Islands, and that I would visit the Dutch island of Texel to experience a still-vibrant beachcombing culture. I would never have imagined becoming a dedicated sender of messages in bottles, or the comfort that this would bring. I could not have dreamt that pieces of plastic litter found on the shore might mean treasured connections with people living on the other side of an ocean. Most of all, I could not have imagined that the search for a sea bean of my own would lead me to a centuries-old Shetland story – the story of a woman and the brutal injustice that she faced. When we moved to Shetland, I did not foresee that I would become a writer and that I would tell the story of this Shetland woman, alongside the story of my own body and mind. But all of this is yet to come and my journey begins in the northernmost island of the Shetland archipelago, the strangely beautiful island of Unst.

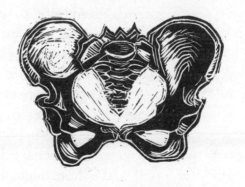

Sea Bean

And, when in storms we founder,
We, too, may leave behind
Some broken bits of flotsam
For other men to find.

From 'Bound is the Boatless Man' by Vagaland

There are many words which are used to express
shades of meaning: –

stramp   to walk
staag   to walk stiffly
harl   to walk with difficulty

From *Nordern Lichts:*
An Anthology of Shetland Verse and Prose, 1964

I have been searching for more than two years and on
beaches of many kinds, but I have not found a drift-seed
of my own. The shell-sand beaches of the south Mainland
are vast and sweeping and teasing. I always feel more certain
of finding a sea bean in these places, but each search ends
in disappointment. The boulder beaches of the west and
north Mainland seem less promising, but slowly they are

growing on me. They are stark and often gloomy, slippery and difficult to cross, but they seem to gather in all sorts of curious debris, both natural and less so.

To improve my chances, or so I think, I decide to travel to the island of Unst before the calmer months of spring and summer arrive. It is the first day of April in 2017. All my hopes are pinned on a beach called Woodwick, which is renowned among Shetland beachcombers for gathering in considerable quantities of jetsam and flotsam. Drift-seeds have been found on this beach and I dare to hope that I might find one there too.

Woodwick, as its name suggests, is a bay where driftwood collects. It is said, in these mostly treeless islands, that wood is a product of the sea and not of the land. A beachcombing friend told me that she had renamed the beach Plasticwick, but then if we were to rename coastal sites in Shetland now, the word 'plastic' would litter the map.

To reach Unst from the Mainland of Shetland you must first travel to, and then through, the island of Yell. There are two car ferries that work Yell Sound between the Mainland and Yell, and they pass each other mid-channel. One is called *Dagalien*, which in Old Norse means 'evening twilight', and the other is called *Daggri*, which means 'the dawn of day'. And so, in Yell Sound each day, dusk meets dawn, and this is how it is in Shetland in midsummer, when the dark of night is almost over before it has really begun.

By the time May arrives there will be sixteen hours of light and then the *shalders* and *sandiloos*, oystercatchers and ringed plovers, will return to the beaches to lay eggs in shallow shingle scrapes or among the shattered rock of storm beaches. The end of April is a time to relinquish many good beachcombing spots back to the birds, and so this journey to Unst feels like this winter's last chance.

I cross Yell Sound on *Daggri*. The ferry lounge is busy. A pair of fractious parents snap at their young daughter as she continues to ignore their instructions. I've left my family behind in the Mainland and am free to do as I please. Out of the ferry's windows, the mist-dampened outline of the small island of Samphrey appears. A pair of elegant razorbills dive under the sea's surface at the ferry's approach.

The shell-sand beaches of Yell are stunning and always divert me on the way to Unst. I break the journey through Yell at West Sandwick, a gathering beach where there is always something of interest to find. Even at the height of summer, when little washes ashore, the sand itself is reason enough to visit this beach. It is rich in mica, *craws-siller*, the silver of crows.

I sat on this beach the year before, on a sunny summer's day, wrapped in a warm jacket while my husband and children swam in the sea. I searched through the sand for mica – pieces the size of my fingertip and shaped like fish scales. Smaller grains of mica fell through the gaps between my fingers, shining like glitter in the sun. My children and husband returned to the shore and wet sand clung to their skin and mica gilded their bodies with gold.

When my mind is racing too fast to allow sleep, or when my body keeps me awake in discomfort, I sometimes reach for a translation of the Finnish folk epic, the *Kalevala*. The runes, or poems, of the *Kalevala* are octosyllabic, a rhythm that is somehow soothing in small doses. The stories brim with beings other than humans. These creatures often have their own agency, and sometimes trees are animate too. There is much possibility held within the words of this text. A woman wanting to escape her entrapment by an unwelcome suitor can wish herself into another species, a whiting or a hare, and in this changed form she can evade her fate.

The *Kalevala* is most often defined by the stories of its heroes, but I read it more for the many heroines. It is a creation myth that begins, after all, when the daughter of the ether, Ilmatar, falls from the air and into the ocean. Storm winds from the east turn the ocean into a wild place of white water and, through force, impregnate her. She must endure a pregnancy that lasts seven hundred years. While she is held in the ocean by the weight of her condition, a duck makes a nest on her knee. In one translation the duck is a teal, in another a scaup, and in a third it is simply described as beauteous. The duck lays six eggs of gold and one of iron. Beneath the nest, Ilmatar's knee begins to burn with heat, and it seems to her as if the fire is threading through her veins. She flinches. The eggs fall from the nest and, when they shatter, they form the earth, the heaven, the sun, the moon, the stars and the clouds.

Part way through the *Kalevala*, there is a rune in which the hero Lemminkäinen is restored back to life by the tenacity and knowledge of his mother, who is not honoured with a name. She takes a rake made from copper and scours the river of the underworld to gather up the scattered pieces of her dead son's body. A raven counsels her to stop. Lemminkäinen's body is food for eels, the raven argues; his eyes have already been nibbled by a whiting, and it is better that his flesh becomes a walrus, a seal, a whale or a porpoise. But the woman ignores the bird and calls on Suonetar, the goddess of veins, to

> Bind the flesh and bone securely,
> In the joints put finest silver,
> Purest gold in all the fissures.

Lemminkäinen's body is restored to life.

I wished, as I sat on the sand and watched my family dry the sea from their skin, that I could be restored to my body. I wanted to swim in the sea and to cover my wet skin in sand that glistened. I wanted the fire-like pain that threaded through my body at times to be extinguished by the cold of an ocean. I did not know how to adapt to my changed body. I could not see beyond what I had lost.

Now, the mica of West Sandwick stays hidden in the absence of sunlight on this dull April day. Offshore, the Ramna Stacks, the sea stacks of the raven, drift in and out of view with the passing of showers, and a tanker sails south towards the oil terminal at Sullom Voe.

The prints of an otter lead from the dunes to the sea, and vanish into the surf. I ignore the pull of the otter's path and search the back of the beach. Dunes catch the small things that have been carried in by the sea and then blown further inland by the wind, and sure enough, I spot a bright blue lobster trap tag half buried in the sand. It is imprinted with a code that tells me that it has floated across the Atlantic Ocean from Canada. I slip the tag into my pocket. It is a treasure of

sorts – a token of a far shore that now seems a little closer. I
head back to the car and make my way to the ferry that will
take me to the island of Unst.

I've rented a holiday cottage in Unst that is a short walk
away from a large sandy beach called Eastings. I drop my bags
inside the door and, though I am weary from the journey,
head straight for the shore. My expectations for this beach
are always high; the seed pod of a flamboyant tree, a species
that grows in the tropics, once washed up here.

The wind is strong, and sand flows in fast streams over
the surface of the beach. Two snow buntings forage in the
shelter of sea-heaped kelp. A posy of fresh plastic flowers
lies half covered in sand, perhaps taken by the wind from
the nearby burial ground that is still used even though it
cannot be reached by road. Coffins are transported across
the fields on a trailer towed by a tractor. Within the burial ground's walls there is a long keel-shaped stone that sits
like an upturned boat and marks the grave of a Viking. The
graves of Picts have been found at Eastings too, uncovered
by the work of a rising sea. Pebbles of quartz were placed
alongside one of the bodies. The osteology report for this
person details lesions on the spine, a detail that I would once
have overlooked, in the days when I took the functioning
and health of my body more or less for granted.

I return to the beach at first light, impatient to know if the
sea has left anything new for me to find. The wind is cold
but the sun shines, and the sky and the sea are deep blue.
Offshore, the *Norröna*, the white block of a ferry that sails
between Denmark, the Faroe Islands and Iceland, works

her way north. Inshore, a group of long-tailed ducks sit just beyond the breaking waves. They are busy foraging, diving in synchrony but bobbing to the surface one or two at a time. I wish that they would pause a while to court and to call. Their Shetland name, *calloo*, is the sound of their call. The Latin, *Clangula hyemalis*, means 'wintry resound'. The wind whips the thin tail feathers of the drakes. They will leave soon for their breeding grounds in the Arctic of Scandinavia and western Russia. I cannot picture their summer places, just as I once could not picture the land and seascapes of Shetland.

I find nothing of note on the beach and turn my attention to the rock pools, where a robin follows me about. It will soon fly across the North Sea to Norway. Robins overwinter in Shetland in some places but depart in the spring for Scandinavia. Birdsong is scarcer in Shetland. Spring is heralded by the song of the Shetland wren and, if you are lucky, the melodious power ballad of a blackbird, but otherwise the islands are mostly a place of the haunting calls of curlews, or the jarring piping of oystercatchers, or the strange utterances of seabirds. This is the first robin song that I have heard since moving here. I urge the robin to take flight, to head out over the vast expanse of the North Sea, but it stays put and sings as if it is singing to me, and it is this rare sound that I take away with me from the beach at Eastings.

I leave the North Sea shores of Unst and drive to the end of the road at Baliasta, where the walk to the Atlantic-washed beach at Woodwick begins. It is still sunny, but mares' tails — the white hooked wisps of cirrus uncinus clouds — stretch through the deep blue of the sky like a warning. The wind is strengthening. The rain that was forecast for later will probably arrive sooner. The prospect of wind-driven rain does not concern me but I worry that the walk to Woodwick will be too far. I'm torn between wanting the freedom to explore alone and wishing that my husband and children were here with me too, just in case I need their help.

At the base of the human spine, and at the base of many non-human spines too, there is a bone called the sacrum. It forms when vertebrae fuse in our late teens and early twenties. The word derives from *os sacrum* or 'sacred bone'. It is thought that the sacrum is so named because it was the part of an animal that was offered during sacrifice. The wear-and-tear damage to my sacroiliac joints, the joints between my pelvis and sacrum, is more typically found in people who have endured many pregnancies. Why it has occurred in me, I do not know. Sometimes I ask myself whether I would have sought to have children had I known that it might limit my ability to walk far. It is not a question that I can answer.

Experiencing such an injury or developing a chronic illness can damage women and girls in other ways too. Medical settings can enable the male gaze to transmute into the male touch. Of the male doctors that I have met, most have been reputable, but not all.

When I was a teenager, I dislocated and broke my kneecap. In the Accident and Emergency department of the nearest hospital, I lay on a gurney, immobilised and speechless from the pain and from the painkillers. A male doctor stood and stared hungrily at my body while slowly stroking my injured leg up and down.

After the cast came off, I spent a week in hospital so that physiotherapists could coax my leg back to mobility. There was another teenage girl on the ward. I learnt to tense like all the nurses did when one particular doctor did his rounds, and to ignore the porters who came into the ward just, it seemed, to stare at us.

In my twenties, I caught a cold virus that would not shift. It settled in my chest, and my lungs became sore. The doctor who examined me asked me to take off my top. I sat in my bra for a length of time. He did not look me in the eyes as he slowly questioned me. Eventually, he listened to my lungs with his stethoscope, and only then was I free to dress again.

Once, in an operating theatre, lying on my stomach and woozy with sedation and immobilised by pain, I heard the male doctor tell the nurse to remove my pants. It was not the first time that I'd had this procedure, and each time I'd never had to remove my pants. While the nurse was busy monitoring a machine near my head, and the radiographer was also similarly occupied, I felt the touch of a finger.

During an early appointment to determine the cause of the damage to my sacroiliac joints, there was a physical exam. I took off my top and was glad to have remembered to wear a vest. The doctor's hands lingered on my skin in a way which made it crawl. He joked that the next step of the examination would be to strip me naked. I exchanged a look of alarm with the young medical student, a woman who had stood in the corner of the room as still and silent as a statue throughout the appointment. The consultation had begun with a provisional diagnosis that my autoimmune system was destroying the joints of my spine. My mind was in freefall. I had no capacity to object to the doctor's behaviour.

In the afternoon after this stressful appointment, the joints of my wrists and hands suddenly became much weaker. I lost the ability to grip cutlery and turn handles. The gentle touch of water was agony. Pain seared if I tried to hold the hands of my children, or my husband.

Doctors focused on discerning the reason for the damage to my sacroiliac joints. With no clear markers in my blood, the cause of the pain and loss of function in my hands was left undiagnosed. At a later appointment, one doctor suggested that motherhood, and specifically the strain of lifting young children, probably explained the problems that I was having with my hands. He told me not to go looking for something that was not there.

In desperation, and at great cost, I sought a second opinion from a private doctor. His professionalism in the physical exam was reassuring, but he too attributed the pain in my hands and wrists to lifting young children, even though I was adamant that I was experiencing an entirely different type of pain.

It is almost as if both of these doctors were reading from the same script: a diagnostic key which concludes that if the patient is a woman with young children, then there is no need to investigate further. But I know from speaking to women who do not have children that their pain is readily dismissed too. I soon learnt that if I took my husband along with me to an appointment, even if he sat there and said nothing, I would be listened to more.

Two years after first reporting the joint pain in my wrists and hands, I was diagnosed with palindromic rheumatism, an autoimmune disease of the joints. In this condition, pain migrates between joints and inflammation waxes and wanes; it is called palindromic because it is supposed to come and go. Though it can be painful and disabling, this type of arthritis does not erode joints. The coincidental damage to my sacroiliac joints was confirmed, as far as is possible, as nothing more than wear and tear.

By the time I began treatment for the autoimmune disease it had spread throughout my body. My eyes had become dry and gritty and I experienced debilitating fatigue after each flare of pain. I learnt the ways of different types of pain. Some I could ignore, others I could not. Early diagnosis is critical in the treatment of autoimmune forms of arthritis – but perhaps more critical, for women, is finding a doctor who will listen.

I see a new rheumatologist now, one who is meticulous and listens as much as she advises. The first time I met her, she asked me to describe the types of pain that I encountered. My mind went blank. It is difficult to find the words for pain when it has been continually denied. With her help, I have been able to dampen my autoimmune system's misplaced attention with a carefully tailored dose of 'disease modifying anti-rheumatic drugs'. This has meant less painful and inflexible joints but also nausea and headaches. Along with injections of steroids into my sacroiliac joints, the medication has returned me to places that had become difficult to reach – including, at times, the upstairs of our house.

*

In the cold of the April morning in Unst, the walk to Wood-wick does feel possible. I have not yet met my enabling rheumatologist and my autoimmune disease is unmanaged. But today it is quiet, and the pain of my sacroiliac joints has been lessened by steroids. The sun emboldens me even though the easterly wind has flensed all warmth from its light. It is a relief to see that no other cars are parked at the end of the road. I do not want to walk to the beach to find someone else already there, taking the pick of all the jetsam and flotsam. My spine tingles with the possibility of what I might find.

A deeply rutted track leads up the slope. I quickly tire of its unevenness and switch to a neat trail of tiny Shetland-pony hoof prints guiding me on an easier path through the boggy ground. At the top of the hill, a long and deep dale fills the view. There is no sea in sight and my heart sinks. But the path down is gentle, and the lower I drop, the more certain I become that I will be able to reach Woodwick.

A fast-falling movement at the edge of my field of sight stops me in my tracks. A merlin, the smallest of falcons, sweeps down the steep slope to my right in an almost-vertical stoop. It levels out to clear a fence by a narrow margin and then glides up the far incline until it loses all lift and drops down into deep heather. I envy it the ground that it can cover in the shortest of moments, but at the end of the valley there is a bright point of colour that hastens me on. Someone has constructed a cairn of yellow and orange trawl floats – a waymarker to a wrecker's paradise. Beyond the cairn, a small stream meanders through flat ground and disappears into the boulders of a storm beach. In the shelter of the flowing water, aquatic plants have begun to grow, and the brightness of their green is startling within a landscape that is still dulled by winter.

A low stone circle, more gaps than structure, encloses an area of flat ground before the beach. A tumbled-down old *pund* perhaps, a pen for sheep, cattle or ponies. I enter the circle between the two tallest stones and break the silence by laughing at the ceremony of it all. I have made it to Woodwick and will be able to hold my own in conversations, now, with other Shetland beachcombers. I voice a thank you, and the east wind carries my words away.

A sea bean can travel far and remain unscathed because the seed coat, the testa, is hard and impermeable yet light and buoyant. The dormant embryo that it contains is so well protected by this testa that viable sea beans can arrive on northern shores after floating on the surface of the ocean for thousands of miles. A sea bean that rattles is unlikely to grow, but as E. Charles Nelson warns in his book, *Sea Beans and Nickar Nuts*,

> The only way to test whether a drift-seed is viable – capable of germinating – is to sacrifice the specimen and attempt to germinate it. It is a decision that you must make yourself, remembering that once the seed is prepared and planted it will produce either a rather a vigorous plant, probably requiring a massive, continually heated greenhouse in which to live, or *nothing* and then it will be so rotten that you will want to dispose of its putrid remains. Whatever the outcome, your lucky drift-seed will be lost for ever.

I would not risk mine.

Perhaps the sea bean that I will one day find is still growing. Maybe it sits cradled, with others, within a seed pod that stretches a little over a metre in length and which dangles from a forest canopy. I have begun to imagine its journey, to think of the rainforest in which its vine grows. At some point the seed will slip from the pod. I do not know how the seeds are scattered – if the pod first falls and then breaks, or if it splits while still aloft. It does not matter; the seed is light and easily lifted from the forest floor by the rivulets of rain that snake through the leaf litter after a torrential downpour. Or maybe the pod hangs over a stream and the seed will not need to wait for the rainy season to begin its journey. Afloat, it becomes a drift-seed, and soon enough the stream will empty into a river and the river will empty into the sea and then the sea bean, my sea bean, will begin its ocean voyage.

I wonder where it is growing – in the American tropics or in the forest of an island in the Caribbean Sea. I prefer the thought of an island forest. Islands are easier to imagine now that I am, in some ways, becoming an islander. I know from *Sea-Beans from the Tropics*, by Ed Perry IV and John V. Dennis, that, if it enters the Caribbean Sea, it will drift north, on the Yucatán Current, and into the Gulf of Mexico. It will circulate in a clockwise direction past the shores of Mexico, Texas and Louisiana, passing by some of the many oil and gas platforms that occupy this body of water. It might even pass the place where the *Deepwater Horizon* once towered above the surface of the sea.

If it passes through the Gulf at a time of bird migration, the sky could be filled with birds of many kinds – or maybe this is too nostalgic and the days of endless flocks have gone, but still there will be birds in the sky. The weaker of the birds seek refuge on the oil and gas platforms, where peregrine falcons have learnt to wait for prey. In poor weather, at night, the lights of the platforms disorientate the birds. They fly in circles; some collide with steel and others fall exhausted into the sea. Migrating birds also succumb to the sea in storms and this is how songbirds, like house wrens, have come to be found in the stomachs of tiger sharks.

My sea bean will need to find its way through the Florida Straits, a gap of ninety miles between the tip of the Florida Keys and Cuba, and then it will join the Gulf Stream. This will carry it north, along the coast of Georgia, South Carolina and then North Carolina. Just beyond the sandy barrier island of Cape Hatteras, the Gulf Stream leaves the continental shelf and begins to cross the Atlantic. Here my sea bean will be joined by drifting debris that has been carried south, from the north, on the Labrador Current – birch bark from the forests of Canada and cigarette lighters from Greenland.

The Gulf Stream does not reach Shetland; instead, it turns south part way across the Atlantic Ocean to eventually encircle the Sargasso Sea. Some drift-seeds will be carried southwards too, to circulate for years on end within this subtropical gyre. This is the place where young sea turtles drift, in water thick with plastic and sargassum seaweed, until they mature and break away to swim to their breeding grounds. The son of my neighbour captained a container ship of bananas through the Sargasso Sea. He said that it was eerie, that the sea smelt oddly like land and that, yes, it was visibly choked with plastic.

Before the Gulf Stream turns south, surface layers of warmer water – a current called the North Atlantic Drift – peel away to continue north, and this is why Shetland is not encased in ice each winter, even though these islands lie at a latitude of 60 degrees north. My sea bean will be carried towards Shetland by the North Atlantic Drift and will be blown by a westerly wind to a local and inshore current. Other drift-seeds will continue further north on diverging currents, and so some will travel west to be found in the Faroe Islands, Iceland and Greenland, while others will head east to wash ashore in Arctic Norway and Russia.

It is still a cause of speculation – the length of time that it takes for a drift-seed to arrive on a northern shore. Drift bottles released from the north-eastern islands of the West Indies reached the beaches of Europe, on average, fourteen months later. This finding has been used as a proxy to estimate the time it takes for a drift-seed to reach beaches in the north. But drift-seeds grow south of this release point, and it is not clear that the bottles arrived as far north as Shetland. The fastest crossing of a bottle, travelling over 4,000 miles from Hispaniola, in the Greater Antilles, to south-western Ireland, took 337 days, but bottles can catch the wind in a way that drift-seeds do not. It has been found that a sea bean can float in a tank of still water for at least nineteen years.

When I find my sea bean, I will not know how long its journey took. I try to picture in my mind the moment of discovery – will it be lying among pebbles, resting on a strandline of tangled seaweed or maybe lying in plain sight, a deep brown on the pale white of shell sand? Sometimes now, when I am unable to sleep, I am comforted by the thought of a sea bean floating northwards, towards Shetland, on the dark surface of the ocean.

There is no sand at Woodwick; it is a beach of large unstable pebbles that shift with a sharp crack of sound as you cross them. Boulders have been tossed high up onto the grass at the back of the beach by the waves of a storm. Patches of bare earth suggest that they were rearranged by the sea this winter.

The two drift-seeds found at Woodwick – a sea bean and a kind called a sea purse – belonged to Joy Sandison. They now lie in a National Trust for Scotland warehouse somewhere in Edinburgh. In the typed note that accompanies a photograph of the drift-seeds, Joy recalls that they had 'lain amongst Mother's sewing things as far back as I can remember'. Joy was born in 1929, and it is possible that both drift-seeds were found more than one hundred years ago. Her note explains that sea beans found on Shetland beaches are thought to be lucky, but she does not elaborate any further.

Joy Sandison's sea bean was found by Tommy Bruce, a shepherd. There is no date for when Tommy found it, but I think of him, strolling along the beach at Woodwick and bending down to pluck it from a strandline. Did he know of their use as charms and, if so, why did he give his luck away? Perhaps Joy's mother, Ida, was a keen collector of natural curios and he was fond of her, or loyal.

I am left contemplating this luck. The absence of drift-seed folklore in Shetland frustrates me. It is so well documented elsewhere along the shores of the north-eastern Atlantic that I don't understand why nobody has ever noted down their use as charms here. There are several records of drift-seeds washing up in Shetland, including for the parish in which I live, but these are perfunctory descriptions at best.

Scouring the shores of the Internet one day, I find an academic paper on drift-seeds that might hint at their former importance in Shetland – a place that was once part of the Norse realm. It is written by Torbjørn Alm, from the University of Trømso's Department of Botany. I read through his words in a hurry of greed, and learn that he has documented the folklore of drift-seeds in Norway, as relevant to Sámi, Finnish, Roma and Norwegian communities. He lists the names that drift-seeds have been given and the ways in which they have been used as charms. Men have taken drift-seeds out on boats as a charm against drowning, he explains, and women have used them in childbirth as a charm against dying. Drift-seeds have been used to cure illnesses in people and in cattle, to steal the milk from a neighbour's cow, or to stop a neighbour stealing milk from one's own cow. I read all this and it seems even stranger to me that their use as charms in Shetland is, as far as I can tell, unrecorded.

In terms of extant knowledge, Alm is less than encouraging: 'Although I have carried out extensive ethnobotanical field work in north Norway, I have so far failed to find more than a dozen persons who had first-hand knowledge of drift seeds and their traditional uses.' I have not yet met anyone in Shetland that can tell me about the folklore of drift-seeds. When I ask my crofter naturalist friend Oliver Cheyne, who has a drift-seed found by his late father, he scratches his head and tells me that, now that he thinks of it, it does stir a vague memory of drift-seeds being used as good-luck charms.

Alm reports that it has become more difficult to find drift-seeds on the shore. In the late 1500s they were plentiful and could be found both floating and stranded on Cornish beaches. They were still abundant in the 1800s: 'Norwegian fishermen, like those of the west coast of Scotland, collect these seeds in fairly large numbers.' But Alm cautions that habitat loss, the felling of tropical forests, means that fewer drift-seeds enter the ocean.

My chances of finding a sea bean are reduced; I will need more luck. I revise my sea bean's origins. It is enclosed in a pod that hangs from a vine in a small scrap of secondary forest in an island that was mostly cleared of its forests following the arrival of European colonists. This scrap of forest in which my sea bean grows is vulnerable to felling by the hurricanes that are becoming ever more frequent and ever more devastating now that we are within a climate emergency.

In *Sea Beans and Nickar Nuts*, I read that drift-seeds found on the shores of the Azores, Madeira and Porto Santa encouraged Columbus to sail west across the Atlantic, and that in Portuguese they are called *fava de Colom* (Columbus's bean) and *castanha de Colombo* (Columbus's chestnut). The *Entada gigas* vine is also known as the monkey ladder vine, names that lose their charm if we care to remember that English is a colonial language and that the binomial naming of plants in Latin has eradicated many indigenous names. I learn that sea beans are called *cacoon* in Jamaica. In my romanticisation of the use of drift-seeds as protective charms along the shores of the north, I had not taken the time to consider that sea beans grow in places that are still subjected to colonial harm.

The large pebbles at Woodwick unsteady me but I can lean, in places, on the vast hulks of drifted trees that give this beach its name, each far thicker in circumference than any tree now growing in Shetland. Some still have the stumps of roots attached, and these would have fallen into rivers during storms. Others have been cleaned of roots and branches – which makes me wonder if they might have been deliberately floated down rivers by logging companies? I sometimes wish to pinpoint drifted trees to the exact place where they grew, and then I could learn about the birds that might have flitted around their branches. Other times, it is enough to just place an ungloved hand on wood.

This clutter of drifted trees is impressive, but my eyes are already beyond their thick trunks. There is so much jetsam and flotsam on the beach that I struggle to choose a place to start my search. I make for a black mound of fishing net decorated with small green Galician floats, where the gold shine of an ornate tin has caught my attention. On the tin, there is a picture of a white woman dressed 'in costume': a turban and 'harem' pants. She reclines languorously on cushions; one of the straps of her top has fallen from her shoulder and a wisp of smoke from her cigarette rises into still air. The tin is now empty but is labelled 'La Odalisca', and it once contained smoked Spanish paprika. *Odalisca*, I learn, is a term that in Turkish originally described a chambermaid but came to mean, in western usage, a concubine.

In the eighteenth century, in the western world, it evolved further to define a genre of erotic art in which an 'exotic' woman would lie, on show, for the white male gaze.

A Shetland wren starts to sing in short bursts, the first wren song that I have heard this spring, but I am too distracted by my feverish beachcombing greed to pay the bird any attention. There are many cartons: banana milk from Ireland, Belgian cream and Faroese sour cream, all probably jettisoned from fishing boats. A glass bottle of Icelandic vodka lies empty and smelling only of the sea. I check all the intact plastic bottles and only one contains what could have been a message, but the paper has been pulped by the sea and the ink is smudged and unreadable. In the middle strandline, a cetacean vertebrate sits upright and obvious as if some sort of consolation prize, an offering made in the absence of a sea bean.

The wind grows stronger and scalps the crests from the waves. Rainbows fall from wind-scattered spray. I pull the hood of my jacket over my hat. The noise of the wind on my waterproof drowns out the song of the wren, but I can still sense the low thrum of a helicopter passing high overhead. The helicopter returns my thoughts to my husband.

We met in 2008, and in the time that I have known him there have been several oil and gas helicopter accidents. In 2009, mechanical failure caused a helicopter to crash into the sea off the coast of Newfoundland. Only one of the eighteen people on board survived. In 2013, one woman and three men died when pilot error caused an oil and gas helicopter to crash into the sea two miles west of Shetland's main airport. In 2016, mechanical failure caused an oil and gas helicopter to crash into a small rocky islet off the coast of Bergen, killing all on board. There is a lifeboat stationed at the harbour in the community in which we live. When my husband is out flying, I experience a lurch of panic each time I see it launch. It is a relief, standing here in the cold east wind at Woodwick, to remember that he is at home caring for our children.

In the north of Unst, at a beach called Skaw, I once found a clump of juvenile glaucous gull feathers pinned upright in the sand. They were very soft, white and lightly flecked with pale brown. These white-winged gulls of the Arctic visit Shetland in small numbers in the winter. I stood on the beach, with the gull's feathers in my hand, and looked due north, to the clear expanse of sea that stretches, uninterrupted, all the way to the Arctic. I exulted, even, in being the most northerly person in Shetland and Britain, forgetting about the men and women on the steel island of the Magnus. It lies to the north-east of Unst, just one of many oil and gas installations that surround Shetland, most of which are conveniently beyond sight.

I watch the helicopter pass overhead and then return my gaze to the beach. A red and white lifebuoy lies on a strandline of filmy, wine-red dulse. The markings on the buoy have been scoured away by the sea. Further along, a bright yellow lifebuoy light looks freshly ashore. Its label is clearly readable; it did not spend long in the sea. Later, I search for its kind on the Internet. This exact model costs just over £100.

The cold wind reaches through my jacket and chills me to the core, and the sight of the emergency light extinguishes any further wish within me to continue beachcombing. There could be a sea bean hidden somewhere among the jetsam and flotsam of this beach but it is not mine to find. I take a teal-coloured Galician float and turn inland, away from the sea.

Part way up the dale, a flurry of tiny red-brown feathers swirl across the bare soil of the path. I grab some before they are all taken by the wind. Nothing else is left of the Shetland wren and there is no sign of the merlin that killed it. Just as a wrecked ship once provided welcome spoils for a beachcomber, I hold the wren's feathers in the cage of my hands and the elation that I feel is tempered by a hint of unease.

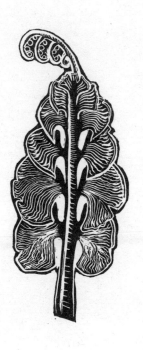

Alamootie

Storm Petrel

Beachcombing returned me to myself, but a tiny seabird helped me along the way. I first saw a storm petrel when my daughter was a little more than a year old, when I still believed that my body would recover from pregnancy. I had flown to Fair Isle for two nights on my own, to prove to myself that I could still exist beyond motherhood.

The island, placed as it is between the archipelagos of Shetland and Orkney, is a resting place for migrating birds in spring and autumn. I stayed at the Bird Observatory, a large building that hosts ornithological researchers alongside paying guests. The staff were welcoming and it was thrilling to briefly experience life in a building dedicated to the study of birds, but it was also an unsettling reminder of who I used to be and no longer was. I was slowly beginning to get to know people working in the fields of ecology and conservation in Shetland. And when my husband wasn't working and could care for our children, I surveyed birds as a volunteer. I enjoyed making these connections and completing the surveys, but part of me resented being back at square one, working for free to get a foot in the door.

I had known that moving to Shetland would limit my chances of finding paid work in the field of nature conservation, but I had not realised just how difficult it would be to return to work at all. I scrutinised the situations vacant pages of the *Shetland Times* each week, and each week the jobs that I could plausibly apply for came with salaries that would not cover the cost of childcare. There was no flexibility in my husband's salary to subsidise my return to work.

In the days after my daughter was born, a health visitor had come to the house to assess how we were both doing. We sat at a table as she filled out a long form. It felt like an exam – how could it not? I tried to give an impression of competency. But when she reached the section related to occupation, I was more open and honest. I gabbled out my frustrations. I explained that I had worked in nature conservation and that this was my vocation and that it was not my choice to stay at home and that I had looked for other forms of work too but that the cost of childcare was always too high and that, in all honesty, I felt a little trapped. She listened to all this and then dipped her head and wrote 'home maker' on the form, as if there had been no past and there was no future.

It was a happy few days in Fair Isle, rekindling my interest in birds. My sense of self had been eroded by unemployment and staying at home with young children, but in Fair Isle I found that, deep down, it was still there. Though I did note that all of the ornithologists at the observatory were men, and most of the visitors too. I found women busy juggling logistics in the office, or cleaning the rooms, or minding the children. And important though these jobs are, there were no men in these roles. It reminded me of the academic conferences I had attended. It had been a rare sight to see a woman in her thirties or early forties. I was beginning to think of women with young children as having clipped wings.

Each morning, I rose early to join the ornithologists in checking the many Heligoland funnel traps for migrant birds. In one, there was a Fair Isle wren, a subspecies that is endemic to the island. Fair Isle wrens are much larger and darker than the tiny wrens of Britain and Ireland. In the observatory's library, I read that the population of this North Atlantic island subspecies fluctuates each year between ten and fifty singing males. I thought of this in terms of fragility and vulnerability until an ornithologist suggested that, actually, we can think of this small island population in terms of resilience too. I later saw one scurrying along the lip of a vertiginous cliff in the north of the island, and this cemented my impression of the hardiness of this tiny bird.

One evening, all of the observatory guests were invited to a storm petrel ringing session. After dark, we gathered down at the ringing shed, near a narrow isthmus that separated a beach of sand from a beach of pebbles. In the still evening air, it was possible to hear the detail in the wash of every wave. Flashes of torchlight came from the strip of grass behind the pebble beach, where some of the ornithologists were setting up mist nets that looked a little like volleyball nets. Their fine mesh was invisible in the dark.

Once the nets were all in place, a recording of a storm petrel call was blared out over the ocean, on repeat – a lure to bring the tiny seabirds to land. It was the strangest of sounds, a sharp shuddering: a purr so fast that it became a rasp that was interrupted, at regular intervals, by a hiccupping noise. It made me think of the sour taste of bile.

I would later learn, from the seabird ecologist Will Miles, that a storm petrel's call acts as a sonic lantern that guides their mate back to the nest in darkness. If they returned in daylight, they would be preyed upon by gulls and skuas, and so they hide within the dark. When the moon is full and the sky is cloudless, and there is enough light for these predators to hunt, storm petrels stay out at sea. Their nest-bound mates, incubating a single white egg or tending a chick, must wait longer than the usual two or three days to be relieved. It must be strange to be so confined to a nest, and surrounded by rock, when you are used to the space of an entire ocean, but I think I know a little of how this might feel. Storm petrels make their nests in fissures of rock, on cliffs or boulder beaches or in the slender gaps in drystone walls. They navigate their lives through rock and waves. I could not wait to meet one.

I stood outside by the ringing shed in the thick darkness, and soon a person emerged from the gloom carrying a small drawstring bag of cloth weighted with the body of a storm petrel. They are starting to come in, he told us, and sure enough a steady stream of people followed him, all tasked with disentangling the birds as swiftly and gently as possible and then transporting them in cloth bags to the ringing shed.

It was snug inside the shed, a huddle of human bodies watching eagerly for the first storm petrel to be pulled from its bag like a rabbit from a top hat. It was smaller than I expected, the size of a swallow and a deep brown in colour. The ringers worked deftly. One closed a metal band around a leg and the other noted the band's code on a paper form. As they worked, they talked us through the purpose of this ringing. Some of these ringed storm petrels would be recaptured, and the date and location of their recapture would give an insight into their life history and movements.

Many of the storm petrels that will be caught tonight are wanderers, they explained; they are young and not yet breeding. During the northern summer, they roam the north-east Atlantic prospecting for nest sites, flitting between archipelagos and rocky coastlines and isolated islands like silver balls ricocheting around a pinball machine. In late autumn they migrate south to winter off the coast of South Africa, where they share the Southern Ocean with albatrosses which must seem to them something like giants.

Then the ringers asked if anyone would like to release the bird back into the dark. I stepped forward and it was placed in the cup of one of my hands. They showed me how to rest the other hand over its body, to fork two fingers around its neck so that its head could poke through the gentlest of restraints. I took it, nervous that I might flinch in fright if the bird moved, and drop it in its slightly subdued state. But it stayed perfectly still as I walked it back outside.

Its head was a little strange-looking, steeply domed. I would later learn that the part of their brain that is concerned with smell is enlarged. Storm petrels smell their way to food: bioluminescent plankton, insects that have been blown out to sea, by-the-wind sailors, fish guts, the corpses of whales. In the days of the *haaf* fishing, Shetland men would row open boats out into the deep sea, where they would stay for two or three days to catch fish using long, hand-hauled lines. At night, they would clean the fish and tip the guts overboard. Storm petrels would gather and feed, pattering their feet on the water. In *Fauna Orcadensis*, published in 1813, George Low notes: 'Our fishermen often fall in with the stormfinch at sea, but they do not like them, for they are sure of a gust of wind immediately to follow as often as they approach the land.' Some thought them to be the souls of drowned sailors 'seeking the prayers of the living, or they are devil-birds, flitting over the corpses of the lost'. They have been called many names: Witch, Water-Witch, Bird of the Devil.

Standing in the dark on the shore of Fair Isle with a storm petrel in my hand, I did feel a little bewitched. It was so light, almost too light for the nerves in the skin of my palm to register its presence. I felt the bird's touch more in my heart than on the surface of my skin. It roused a little, shivered and took flight, leaving my hand scented with a pleasantly sweet and musty smell. When I returned to my ordinary life, I would think of this storm petrel often. It formed a memory that remained vivid, however busy and difficult life became. The thought of being close to a storm petrel was often strong enough to draw me out from a melancholy state.

In 2017, I win an award for a piece of writing. I still have not found regular employment but I have begun to find sporadic work as a freelance writer. I started to write when my daughter was still a baby. I saw an advert in a wildlife magazine calling for people to write an online nature diary, and my application was successful. My writing was tentative to begin with, but when I start to write longer pieces and they are published, my confidence grows. The process of researching and drafting is absorbing enough to distract me from low-level pain. I begin to regain a sense of self that I lost in unemployment.

I decide to use the award money to spread my wings a little further than the islands of Shetland. There is only one place that I wish to visit: the island of Nólsoy in the Faroe Islands, home to the largest storm petrel colony in the world.

The woman sat next to me on the Atlantic Airways plane is chatty with nerves and confides in me that she is a little anxious. It is her first trip since completing a course of chemotherapy. Her skin is pallid and she looks as if she has been through the mill. She tells me that cancer has made her lose her confidence and that she is travelling in an attempt to regain it. I question if I am doing something of the same, though I keep this thought to myself. I have been through much but I have not had to face my own mortality.

Developing a chronic illness means developing an instinct for when to speak about it and when to remain silent – if you have this choice, meaning if it is not visible or if you are not in a situation which forces disclosure. I do have the choice but mostly I remain silent. Experience has taught me that few people make the effort to understand. More often than not, I make excuses for not attending social gatherings that are held in the evening. It is easier to explain that you cannot get a babysitter than to describe how attending the gathering would mean two days of incapacitating fatigue. Friendships with people who also have unreliable bodies are invaluable; there is rarely ever a need to explain.

I ask the woman next to me on the plane where in the Faroe Islands she will visit. She does not know exactly because she is joining a tour group and a guide is taking care of all the details. I envy her a little. This trip to the Faroe Islands is my first solo journey of any length or distance since having children and encountering two types of arthritis. In the weeks before the trip, I was due to receive injections of steroids to relieve the pain in the joints between my spine and pelvis, but the appointment was cancelled at short notice. I had banked on having these steroids. Now I will not be able to walk very far. I worry that I have wasted this gift of money. I am stressed by the thought of being in pain and away from home. I coped well without the support of my husband on my trip to beachcomb at Woodwick in April, but it would have been easy to return home if I had needed to.

But as soon as I arrive in the island of Nólsoy, I know that everything will be okay. The guesthouse is warm and inviting, its walls decorated with the artwork of Tove Jansson, and my hosts are a Swedish-speaking Finn and a German. Their young son switches with ease between languages. He has the smiling eyes of his mother. His father's eyes are sleepy from working night shifts in Tórshavn. A dog wags its tail in welcome and the boy's maternal grandmother, who is visiting, ushers it outside for a walk. The other guests are two young Canadian women on their honeymoon. Over a cup of tea, I listen with wide eyes as one of them tells me, matter-of-factly, about the time she was stalked by a grizzly bear.

As much as I am enjoying the warm company, a beach is calling to me – a small slither of sand that I spied down at the harbour. I leave the guesthouse dressed in a jacket and hat. The northerly wind is cold and the sky is clouded, but strolling through the settlement is cheering. Many of the houses are painted in bright colours – blues, reds, greens and yellows – and some have turf roofs covered in grass and buttercups. I walk through a whale-bone arch and along the road, past the wooden boat sheds that rim a low and rocky shore.

Beyond the harbour walls, the swell is heavy and white-capped. The ferry journey from Tórshavn was uncomfortable but only took twenty minutes. No one else sat outside in the cold wind on the open deck. A smoker appeared briefly but disappeared back into the passenger saloon as soon as his cigarette was spent. Inside the harbour walls, a great northern diver sits alert and wary on the calm water. Eider ducks sleep, heads tucked under wings, on the rocks below the boat sheds, and lesser black-backed gulls peer down from street lamps near a jetty where neat rows of small wooden boats are moored.

There is the familiar smell of the sea, the clutter of boats, and the birds of home. For a brief moment I miss home, but mostly I am elated to have made it to this island. It is unlike any other that I have visited. The harbour is cupped within the curve of a narrow isthmus. On the other side of the isthmus, to the east, a sweep of low cliffs bears the brunt of the ocean's force. Every now and then, a muffled boom signals a wave exploding in the confines of a sea cave. Some of the houses sit close to the cliff edge. In an easterly storm, they must be drenched in salt spray. I'm not sure that I would like to live in an island like Nólsoy, where you are so kept from the sea by cliffs.

A grey wall near the harbour is brightened by a children's mural of storm petrel burrows. Chicks emerge from white eggshells, watched over by proud-looking parent birds. To the south, beyond the narrow pinch of the isthmus, there is a stone wall that reaches from one side of the island to the other, east to west. The wall divides the island into the *hagi* in the south, the hill ground where the coarse-woolled sheep graze in the summer months, and the *bøur* in the north, the infield where hay – winter fodder for the sheep – is grown.

The *bøur* is inviting, with all its lush meadows, but the *hagi* is wild-looking, the dour green of a sheep-nibbled short sward on boggy ground. The upper slopes of a mountain called Høgoyggj are broken by a landform called *hamar*, vertical rock walls formed from the exposed edges of lava fields. The slopes below the *hamar* are covered in scree and boulder fields, and this mess of loose rock is where the storm petrels nest, perhaps as many as 100,000. The sight of the mountain makes me wish to see the land writhe in the dark with the fluttering wings of many thousands of storm petrels – but, in the absence of steroids, I will be kept to the low ground.

I turn my back to the mountain and my attention to the tiny slither of sand that forms the harbour's beach. It is less than ten strides in length and one stride in width, though

I'm not sure whether the tide is ebbing or flooding. Later, I find that there is no beach at high tide and that this is the only place to beachcomb near the settlement. I gather up the gaping orange plastic shell of a Kinder Egg and fill it with fragments of yellow, green and orange sea glass, and by the time it is full I am a little more at peace.

On the northern edge of the settlement, a gentle track leads over higher ground through the hay meadows of the *bøur* and past neat rigs of potatoes. The meadows are brimful with buttercups, ragged robin and yellow rattle. A cluster of moonwort, a tiny fern, grows near an outcrop of basalt. The rock is beautiful, almost jet black and pockmarked with vesicles filled with bright white crystals. The fern is on the cusp of unfurling. I wish that it would open and tell me its secrets.

The peace is broken by the sound of a man on a quad bike driving along a lower track that follows the curve of the shore. A whimbrel takes flight, rises steeply into the air and trails its faltering alarm call from its long and delicate bill. Perhaps its young are hiding in the tall grass. It glides down to land on a low rock at the highest point of the hill, where it stands and stares at the intruder, its neck fully outstretched.

He parks the quad bike on a verge, switches off the engine and climbs stiffly over a wooden fence into a green meadow, where a colony of Arctic terns nest in a pink swathe of ragged robin. The terns lift from their nests and gather screeching at his head. They become a swirling cloud of white that takes on a maleficent form. His black cap is soon streaked with the white of their shit, but he seems unperturbed and never lets his gaze leave the ground as he walks slowly through the long grass. Every now and then he bends down and plucks an egg from a nest. I cannot tell if the egg is intact or just a shell, or an unhatched leftover from a nest of chicks. He examines each egg for a brief moment before slipping it into his pocket. When he leaves the field, the terns soon settle back on their nests as if nothing has happened. I wish I could ask him what it was, specifically, that he was seeking – the perfect form of beauty, perhaps.

At last, I find a place where the grass has been grazed short and I can reach the cliffs without trampling precious hay. It is only a short walk down a gentle slope but first I must negotiate the fence, and I find myself less nimble than the aged egg thief. A ram with huge, curled horns stares at me from within the field. He wears a bright pink creel marker buoy around his neck that stops him from jumping the fence in search of ewes.

I sit some distance from the cliff edge, content to have reached an open view of the Atlantic Ocean. It glowers in the absence of sun, and its moodiness suits the haunting look of the cliffs. Two thick layers of black basalt drop almost vertically into the sea. The rock is smooth and bulges a little. Between the layers of basalt, there is a generous ledge where fulmars sit on nests in a lush growth of grass and roseroot. Below the ledge, the cliff face has been hollowed out by the sea in places and gapes in oval-mouthed caves. A shag in splendid oily greenish-black plumage perches in the entrance of one, the cloak of its wings outstretched as if barring the way to a gold-filled lair.

Arctic terns stream out over the cliffs to go fishing, passing others that are returning to the colony, most with empty beaks. A hooded crow flies above the fulmars' ledge on splayed wings looking for an unguarded egg to steal. In Faroese their name is *kráka*, and *krákumáni*, which means 'a very short time' or 'a crow's time' because these clever birds are never in any one place for very long. The crow's search is unsuccessful and it flies away to try a different stretch of cliff.

Three puffins, their wings short and whirring, fly in from the sea but do not land. They loop past the cliff ledge as if checking that it is safe to return to their burrows before committing to land on their second pass. Each disappears into the long grass that must also hide the entrances to their underground nests. I wait for more to arrive but none do. Ten thousand or so puffins are now thought to nest in Nólsoy. This sounds like an abundance but an estimated 35,000 to 50,000 puffins whirred around Nólsoy's cliffs in the late 1990s.

Until recently, puffins formed a part of the Faroese diet – they were eaten fresh in the summer and salted and dried for the winter months – but they are no longer hunted in Nólsoy because there are now too few to make the effort of their capture worthwhile. A bird once so important in keeping human hunger at bay in these islands is now unable to feed its chicks. The sandeels on which they depend are being displaced by a warming ocean.

Fulmars have a broader diet and have benefited from the fishing industry's waste – the discarding of unwanted fish species overboard. Their chicks are still plentiful and, in the late summer, men take to boats and use nets on long poles to scoop up the young fulmars drifting on the surface of the ocean while they are still too heavy to fly. When I return to Tórshavn I will see some, oven-ready and laid out like plucked chickens on the slabs of the harbour-side open market, next to dark hunks of pilot-whale meat.

It is too cold to wait for any more puffins. I crawl forward, on my belly, to drop a message in a small glass bottle over the edge of the cliff. Not long before I left for the Faroe Islands, I bought a second-hand book, *The Shell Book of Beachcombing*, written by the naturalist Tony Soper. It was published in 1972, two years before I was born and during the heyday of North Sea oil and gas exploration. The cover is decorated with the energy company's unmistakable scallop-shell logo. It is strange to read this book from within the climate emergency. Still, it is beautifully written and rich with details of beachcombing fieldcraft. The section on bottle post piqued my interest and I have brought a bottle with me to the Faroe Islands. The message inside is perfunctory, but I indulge in a fantasy of the north wind blowing my bottle back to Shetland. It falls to the sea and does not shatter.

In the evening, I sit at the kitchen table clasping a mug of hot tea and talk with my Finnish hostess. Her long fair hair is loosely pinned up and a shawl is wrapped around her shoulders. Her husband has left for the night shift and their young son is tucked up in bed. She looks tired and happy. Outside, the rain lashes down and the street lights sway in the wind. The heating is on and I am glad of its warmth. We compare our experiences of the severe storm that struck both archipelagos on Christmas Day the winter before. Gusts of eighty miles per hour shook our house in Shetland. The wind was even more violent in the Faroe Islands.

I ask about giving birth. Do pregnant people leave their home islands to stay near the large hospital in Tórshavn in the weeks before they are due? They do, she replies, but there are also two small maternity units elsewhere in the archipelago. It must be a difficult choice, to risk giving birth in a small maternity unit which is not equipped to deal with an emergency, or to leave older children and partners behind and spend the last weeks of pregnancy alone in Tórshavn. I am not sure what I would have done, if faced with this choice.

Neither of my children came into the world easily. My son's birth was stimulated by synthetic hormones delivered overnight into my bloodstream through a vein in my wrist. This drip and the two sets of heart rate monitors tethered me tightly to the bed. Each time the midwife increased the dose of Syntocinon, the pain would ratchet up. When my son's heartbeat faltered, I was whisked into an operating theatre where he was delivered by forceps after an episiotomy. I had flashbacks for months afterwards.

The birth of my second child, my daughter, was induced in the small hospital in Lerwick. When this process stalled, the doctor and midwife decided that I would be flown south to Aberdeen in the air ambulance. The ambulance plane was already on its way, summoned for a baby who was arriving prematurely in a room along the corridor. A neonatal team were flying north in the plane to stabilise the baby. Then these doctors would accompany the baby south to Aberdeen in the air ambulance, to a neonatal specialist-care ward.

When this happens, the mother is often left behind in Shetland and has to fly south, once recovered enough, on a commercial flight – a separation that can increase the trauma of experiencing a premature birth. There are other heart-breaking separations. Certain complications in pregnancy can sometimes mean that pregnant people from Shetland must stay in Aberdeen before the birth, and this can mean being separated from their families and their older children for many months. Giving birth in an island setting is already complicated enough. The climate emergency will make it more stressful still. If flights are more frequently disrupted, fewer lives will be saved.

On the day of my daughter's birth, I waited in a maternity room on my own while my husband and son drove to the airport to catch a commercial flight to Aberdeen. The two midwives on duty were fully occupied by the emergency in the room up the corridor. The neonatal team arrived but it would take them several hours to stabilise the baby before the journey south.

While my husband and son sat in the departure lounge at Sumburgh Airport, my labour started, suddenly and intensely. I pressed a button and summoned the midwife. She instructed me to call my husband, to stop him from boarding the plane. I managed to dial the number before a contraction came and I could not speak, but my husband heard the midwife bellow, 'Get your man off the plane!' He explained the situation to an airport official, who hastily arranged for his bag to be removed from the plane's hold. Our son, then a toddler, had a meltdown on the airport floor when he learnt that he would not, after all, be going on a plane. My husband made it back to the hospital in time to help me with the birth.

My relief at not having to fly to Aberdeen was marred by the knowledge that pain management in birth in Shetland is limited to Entonox and morphine. I took both. Some weeks later, cradling my baby daughter in my arms, I remarked to a friend that Shetland women are tough. Quick as a flash, she replied, yes, we are, but not through choice.

I ask my Finnish hostess if she has ever heard of drift-seeds being used as birth charms in the Faroe Islands, but she shakes her head to mean no. In Icelandic, the name for drift-seeds is *lausnarsteinn*, and one of the many Norwegian names is *løsningsstein*. Both mean 'loosening stone', as drift-seeds were once thought to loosen the baby from the body of its mother.

In Norway, a labouring woman would sometimes hold a drift-seed in her hand, or it would be rubbed on her stomach or tied to her thigh or, more simply, placed in the bed alongside her. Sometimes drift-seeds were boiled in water, and the woman would then drink this water. In some instances, women drank beer, wine or spirits using the hollowed-out drift-seed as a cup.

It may even have been a drift-seed that hung from the *Brísingamen*, the necklace or girdle worn by Freyja, the Norse goddess of fertility. Women in the Norse realm would have called upon Freyja for help during childbirth. In the Western Isles, a Gaelic name for drift-seeds is *tearna Moire*, which has been translated as 'the saving of Mary' or 'the Virgin's charm of deliverance'. Some of the drift-seed birth charms used in the Western Isles were even consecrated by a bishop or a priest. A labouring woman would hold the drift-seed in her hand and the midwife would circle her in a sunwise direction, incanting a prayer of deliverance. And so the old ways mixed with those of the church, and labouring women felt hope in the face of possible death.

Perhaps I would have found comfort in having a sea bean to hold when I laboured during the births of both of my children, but I'm not so sure. If I could have wished for anything, it would have been the option of more effective pain relief.

The next day, I walk through the village to the house where the taxidermist and naturalist Jens-Kjeld Jensen lives. I've come to ask if he will be ringing storm petrels during the time that I am staying in Nólsoy, and if so, how far up the mountain slope the ringing takes place.

He welcomes me warmly into his house and explains that he will be with me shortly, once he has finished his lunch. I wait in his wonderfully strange workshop. The room smells strongly of the flesh of seabirds. Many fulmars hang from the ceiling, fixed in a perpetual glide. An all-grey bird, a 'blue' fulmar from the Arctic, is noticeable among the flock of white-bodied and grey-winged birds. Puffins line the shelves, sitting in loose groups as they might on a cliff top. A single Faroese wren perches pertly on a rock. The Shetland wren and the Faroese wren, both North Atlantic island subspecies like the Fair Isle wren, once shared a name: *sistie moose* and *músabróðir*, 'brother to the mouse'. I have heard a wren singing in a Nólsoy street, but have yet to see one.

Jens-Kjeld returns to the workshop and we talk about seabirds, the steep decline of puffin numbers and kittiwakes in both archipelagos, and the ingestion of plastics by fulmars. He is tall and slim, with unruly white hair and round metal-framed glasses. A Dane by birth, he moved to the Faroes many years ago. We compare beachcombing notes. He does not recall finding any skate eggcases (mermaid's purses) in Nólsoy, but when I ask him if he has ever found a sea bean he smiles and pulls one from the pocket of his jeans, where he keeps it as a protective charm of sorts. He explains that sea beans are stowed in some of the small wooden boats in Nólsoy's harbour. There is a Faroese saying which Jens-Kjeld has translated as: 'Luck follows the Sea Pearls, they bring wisdom to the finder; a man, carrying a Sea Pearl, will not drown in the sea.' Fewer sea beans are found these days, he observes, perhaps because of habitat loss in the places where they grow. A sharp pang of envy surges through me as he slips his rare and lucky sea pearl back into his pocket.

Jens-Kjeld won't be ringing storm petrels this week, but when I ask him where exactly the storm petrels nest on the mountain, he points to the site of the colony on a map on the wall. It is much closer than I had assumed; I will be able to walk to it. I nearly cry with happiness but manage to hold it together while I listen to his instructions. He advises me to wait until at least 11.30 p.m. and instructs me to stay on the outskirts of the boulder field to avoid disturbing the colony as much as possible.

When I leave the guesthouse at 11 p.m. it is still dusk. I walk out of the village, past the small slither of the harbour beach and through the gate in the wall that leads to the *hagi*. It is a thrill to walk in the twilight. It seems safe enough, as a woman, to walk alone here. The ground is familiarly boggy and cushions each step. To the east, large waves crash into the island's cliffs. To the west, over the sound that separates Nólsoy from Streymoy, the lights of Tórshavn burn brightly. Høgoyggj looms ominously and boulders take on the shapes of the *Huldufólk*, the Faroese relation of the Shetlandic *trow* or troll; but, more worryingly, I can see the dark forms of skuas and great black-backed gulls still patrolling the mountain's steep slopes. The sky is unclouded and too bright. The storm petrels might not come in. In the twilight, I don't notice the whimbrel until I am almost upon it and it bursts into flight, shrieking loudly. I walk on more carefully and it takes a while for my nerves to settle.

On the outskirts of the colony, at the edge of a vast slope of scree, I hide from the north wind in the lee of a large boulder and pull my hood over my hat. I wish to tell my husband that I have made it after all, to the colony, but he will be fast asleep by now.

The sky darkens by increments but it is still too light for storm petrels to risk returning from the sea to their rock-crevice nests. A mountain hare, dark with summer, ambles over the scree and pokes its nose into the crevices as if sniffing out a mate. Thanks to Jens-Kjeld, measures have been taken in Nólsoy to protect the storm petrels from the predations of rats and cats. Elsewhere in the North Atlantic, some islands have lost their storm petrel colonies to these creatures. Nólsoy islanders must neuter their cats and can keep only one per household. At first, this cat edict caused a 'mini civil war' in the island, but now the rule is wholly respected. Any cats found in the vicinity of the colony are shot. The bin lorry that comes on the ferry from Tórshavn is carefully checked for rat stowaways.

The sounds of an open-air pop concert drift across from Tórshavn. A small wooden boat motors unlit over to Nólsoy. It seems dangerous that they don't make their presence known with lights and I wonder why they would risk not being seen by a larger vessel. But maybe a sea bean is stowed on board and the person at the helm is emboldened by a sense of invincibility.

The Faroese word for storm petrel, *drunnhvíti*, means 'white rump'. The Shetland name is *alamootie*. In Old Norse, a *motti* is a moth, mite or tiny insect. *Mootie*, as it is used in Shetland now, is a term of endearment for small things, like a lamb or a child. The Faroese linguist Jakob Jakobsen suggested that *ala* might be a derivation of a Danish or Swedish word, *adel*, for urine or liquid manure. Storm petrels can eject a yellow oily liquid, through their mouth, in defence. In Foula, storm petrels have sometimes been called *oily mooties*.

It is this oily, lipid-rich liquid that adult storm petrels feed to their young. And it was the young storm petrels that once lit up the dark winter nights in these northern archipelagos. In his book *The Atlantic Islands*, Kenneth Williamson wrote of how, up until the mid-seventeenth century, the people in Mykines – the westernmost island in the Faroese archipelago – would take and kill many of the fat and oily young of storm petrels and use them as candles. The birds would be plucked, decapitated and dried, and a wick would be threaded through their bodies. People would gather for an evening of storytelling, and it is said that the session would last as long as it took for the storm petrel to burn.

The concert is still in full flow long after midnight. The cloud cover increases. A movement at the edge of my vision, a blur of whirring wings flying here and there around the boulders, a flicker of flight so quick in the midsummer twilight that the bird seems to appear and disappear in almost the same instant.

A storm petrel!

I watch the bird weaving, low, through the boulders. I wait longer and more appear but my eyes struggle to keep hold of them and they tease me, 'Now you see me, now you don't.' Strangely, I hear no storm petrel calling from the boulder field. Perhaps the light levels are still too high. They nest later in the summer in the Faroes than they do in Shetland, to give their young more chance to fledge in darkness. A Faroese storm petrel emerges from its nest in October or November, straight into winter. If it is lucky enough to fledge when the north wind blows, its migration south will gain a good start.

I stay for an hour or so more and then head back to the village happy-hearted, leaving the storm petrels to flutter furiously through the boulder field in the near-dark.

A year later, I am under the care of a compassionate and professional rheumatologist and have been taking a tailored dose of an immunosuppressant. Three months in and the drugs are working, and most days I'm coping okay with their side effects. I see notice of a late-night storm petrel ringing session at Sumburgh Head, and book my place without my usual hesitation.

The event is being hosted by the Shetland Nature Festival, and starts in the lighthouse café with a talk by the seabird ecologist Will Miles, who coordinates the monitoring of Shetland's seabirds now that Martin Heubeck has retired. Will studied the Leach's petrels of St Kilda for his doctorate and is a self-confessed 'petrel head'. Every seat is taken. I am next to a petite white-haired woman who is on holiday and lives in London. She sits bolt upright and is so excited that she barely stops grinning. I share her excitement – it seems that everyone in the room does, because Will's love for petrels is immediately infectious. He is in his thirties, tall and neatly bearded. Quietly spoken, he smiles the whole way through his talk, his eyes alight with enthusiasm. We all sit rapt as he brings the oceanic world of these birds to life.

Will shows us a photograph of a petrel flying along a deep trough between the crests of towering waves. In storms, or the heavy swells following storms, these small petrels can still find passage through mountainous seas. The photograph makes me think of shelter differently, of what it can mean and how it can be found in unexpected places – in the memory of the touch of the storm petrel I briefly held in Fair Isle, for example. The way this memory kept something alight in me, helped me to pay attention to birds at a time in my life when I was struggling to stay afloat.

But storm petrels are not, Will explains, invulnerable to being blown off course. He describes the research of Mark Bolton, who works for the Royal Society for the Protection of Birds. Mark is investigating the flight paths of the storm petrels that nest in the small Shetland island of Mousa. In summer, when dusk falls, a boat takes people out to Mousa to see the hundreds of petrels that swirl in a dark vortex around the huge round tower of an Iron Age broch. Single birds break away from the circling flock to dissolve, ghost-like, into nests hidden in the structure's drystone walls.

Mark has attached tiny GPS tags to some of the Mousa storm petrels, to understand where they forage. If this area can be identified then measures can be taken to secure its protection. Off the coastline of Newfoundland, Leach's storm petrels are known to crash-land on oil and gas instal-lations on moonless and foggy nights. Some are even incinerated in the flames of the gas flares. The GPS data from the Mousa storm petrels indicates that they fly to an area south-east of Shetland and that there is some overlap with the location of oil and gas wells and platforms.

The reasons why they forage where they do remain a mystery, but in one instance the GPS data revealed that a single storm-caught storm petrel was blown all the way to Stavanger in Norway. It waited the weather out in the shel-ter of a fjord before returning to its nest in Mousa. When I listen to Will talk, I think of two young Shetland women who were blown across the North Sea to Norway in the mid-1700s. Both survived but they never returned.

The two women were servants of the laird of Uyea, a small island off the coast of Unst, and were rowing back from milking the cows of Haaf Gruney when a storm blew in from the north-west. They had no choice but to let the boat run before the gale. It is said that when they arrived at the coast of Norway eight days later, the locals feared they might have otherworldly powers. One of the two young women stood and made the sign of the cross, and only then were they allowed ashore. The women settled, it is thought, in the island of Karmøy, where they married local men. They asked a Dutch sailor to carry a letter home to Shetland, informing their families that they had survived.

When the talk finishes, we drink tea, eat cakes and then gather outside, under the tower of the lighthouse. It is nearing midnight and it is already a thrill to stand on this precipitous headland, high above the dark surface of the ocean. The beam of the lighthouse sweeps a wide arc over our heads, three white flashes every thirty seconds. Away in the distance, the North Light of Fair Isle blinks back as if in polite response, two white flashes every thirty seconds.

Hidden by the dark and unseen by us, thousands of storm petrels are flying out over the surface of the sea to forage, passing those that are returning to land to relieve their nest-bound mates. The mist nets are set and storm petrels are already being lured in by a recording of their call. A pair of ornithologists ring the birds in the back of a specially adapted van. In front of me, in the queue to hold and release a storm petrel, two teenagers – both dressed in black with hoods pulled over their heads – discuss the most recent *Star Wars* film. The queue moves forward and I watch the ringers work deftly and with great care.

The teenagers fall silent when they reach the van. They both handle the storm petrels with assurance, as if this is something they do every day. At the release point, a low wall, they stand in silence, heads bowed as they focus only on the birds in their hands. Slowly, they remove their fingers from around the petrels' necks. The birds sit for a while and then one shivers and takes flight, followed by the other, and they

swerve and flicker away, the dark of their plumage meld-
ing into the night, the white on their rumps marking them
for a moment longer. After a brief moment, the teenagers
reanimate from their deep stillness. They resume their conversation and return to the back of the queue.

When it is my turn, the petrel that I am due to hold is
pulled from the cloth bag with a ring already on its leg,
stamped with a Faroese code. It is possible that this bird
was ringed in Nólsoy by Jens-Kjeld. I peel away from the
queue and walk to the wall. The bird bites my finger, not
hard enough to draw blood, and I keep my hold steady and
do not flinch. I lift my fingers from its back. Two sweeps
of the lighthouse beam pass before the bird rouses and disappears into flight, presses on into the dark, finds its way
back to the waves.

Message in a Bottle

The message in a bottle that I dropped into the sea from a Nólsoy cliff was the first of many. I keep my notes short and to the point, not believing that they will be found. It started as a bit of fun, but now I cast sea post adrift as a deliberate counter to the fast pace of digital communication. I don't wish to part completely with instant messaging and the connections that the Internet allows, but I do want to lessen their hold on me. I like the uncertainty of not knowing how far each bottle will travel and where it will end up, or whether it will be found at all.

On a sunny summer's day in 2019, I leave my family at home and catch a small car ferry to the Out Skerries, a tight cluster of tiny islands that lie in the North Sea to the east of the Shetland Mainland. The forecast for the coming days looks favourable for sending sea post. There is a chance that the south-west wind will blow for long enough to carry my bottles across the North Sea to Norway. But the wind is yet to rise, there is no swell, and the fulmars sit on the surface of the sea looking bored. I stand on the car deck in the sun, next to a pile of supplies topped by a punnet of brown hens' eggs.

As we sail closer, the Out Skerries appear to rise out from the sea. The white tower of the Stevenson lighthouse on

Bound Skerry gleams in the sun. Chimneys stretch upwards like arms waving to confirm the presence of people, and I feel like waving back. I have fallen for this place deeply. It is where my thoughts turn to when I wish to remove myself from the routine of daily life.

Viewed from the Mainland, or approaching by boat, the Out Skerries look rocky and inhospitable, but only because they hide their secrets well. When the ferry slips through an inlet and into the interior of this small huddle of islands, the gentlest of scenes unfolds: a harbour with calm water, moored boats, and a fertile green shore strung with white-washed houses. Only Bruray and Housay (or West Isle, as it is more often known) are now inhabited. The lighthouse keepers' cottages of Grunay are abandoned and falling into ruin.

Together, the islands of the Out Skerries cover little more than two square miles. I've heard it said that there is only one place in the Out Skerries, a hollow of some kind, where the sea cannot be seen. I have not found this hollow but I have never felt so at ease at being this surrounded by the sea. Though it is true that I have never spent time in the Out Skerries during a storm.

I think that I feel so at ease here because the scale of the Out Skerries suits the capabilities of my body. It is a short walk from the harbour to the highest point on Bruray. I can stand by the hilltop cairn and spin the view 360 degrees – like a sailor in a crow's nest, high up on a ship's mast. I can walk the circumference of Bruray and believe that I have walked far, though the distance I have travelled is small. If my body is too sore for this, I can drive across the bridge to Housay for a change of scene. But on this visit, I am feeling carefree. A long course of immunosuppressants has worked well enough for me to stop taking the drugs. I am clear of their side effects and can walk quite freely if I don't walk too far.

The *Filla*, the usual Out Skerries ferry, has been replaced on this weekend by a larger ferry called the *Hevda*. It is the day after the Out Skerries *eela*, an inshore fishing competition. Thirty or so people now live in the Out Skerries, but many people connected to these small islands return for the *eela* and its celebrations. On the afternoon ferry sailing back to the Mainland, the deck will be packed with cars, and once the ferry pulls away from the Bruray pier, the Out Skerries will seem just a little too quiet again.

Only one other vehicle sits alongside mine on the car deck. Its occupants are a teacher and her husband, a Church of Scotland minister, and they join me when I point towards the glinting dorsal fin of a minke whale. They both wear short-sleeved shirts and have matching ichthys tattoos, the fish symbol of their Christian faith, on the freckled skin of their arms. They explain that it is Sea Sunday, the annual service in honour of seafarers. We stand in the warm sun and watch for the minke whale to surface again. A fishing boat, one of three whitefish trawlers registered in the Out Skerries, sails away from the islands. In the distance, an oil and gas vessel moves out towards the platforms hidden beyond the eastern horizon. Puffins line the grassy cliff top of the tiny island of North Benelip, their heads turning back and forth as the ferry passes. And below the cliffs, guillemots and their newly fledged young sit on the calm surface of the sea.

The *Hevda* pulls into the pier at Bruray and I follow the

only road that leads, by way of a narrow bridge, to Housay, where Alice Arthur lives. I'm looking forward to a big bear hug with Alice. She radiates an energy that is infectious, and I always feel more capable in her company. I'm a little bit in awe of her too. She was an art teacher at the school here and worked in the local fish factory. She was also the Out Skerries' most senior firefighter and chair of the local development trust. In the hallway of Alice's house there is a photograph of her dressed in her firefighter's uniform, stood in Buckingham Palace, an MBE medal freshly pinned to her jacket.

I yell a hello before I enter Alice's house and find it filled with four generations of her family. Her children and grand-children have returned for the *eela* and her husband, Gibbie, is home from the Mainland where he works during the week. The children swirl around the house between groups of grown-ups catching up on news. Her mother, Anna, who lives nearby, calls in on her way to the service in the kirk and invites me to visit later in the afternoon. Anna's late hus-band, Donnie, was a fanatical beachcomber and a sender of sea post. She promises to show me the way to Vogans Point, where Donnie set his bottles adrift.

I never met Donnie. I wish that I had. Alice describes her late father as 'king of the beach', and I would like to have asked him what it was, exactly, that he searched for in the strandlines of the Out Skerries, and what he wrote in all those messages. Before I leave, Alice shows me a silver coin that he once pulled from a narrow cleft in a rock in a Mioness geo, treasure from a centuries-old wreck.

*

When I reach Anna's house, I find her resting in a high-backed chair in her sunroom. At first I think she is asleep and I hesitate to go in, but she sees me and calls for me to enter. She looks comfortable in her chair. The room is warm and she wears a light cardigan over her shoulders. The waves of her thick white hair are neatly combed. She has the same brown and twinkling eyes as Alice.

We both sit in easy silence for a while and scan the wide view. The afternoon ferry is pulling away from the pier, fully loaded with cars, and the VHF radio on Anna's wall begins to crackle. The voice of the ferry's skipper is loud and clear as he reports the number of people on board. The Coastguard confirms that the skipper's message has been received. Anna nods as if to say, good, all is well. A pair of large binoculars sits on the table. I pick them up and scan the sea. A man rows a small wooden boat across the tranquil surface of Böd Voe, and a cruise ship, white and towering, sails past in a north-easterly direction, perhaps leaving Shetland for Norway. Out beyond Stoura Stack, a Skerries trawler rolls with a gentle swell.

In December 1664, a Dutch East India Company ship named the *Kennemerland* wrecked on Stoura Stack after being driven ashore in a southerly gale. She had left the Wadden Sea island of Texel a week before and was taking supplies to a Dutch colony in Indonesia. The weather that night was wild, and the four crew members on lookout duty at the top of the foremast did not see the waves breaking on rocks until it was too late. Three of the lookout men were flung ashore when the ship keeled over. They survived but two hundred perished. The ship's drummer boy was buried near the shore but there are no other known graves from this wrecking. In her book on the Out Skerries, Joan Dey explains that it would have been difficult to bury so many bodies in a place where soil lies so thinly over rock, and so those that washed ashore 'may have been more summarily dealt with'.

The *Kennemerland* had taken a northern route, through the North Sea, to avoid sailing through the English Channel. Navigating such a heavily laden ship through the Channel's narrow confines would have been challenging in the prevailing winds of winter, and war was about to be declared between the British and the Dutch; the English Channel had become a doubly hostile place. A further two Dutch East India Company ships are known to have wrecked on the rocks of the Out Skerries on their outgoing voyages. The identity of one is uncertain but the other, *De Liefde* ('The Love), wrecked on Mioness in November 1711, four days after her departure from Texel. More than three hundred people were on board and only one survived. It is said that this sole survivor had to stay with the islanders for a year before finding a passage home.

I sometimes catch myself hoping to find a piece of gold or silver when I beachcomb in the Skerries, but I fear that the sea might reward my greed with a piece of human bone. The silver coin that Donnie found wedged in a fissure of rock in a Mioness geo may have been lost from *De Liefde*. She was built in 1698 – the third ship of the Dutch East India Company to carry this name. She does not seem to be listed in the Slave Voyages database but there are several entries for her namesakes.

Anna is pleased to see the gulls fussing over the Out

Skerries fishing boat as it hauls in its green trawl net. It is a sign that fish have been caught. In the time after the Second World War, her mother would sometimes send her to the height of the hill in Bruray to watch for the return of her father's fishing boat. Mines still floated in the sea and were much feared. As a child, she remembers her parents tending to the wet-clothed survivors of wrecked ships. Her earliest memory is of a Canadian reconnaissance plane crash-landing on the rocky ground of Grunay. Her father rowed out to look for survivors and found none.

Some mornings, before she left for school, Anna would sit with her siblings and bait fishing hooks with limpets or mackerel. She looked forward to Sundays. In fine weather, her family would row over to Grunay to take tea with the wives of the lighthouse keepers and Anna would play hide-and-seek with their children. To save the batteries of her torch at night, she would play grandmother's footsteps with the dark, only moving forward during the sweep of the lighthouse's beam.

Anna always travelled to the Shetland Mainland to give birth. She would leave the Skerries a few weeks before her due date and lodge somewhere in Lerwick. There was no ferry to the Out Skerries at that time, and so she would return on a fishing boat. She would sit outside the small wheelhouse, her and her newborn swaddled in oilskins. It was a worry, she explains, and pregnant Skerries women would always be preoccupied with the logistics of birth.

I ask Anna if she fears storms. She smiles and shakes her head to indicate no. She enjoys south-westerly gales, when the waves crash over Stoura Stack and race in through the

South Mouth and across Böd Voe. I imagine her company would be comforting in a storm; she is a person of quiet self-assurance. As we sit and talk, she casts her eye over the sea. The wind has picked up and ruffles the surface. She tells me that it is a good day to send sea post. The wind is from the south-west as forecast, and the bottles will be blown away from the shore and out towards Norway.

I ask Anna about Donnie. She laughs fondly as she recalls the depth of her late husband's beachcombing obsession. He would often rise at 5 a.m. to go to the beach before work. Evenings would be spent writing messages and inserting them into bottles. She is not sure what he wrote in the messages but she remembers that he used glass lemonade bottles at first – though, fearing that these would smash on rocks, he soon switched to plastic lemonade bottles instead. He would wrap the message in a clear plastic freezer bag and seal the lid of the bottle with tape. When a sustained south-westerly wind was forecast, he would carry his sack of sea post to Vogans Point and release his many bottles into the sea.

Donnie would then wait impatiently for a letter with a Norwegian stamp to arrive. In the back room of Anna's house there is a faded map of the coastline of Norway hanging on the wall. It is dotted with more than fifty tiny yellow, blue, green and gold stickers. Anna explains that some of the stickers have fallen off and that she cannot remember the significance of the different colours. Each pinpoints a place where one of Donnie's bottles was found. One marks a spot near the Nordkapp, the most northerly point in mainland Arctic Norway. It is possible that others sailed beyond the Nordkapp and into Russian coastal waters. Perhaps one of Donnie's bottles still waits to be found, somewhere on the shore of the White Sea.

Donnie and Anna travelled to Norway to meet some of the people who found his sea post, and warm friendships formed. They hosted their new Norwegian friends in the Out Skerries too. It was easier in those days, as a boat sailed regularly between Shetland and Norway. I wish that it still did. I dream of boarding a boat in Lerwick on a calm summer's day and staying on deck, or by a window, all the way to Norway. I would like to experience the North Sea where land cannot be seen, and to sail past the steel structures of the oilfields that my husband visits each day for his work. It would be strangely wonderful to leave the wind-scalped islands of Shetland behind and arrive in a place where trees clad islands and hillslopes and clutter the cities.

We head outside and Anna points out a route to Vogans Point. I have only three small glass bottles – two vinegar bottles and one whisky bottle – each containing a brief message with my name, address and a greeting. She eyes my three bottles and tells me to make more sea post when I get home, and to put a sack of them on the Out Skerries ferry. She will ask someone to cast them into the sea for me, when the wind is favourable. Before we part, she reminds me that the coast of Norway is a maze of innumerable rocky holms and skerries, places where a bottle could lie undetected on a shore for years – assuming it does not smash when the waves bring it ashore. I know that my chances would improve if I used plastic bottles but I cannot bring myself to throw these into the sea; the shores of Shetland are already strewn with them.

I leave Anna sat in her sunroom and set off along a path that leads past the Lambie Hoose – the Lamb's House – with its drystone walls and its roof made from an upturned wooden boat, once the lifeboat of a herring drifter. The drifter was sunk by a German submarine in 1915, but the crew were given time to launch the lifeboat and made it ashore. The sward is high; there are few sheep on the island now and the last cow was slaughtered in 1968. The grass is thick with the white of yarrow and the pink of ragged robin, and my steps flush out painted lady butterflies into the air. A single butterfly heads out to sea and I wait for it to return to land, but it continues on, in the direction of Norway.

Beyond Skeo Houll, there are traces of many rig systems – the divisions of arable land where bere barley, oats, hay and tatties would have been grown in long strips in a rotational system. Joan Dey notes that the cultivatable land would be divided equitably, and each household would be allocated parcels of good and parcels of poor land. Dey collected all the names of the different Out Skerries rigs before they passed from memory, and on her meticulous map they read like a found poem: Bagahoola, Raga Marks, Runkholla, Sneckrins, Kloonger and Daalawil.

Rabbits have burrowed into the site of an old midden, and limpet shells spill from the soil. Sting-tailed gannets and kink-necked shags fly overhead. I stop at Flinty Beach and search among the pebbles for the flint that gives the beach its name – ballast from a French boat returning from Russia. It wrecked on a rock near the Hevda Skerries in 1625, spilling a cargo of timber and tar. I find no flint and continue on, revelling in walking; the ground is uneven but my joints are loose and free from pain. The sun is warm and there is nowhere I would rather be.

The view from Vogans Point is vast. The sea is a deep blue and the dark rocks of the shore are bright with lichens the rich yellow-orange of egg yolk. To the east, there is only sea. To the west, the gas flare of the oil terminal at Sullom Voe burns in a hazy blue sky, and to the north, the white radar domes on top of Saxa Vord in Unst shine softly in the sun. By my feet, a spray of pink thrift grows through the spinal canal of a seal's vertebra.

I wonder where, exactly, Donnie would have cast his bottles adrift; perhaps from the beach a little further along the shore. But I stay on the low cliffs and choose a spot where the land falls abruptly away, and I throw one of the bottles into the sea. In my haste, I fail to spot that the water below the low cliff lies slack and sheltered from the wind. The bottle floats but does not move. It is trapped for now, but there is a chance that it will be carried away on the tide.

Further along, the wind frets the surface of the sea, and the second and third bottles arc high and reach beyond the lethal apron of rock that skirts the cliff. They land with a slosh and bob back to the surface intact. My littering does not go unnoticed. A grey seal emerges from the sea to nose the larger of the two bottles. She turns to look over her shoulder in my direction and my cheeks flush. When I sneeze, she slaps her way back under the surface. She appears again, a few metres further out, and noses the smaller of the two bottles. After one more glance in my direction, she swims away. I sit a while and watch both bottles drift through the narrow gap between the Hevda Skerries and out across the surface of the North Sea. A gannet flies in and dives very close to shore, or perhaps it is more that the land in the Out Skerries is very close to sea.

The next morning, I wake to find that a thick haar engulfs the Out Skerries. The walls of the whitewashed houses disappear, leaving dark slate roofs suspended in mid-air. On the high ground by the airstrip, a red warning light bleeds into the mist. The sea is missing and seems more dangerous. Anything could be passing the Out Skerries unseen. I begin to imagine wrecked ships rising from the depths, crewed by the ghosts of hundreds of drowned sailors. I would like to stay inside but have arranged to clean Trussi Geo with a magician called Crazy Chris.

My lovely neighbour Susan, who is from the island of Whalsay, uses the word *truss* when she is telling her grandchildren to put their crisp packets in the bin. *Trus* in Old Norse means 'rubbish' or 'mess'. Trussi Geo may mean the geo (the inland cleft in a cliff) that gathers in a mess of driftwood. Above the geo there is a short section of drystone wall – a possible *skjogg*, a crude type of shelter once used in Shetland for scanning the sea for incoming driftwood. The last time that I visited the Out Skerries, I was shocked at how much plastic litter had collected in this one small geo. When I mentioned to Alice that I would like to clean it, she told me that Chris would help me, and sure enough, he agreed.

By the time I reach the Old Schoolhouse, where Chris lives, the mist has lifted and a fine rain has begun to fall. The view returns and the sea seems innocuous enough. I wait in the garden near the shipping container that Chris has converted into a gym with a hot tub. He moved to the Out Skerries in 2016 and renovated the derelict schoolhouse, furnishing it with a small cinema and a candy floss machine to be used by Out Skerries residents and visitors alike.

Chris emerges from the Old Schoolhouse with a cheery greeting. He is tall and wears his long white hair in a neat ponytail over a closely shaved undercut. It is easy to imagine him as a modern-day wizard. Clutching black plastic bin bags, we leave the tarmac of the road and take a track towards Trussi Geo. I feel guilty dragging Chris out in the rain and suggest that we could wait for better weather, but he laughs at my lack of commitment and so off we go.

As well as being a magician of note, Chris is also employed by Scottish Water to monitor and maintain the Out Skerries water treatment plant. Fresh water is not plentiful in these small islands, and in the 1950s a small aqueduct was built into the side of the Bruray hill. Rainwater flows down the aqueduct into a reservoir that can store enough water to last the community for a month. Below the reservoir is the large water treatment plant, which hums and ticks with computer-controlled machinery. The pressure on the Out Skerries water supply is lower now than it was a few years ago, as the school has been mothballed and the community salmon farm and processing factory has closed down.

These two closures are connected. The Out Skerries farm produced salmon under contract for a Norwegian company. But the company decided not to renew this contract, and in 2015, with no other companies interested, the salmon farm was forced to close. The population of the Out Skerries suddenly fell from around seventy to thirty residents. Young families had to leave their newly built homes to find work elsewhere in Shetland, and now there are no children in the Out Skerries during the week, though families return at the weekends and during holidays. The departure of some of the trained firefighters meant that the flight service to and from the Shetland Mainland was withdrawn. In summer, the gravel of the airstrip now becomes overgrown with eyebright and gentian, and though this is beautiful it is an unwelcome rewilding. On the airstrip fence posts, someone has put up nest boxes for *linties* (twites). The island's ravens have learnt to hang by their claws from the nest-box hole and pull out the writhing chicks with their long beaks.

Before the loss of the salmon farm, the Shetland Islands Council closed the secondary department of the Out Skerries school, forcing older students to board in Lerwick against their parents' wishes. If the secondary department had stayed open, it is more probable that women and children would have remained in the Out Skerries after the salmon farm closed. Their partners would have sought work elsewhere in Shetland and returned home at the weekends. The Council could have based the Out Skerries ferry in the islands, and this would have replaced some of the lost jobs, but the ferry continues to be moored up each night at the pier in the neighbouring island of Whalsay. It is uncomfortable to see it swing in and then swing out of the Skerries harbour but never stay. It appears a little like a rebuke.

The Out Skerries islands are owned by an English man whose business interests include a weapons testing and storage facility. He has bought some of the salmon farm's assets, cages, feed barges and a processing shed. An article in the *Shetland Times* from 2018 reported that the Out Sker-ries inhabitants hoped that his investment in their islands might restore some of the lost jobs and enable young fam-ilies to return and the primary school to reopen. But on this visit, the salmon farm equipment lies rusting and the school remains mothballed. Perhaps his ownership may yet breathe life back into the islands. I hope so. It would be heartbreak-ing to see the place wither when there are young Skerries families who would live there again, if only they could.

Chris and I trudge over the low hill and down to the beach at South Mills, where we find a strandline of seaweed sticky with viscous oil. Spots of it speckle the pebbles like the first drops of heavy rain. A clear plastic bottle labelled in a Cyril-lic script lies covered in this sludge. I gather the bottle into a bag with an oil-covered pebble.

When I return home, I post the oil samples to Will Miles, the ecologist responsible for monitoring Shetland's sea-birds. Months later, he will call me with the results of the molecular analysis: it is crude oil from the East Shetland Basin but, strangely, it matches none of the samples from the investigator's database. Its exact source remains a mys-tery and, as such, no further investigation will take place. This rarely happens, as oil on the shore or on the feathers of seabirds can usually be attributed to shipping or to a specific oil well. The polluter then becomes responsible for cleaning the spill up. In time, the oil on this Out Skerries beach will be dispersed by the action of the waves. I think of the guillemots I saw from the ferry the day before and hope that none have been harmed.

From the beach we walk up a slope towards Trussi Geo, stepping over creeping willow and tiny frog orchids. I am excited to return. On my first visit to the geo, the year before, it seemed an otherworldly place. Someone had stacked the driftwood neatly and left their saw nearby. There was a sign saying 'Access Forbidden' in English, lost from a Norwegian oil and gas platform, as well as a tree trunk covered in fresh-looking fungi, moss and grass.

Scattered around the geo's floor, in among all the plastic, there were many starry skate eggcases. A white RNLI helmet bobbed along in the sea. I sat on the tongue of rock that cleaved the geo in half. Pale-pink moon jellies pulsed through the gloomy water, past tiny fish that hung motionless but moved with each wave.

But this summer, the sight of the geo is dismal and it is not even the rain's fault. Winter storms have formed the pebbles into a dam that traps a pool of water. The surface of the pool is entirely hidden under a thick layer of plastic: bottles, containers and shards. The interstices between these larger pieces of plastic are completely filled by a fine white layer of polystyrene spherules. The damp rock walls are white with these spherules too. The pool looks like a toddler ball pit, but one filled with rubbish.

The sight of the spherules defeats me, but Chris wades straight into the stagnant mess, cold water spilling over the tops of his wellies. I teeter at the edge of the pool and scoop rubbish into a bag. We find more bottles slicked in crude oil.

It is overwhelming. There must be several thousand individual pieces of plastic in a pool that is less than two metres wide. We gather more than sixty bottles. Just as I am scooping up the last of them, I see that one contains a message. It seems like a thank you of sorts.

The paper inside is wet but it has not been pulped. Back in the warmth of the cottage, it dries nicely and the message is decipherable even though some of the words are missing.

> My name . . . Ole A Andersen . . . I'm sending this from the Tugboat . . . Worker . . . North Sea . . . On our way to Norway . . . N 59° 34 51, E 001° 13 15 . . . Looking forward . . . from . . . Ole A Andersen Kråkerøy

I buy a stamp for Norway and slip my reply to Ole into a storm-proof postbox.

At first, I did not pay much attention to the mass of plastic bottles that litter Shetland's shores. But one day, my husband found a message in a bottle that had been cast adrift by a Norwegian called Terje Nordberg, an engineer in the oil industry. I now give every plastic bottle a cursory look, to see if there is a note inside.

Terje's bottle was sealed tight and weighted. We made a note of his email address and followed the instruction to place the bottle back into the sea. He was quick to reply and explained that he had dropped the bottle into the River Dee in Aberdeen. It had been found only once before, to his knowledge, in the harbour in Aberdeen, before being cast adrift again into the North Sea.

Terje, like the late Donnie Henderson of the Out Skerries,

is a fanatical sender of messages in bottles. He collates a newsletter of his bottles' progress and sends his findings to the oceanographer Curtis Ebbesmeyer, who has spent a lifetime tracing ocean currents through the findings of beachcombers. In his book *Flotsametrics and the Floating World*, Ebbesmeyer guesses that only one bottle will be found and reported for every ten sent. My family and I have sent more than ten bottles but only one has been found, so far. We cast it adrift from a beach in Foula. It floated straight back to shore, where it was found by Fran and her children – who live in the island. Even though it had not travelled anywhere, they were excited to find it. They opened it and added their own message before sealing it back up and casting it adrift again.

In 1892, two bottles were found on the shore of the Shetland Mainland, both sent by Foula islanders, and the message in one, dated 27 January 1892, reads:

> We have had no communication now for five weeks. Our provisions are almost exhausted – flour, oatmeal, sugar, tobacco done. Tea nearly done. Natives' meal and potatoes scarce and bad. One death – an old man on 6th instant. All rest well. Very bad weather. [Signed)] George Morrison, Minister.

A third message, also requesting provisions, was sent by Foula islanders during this desperate time, and it reached the Mainland of Shetland, but not in a bottle:

> Sir, – One day last week when me and my boy Mansie wis oot in our boat about a mile from Wattsness, looking for bits of wood for clog-soles, and any other peerie gifts the

Lord might send us, we saw a Norie [a puffin] sitting in the water, and so tired or sickly that it let Mansie lift it into the boat. When we returned home we found a paper tied under its wing. We dried the paper, and although some of the words were washed or rubbed out, we could read the most of it . . .

On 10 February 1892, a boat did at last reach Foula with provisions, the first resupply to the island in almost two months.

Messages in bottles are now mostly sent in fun and not by stricken islanders or desperate mariners on sinking ships. But I have heard of bottles washing up in Shetland that contain tracts from the Bible – dropped into the North Sea by fishermen working on trawlers registered in Banff and Buchan, in the north-east of Scotland.

Sea-cast offerings come in different forms. Andy Gear, in the island of Yell, once found a bottle that contained the plastic arm of a doll and a few Canadian coins. In 2018, a small brown bottle – the kind that once contained medication in tablet form – was handed in to the Shetland Museum. Inside, there was a piece of paper covered in neat Arabic script, and some blue beads. When the curators made enquiries, they learnt that the bottle contained an incantation for the purpose of wishing someone harm.

Meanwhile, a friend tells me that her niece once found a bottle containing a note that simply read, 'You nosey cunt.' But sometimes it pays to be nosey. Another Shetland-found bottle, which had crossed the Atlantic from New York, came with a $1,000 reward. I dare not wish for such a find;

the sea never rewards greed. Tove Jansson knew this. In *The Summer Book* there is a passage in which young Sophia and her grandmother are beachcombing. They find exactly what they need: a gin crate in which to hold a newly dug-up *Rosa rugosa* bush, and an old Russian cap in which to store the mushrooms they have gathered. And when the grandmother is thirsty, Sophia searches the shore and finds a washed-up bottle of sealed and perfectly good lemonade. She is so buoyed by all this that she sets off to find her grandmother a new watering can. But the grandmother has 'a feeling that they shouldn't press their luck', and so they row home.

On my last morning in the Out Skerries, I walk to the Head of Bloshin, the headland of the dark-blue pools, to eke out time alone with my thoughts before heading home to busy family life. The horizon is distinct, but the sky and the surface of the sea are the same turgid colour of grey and the wind is cold. And this is how I picture the North Sea in my mind, somehow more menacing and greyer than the bright and breezy blue of the Atlantic Ocean that I watch from the windows of my house.

I take a seat on a soft cushion of thrift, next to some regurgitated pellets. A pair of great black-backed gulls scold me from the top of Lamba Stack and, at first, I think that I have usurped their resting place. But then I notice a large fledgling gull standing on a ledge below where I sit. One of the adult gulls takes flight and climbs steeply into the air before swooping at my head. It is unnerving but I stay put. The rocks are uneven and it took me ages to reach this viewpoint. After two more swoops, the gull gives up and returns to Lamba Stack, and as it lands a black guillemot launches from the rock and falls on outstretched wings, down to the sea.

The gull pellets are neatly arranged as if photos on a restaurant menu. A meal of a rabbit: a pellet of fur and sinew-wrapped bone. A meal of a *tystie*, a black guillemot: a pellet of feathers and a sharp-beaked skull. A meal of crab: a neat sculptural sphere of crushed shell and folded crustacean limbs. I take the *tystie* skull and later regret this; it smells foul, crammed as it is with partly digested remains.

Through my binoculars, I spy a small yacht on the horizon, sailing in from the direction of Norway. It rolls from side to side in the heavy swell. When it reaches the shelter of the channel between Bound Skerry and the Head of Bloshin, I see that it is called *Lady Hysteria*.

Perhaps on its crossing it passed two, maybe three, glass bottles gently bobbing at the surface of the sea, cast adrift in honour of Anna and in memory of Donnie. Back home, in the midst of raising two children and earning a living, I wait patiently for news that one of my bottles has been found somewhere on a Norwegian shore. I have yet to hear back from Ole A. Andersen, sender of the Trussi Geo found bottle, but maybe, someday, I will.

Eggcase

When I find an eggcase washed up on a beach, the emotion that I feel is more akin to love than to desire and I wake happy each time I find an eggcase in my dreams. But my first memory of finding a mermaid's purse, the eggcase of a skate or catshark, is not a joyful one.

A few months after moving to Shetland I was glad to find out that I was pregnant again. We had hoped for a second child. I lost the sense that I was treading water and that time was slipping away. But then the pregnancy slipped away, before the twelve-week ultrasound scan. It felt like I was failing in all things. I had failed to find employment that would cover the cost of childcare and I had failed to sustain this pregnancy. In the weeks after this loss, I would leave my son with my husband and walk the shore with a vague notion that I could somehow cast my sadness out to sea.

Three months later, a new pregnancy began. A few days before the twelve-week scan I sensed that something was wrong. There was a light spotting of blood but this is not so unusual in the early months of pregnancy. Something else, which I could not pinpoint, led me to call the maternity unit at the hospital in Lerwick. My husband was at work, out flying somewhere over the North Sea. I left my one-year-old son crying in a crèche and drove myself to the hospital.

In the ultrasound room, the midwife sonographer's face

was inscrutable but her search for a heartbeat took long enough for me to know that she could not find one. When she confirmed that my baby had died, I was shocked by the intensity of my grief.

My belly clean of cold gel and my clothes refastened, the midwife sonographer guided me to the privacy of the room where maternity checks are carried out. The walls were covered in posters of smiling pregnant women. The on-duty midwife explained that I was experiencing a missed miscarriage. My body still thought that it was pregnant. Somehow, and without any compelling physical signs, my mind had understood otherwise.

My options, the midwife explained, were to wait for a natural resolution or I could undergo a surgical procedure called an Evacuation of the Retained Products of Conception. A doctor once apologised to me for the cold unwieldiness of this name but I cannot think of an alternative that would be easier on the mind, or on the heart. Under general anaesthesia, the cervix is opened and the pregnancy 'tissue' is scraped and suctioned out of the uterus.

I could also opt to travel two hundred miles by plane or ferry to the large hospital in Aberdeen for a medically managed miscarriage. In this procedure, a tampon-like pessary is inserted into the vagina, and the drugs that it is laced with widen the cervix and encourage the uterus to empty. But travelling to Aberdeen alone in these circumstances was not an appealing option.

I feared the surgical intervention. Though this procedure is deemed very safe, the list of potential complications is daunting and every operation under general anaesthesia has its risks. My body had naturally resolved a miscarriage before and I had no reason to think that it would not do so again.

Two weeks later, I returned to the maternity unit. The midwife sonographer confirmed that my womb still cradled all the 'material' of pregnancy. I opted to keep waiting. A further two weeks passed and another appointment for a scan was made, but this time it took place in the outpatient clinic. It was uncomfortable sitting in the busy waiting room; I would have preferred the familiarity of the maternity department. The sonographer was not a midwife and she avoided eye contact. She coolly confirmed that my womb had not emptied and, as soon as I was dressed again, she ushered me out of the room. There was no midwife or doctor that I could consult. I left the hospital and returned home full of shame and feeling lost; I did not know what to do.

I had bled very little all this time and had been too worried to leave the house in case the bleeding began in earnest. My husband looked after me when he was home, but when he was at work it was exhausting caring for our son. The loneliness was intense.

In the end, it was not my body that decided things. Shortly after the ultrasound in the outpatient clinic, thoughts of self-harm began to flood my mind. I knew that I would not enact these thoughts but I was scared to tell anyone what was going on in my head, in case they thought that I was not fit to look after my son. My husband knew that I was struggling but I kept the full extent of my distress from him.

I rang the maternity department and requested the surgical

procedure, but only if I was allowed to recover in the privacy of a maternity room. Day surgery in Shetland can mean waking up in a tiny and tightly packed mixed ward. I didn't want to meet anyone I knew and it is almost impossible to be anonymous in such a small hospital. The midwives agreed; the maternity unit was quiet and they would be able to spare a room. The theatre nurse was kind but neither the surgeon nor the anaesthetist, both men, talked to me or looked me in the face. I lay on the trolley and quietly cried.

The procedure was successful in the sense that I left the hospital the same day with a tidied womb. The intrusive thoughts of self-harm morphed into something less immediately violent. I would catch sight of the sea from the car window, and a thought would arrive in my mind of what it might be like to wade into the cold water and feel no compulsion to return to shore.

A few weeks later, a doctor phoned to say that nothing of concern had been found in the 'necrotic material' that had been removed from my uterus. I bled heavily for weeks. When it stopped, I began to leave the house again, performing normality as if nothing had happened.

Looking back, it seems remarkable that no one in the medical profession sought, at any point, to assess my mental state. I was reduced to a body without a mind. My body had harboured a life that had died and I was just supposed to get on with it. I was offered a poorly photocopied leaflet that signposted the way to an online miscarriage forum full of anonymised women. I found that they were also broken with grief. There we all were, herded together, our distress corralled in a virtual and hidden place where it wouldn't bother anyone else.

I tried to put this difficult experience behind me by walking alone to the low cliffs at the end of a long peninsula. I said a goodbye into the wind. It did feel like a turning point. But the next time I took the same path, I found a tangle of nine eggcases on the shore – the familiar capsules of the small-spotted catshark. The long wiry tendrils that would usually tether a capsule to seaweed were knotted to one another, as if the mother catshark had thought that this would be anchor enough to keep her young safe. Each capsule contained a lifeless embryo. In my distressed state, it felt as if the sea or the wind, or both, had returned my grief to me. This is my first vivid memory of eggcases.

There is a Shetland folk tale in which Death becomes trapped in an eggcase. I think about it often and sometimes its significance is hard to grasp; at other times I see a meaning clearly. It was told to me by the renowned Shetland storyteller the late Dr Davy Cooper, and it was told to him by the late Lawrence Tulloch, another greatly respected Shetland storyteller from the island of Yell. This is my retelling.

There was a young man who lived by the shore with his mother. His father had drowned some years before, and life since that tragic day had been a struggle. His mother had become ill and the young man could not bear the thought of losing her too. As each day passed, she became weaker, and it was evident to him that she was slipping away. One morning, he had the notion of making a footrest for his mother. He walked to the shore to look for driftwood and was absorbed in his task. So much so that he was slow to realise that a figure had appeared by his side. It was Death, who had come to take his mother.

Quick as a flash, he lunged at Death with a length of driftwood. Death fell to the ground. The young man searched the shore and found a large eggcase, gaping at one end. Bit by bit, he folded Death into the capsule and then sealed it shut with the sticky oil of a tar ball that lay in the strandline. He hid the sealed eggcase away.

When he returned to the house, he found his mother out of her resting chair and at the stove. She was soon well enough to work the croft again. For a while, life settled back into a happy routine. He forgot about the eggcase and its dark secret.

But as the days passed, the young man and his mother found that nothing on the croft would die. The grass grew high but they could not make hay. None of the sheep could be slaughtered, and the fish the young man caught would writhe with life however hard he tried to kill them.

His mother soon realised that something was amiss and quizzed the young man. He immediately confessed to what he had done. With tears in her eyes, she told him that he must free Death. He saw that she was right, and with a sore heart he took the eggcase from its hiding place and released Death back onto the shore. The next day, his mother died. He was distraught. Slowly, things on the croft returned to normal, and the young man lived on, alongside his grief.

*

My next clear memory of finding an eggcase is a happy one. I became pregnant again, not long after the missed miscarriage, and though it was fraught with the usual nausea and vomiting, and the novel experience of painfully inflamed joints, this pregnancy held and my daughter was born in the bright light of late May.

When my daughter was still a baby, two sperm whales stranded at Scollawick in the island of Unst. We drove to see them. It was a bleak day in March. I wrapped my daughter in a snowsuit to keep out the damp air, and my husband carried her down the path to the sea. Our toddler son walked alongside me with his tiny hand warm in mine. We made for the cloud of fulmars that swirled over the point at the shore where the bodies of the whales lay.

A man and his adult son reached the shore before us and together we made a loose fellowship of dead-whale sightseers. The putrid smell overpowered the younger of the two men and he retched into the grass. They had driven for many miles to see the whales but they stayed less than a minute, their curiosity stifled by the stench.

My son and I stood and stared. My husband seemed in shock to be in the presence of such large creatures. One whale was smaller than the other and both were male; their penises bobbed at the surface of the sea. The skin of the larger whale was marked with lengths of pale scars, perhaps wounds inflicted by the teeth of other males. Their lower jaws hung slack and the points of their teeth poked through the wash of the waves. A thick layer of oily spume blanketed the pebbles of the small beach. An offshore wind blew two neat slicks of whale oil far out to sea.

An eggcase, of a kind that I had not seen before, lay caught in the scum below the larger of the two whales. I scrambled down the low bank and snatched it up. It was oblong in shape, brown in colour, ragged-looking and spiked at each corner. It fitted neatly in the palm of my hand.

No autopsies were performed and the deaths of these whales remain unexplained. Both were towed by boat to the beach at Sandwick, where they were buried in the white shell sand, but not before someone was caught in the act of trying to hack off their jaws for the trophy of their teeth.

In the evening, back in the warmth of our home, I took the eggcase from my jacket pocket and sat it on the kitchen table. I opened my laptop and searched for its likeness on the Internet. Using the Shark Trust's key to eggcase identification, I learnt that it was the eggcase of a thornback ray. I was hooked there and then. This eggcase marked a return to the all-absorbing curiosity in nature that I had lost after my second miscarriage. I love eggcases because they are strangely beautiful and because they have helped me, more than any other beachcombed find, to place my imagination in the sea. But I also love eggcases for this deeply personal reason too.

The birth of my daughter marked a turning point, as did the finding of this eggcase. I could look outward again. Stood on the shore with the whales and the eggcase, I was still under the belief that my body would recover from pregnancy. I thought that I had recovered from the mental distress and grief of both miscarriages. I had yet to learn that pregnancy had changed my body in a way that it could not fully recover from, and that this would mean further anguish.

Depression is a common comorbidity, or companion, of arthritis. It remains a point of discussion as to whether inflammation in the brain is directly responsible for this, or whether it is more of an indirect effect – the culmination of a change to a more sedentary lifestyle, increasing isolation, decreasing self-esteem and being worn down by pain. Both causes are plausible and both are possible. More certain is the difficulty of remaining unscathed when the symptoms that you live with are dismissed.

Being transferred to a diligent and professional rheumatologist significantly improved my mental health. I knew that I was being listened to and that I now had access to the treatment that would make a considerable difference to my physical well-being. But still, intrusive thoughts of self-harm lingered. My home sometimes felt as dangerous as a cliff edge. It is exhausting being hypervigilant to risk.

My first visit to a GP to ask for help with my mental health, when my daughter was three, was too bright and breezy and glossed over the detail. It took a redwing, a songbird in the thrush family, to make me seek help again, this time with more honesty. The redwing crashed into the kitchen window at speed while trying to flee from a merlin falcon. I found it lying on the ground with one eyeball dangling by fine sinews from its shattered skull. Boundaries dissolved and, in my mind, I became the broken bird.

I made another appointment with my GP. He listened to me with compassion and saw my shame and lessened it. The support and guidance of two community psychiatric nurses lessened it further still, and with this help a redwing remains just a redwing and the sea is somewhere that I always now wish to return from.

During my time working in conservation, I travelled to many places considered wild. I found out that I was pregnant with my son during a research trip to the Bale Mountains of Ethiopia, and my first encounter with morning sickness was in a tent in the Serengeti, Tanzania. He came with me, *in utero*, to the Carpathian Mountains in Romania. But my mind remains the wildest place that I have ever been.

In February 2019, I coax my family south for a beach-combing holiday in Orkney. My children are not thrilled by this prospect, and so I have bribed them with a trip to the toyshop in Kirkwall. My son chooses some Lego and my daughter picks out a fluffy cat. I feel like a child in a toy-shop too. I hope to find the giant eggcases of the flapper skate, the largest and rarest skate in the world. In several years of beachcombing in Shetland, I have found only five of these eggcases, each bigger than my hand. I have heard that there are beaches in Orkney where they can be gathered by the armful.

On the Orkney Skate Trust's website, the flapper skate is described as being more at risk of global extinction than the blue whale. I have never seen a flapper skate alive. Their wings can span two metres. I would like to meet one in the sea, to watch the tips of its wings curl and unfurl in sea flight. A friend tells me that he has caught them with a rod from his boat, in the *voe* below my house. He released them back into the sea and they swam away. I am not hopeful of meeting one. I spend too little time on boats or in the sea. But if I could wish for a glimpse of any creature in the world, it would be a flapper skate.

In Shetland, the fisherman's taboo name for skate is *hekla*, meaning 'cloak' in Old Norse. A flapper skate once washed up in Lerwick and the sea left it draped over the rocks. It lay belly up and mouth agape. Its teeth looked like concentric rings of neatly embroidered, pearlescent beads, but each tooth was barbed and together they formed a beautiful and lethal armoury strong enough to crush the hard shells of molluscs. It was not so big, at a metre or so in length; too young to have bred.

It is strange to think of fish as being oviparous, as laying eggs like a bird. Only skates, and a few species of shark, lay eggcases. True rays give birth to live young but names can be confusing. The spotted ray and cuckoo ray are actually oviparous skates and produce the most beautiful eggcases too.

Inside a freshly laid eggcase, there is an embryo that is attached to a nourishing yolk. The eggcase capsule wall is tough enough to protect the embryo but permeable enough to allow oxygen to pass through. When the fish outgrows its tight confines, the eggcase neatly splits open at one end and the young skate slips out into the ocean. The 'shell' of a skate egg is made from a keratin-like substance, and it is leathery to the touch and difficult to tear. It can be punctured, though, by the bore of a marine gastropod's predatory tongue. I check every eggcase that I find for these neat piercings and they are common enough. I feel each of these losses, a little more than I should.

Female flapper skates are known to lay their large egg-cases where boulder fields overlie sandy substrates. The boulders shelter the eggcases from tidal flows, and the negative buoyancy of the eggcases anchors them to the seabed. The young develop slowly and hatch after a year or more. But even with this shelter, storms can dislodge and damage eggcases. They can also be torn from the seabed by bottom-trawling fishing gear and scallop dredges. When a flapper skate first emerges from its eggcase it is already large enough to be caught in trawl nets. It must avoid being caught for eleven years if it is to reproduce, and although commercial fisheries have been banned from targeting flapper skates since 2009, adults, juveniles and embryos are still hauled from the sea as bycatch.

There is a Marine Protected Area off the west coast of Scotland – stretching from Loch Sunart to the Sound of Jura – that has been designated specifically for the protection of flapper skates. Dredging for scallops, trawling and long-line fishing have been banned in this MPA since 2016, but by early 2019 there had been twenty-two reports of suspected illegal fishing activity. It is still legal to catch flapper skates for sport in this MPA, but they must be returned to the sea. Anglers are encouraged to take photographs before each flapper skate is released, and more than two hundred individual skates have been identified from the unique constellations of markings on the skin of their backs. As this data set grows, it should become possible to estimate the number of flapper skates in the area and to get a glimpse into their migratory movements.

I'm still haunted by a photograph shared on social media,

taken by a man fishing from a sea kayak. His rod is bent and the line is taut with the weight of the skate that hangs from the hook in her mouth. Her pale belly faces the camera, and an eggcase half protrudes from a slit in her body as if she were aborting in shock. Standing in the local fishmonger's, I cast my eye over the wings of skate lying on ice and think of the body of the fish that these wings were cut from. If the skate was a female, was there an eggcase that sheltered a live embryo in her wingless body when it was discarded onto the waste pile?

In the Mediterranean, an organisation called Sharklab-Malta retrieves eggcases from the dead skates and sharks landed at a wholesale fish market. The eggcases are carefully tended in saltwater tanks, and the hatched young are released back into the sea. It is a drop in the ocean in comparison to the numbers of skates and sharks caught, but I admire this humane effort. It is an example of not giving up, of continuing with the conservation effort, even when the odds are unfavourable.

We catch the early morning ferry from Kirkwall to the island of Sanday, with the new Lego and the fluffy toy cat stowed between my children in the back of the hire car. They are five and eight years old now, and I am grateful that, even during the most difficult times, my bond with them has always remained strong. They are a source of deep joy. My husband and I have somehow weathered the storms of miscarriage, chronic illness and poor mental health. I have been taking immunosuppressants for nearly a year, and though they make me nauseous and tired, they are working well.

I have not needed steroids for a while. I make this trip to Sanday unaccompanied by the constant presence of pain.

The sea is exceptionally still and the sun is warm enough to make me question whether I should buy some sunscreen. Long-tailed ducks, beloved overwintering visitors from the far north, display in tight flocks on the surface of the sea. They seem seasonally out of place, like partygoers who have outstayed their welcome, but it is the warmth itself that is out of place.

Through my Shetland-adjusted eyes, there is a gentleness to the Orcadian land- and seascapes. The low shores of Orkney are rimmed with smooth slabs of sloping rock. These rocks shine in a dazzling ring of silver around the islands when the sun appears after rain. We sail past many holms. Some of these grassy islets are covered in a blanket of grey seals.

The ferry calls in to the island of Stronsay first, and we stand out on the deck and watch all the unloading and loading. A haltered calf is led down the ramp and given to an older man who coaxes the beast into the back of his van. A monk, in long black robes, flags down a disembarking lorry laden with building materials.

The monks of Papa Stronsay are Transalpine Redemptorists, traditionalists of the Catholic faith. I survey the austere-looking monastery with my binoculars. Later, my curiosity leads me to their blog. One post describes their participation in 'pro-life' protests outside an abortion clinic in Lincoln, Nebraska, in 2013. Abortion is described as 'genocide'. The protest was successful, a monk writes jubilantly, and women were turned away. Standing on the ferry,

I note that their island is small and barely rises above the reach of the sea.

When it became apparent that my sacroiliac joints had been damaged by pregnancy, my husband and I discussed what it might mean for my body and for my mind if I were to become pregnant again. I would face a hard choice: abortion, or risk the prospect of further disabling damage to my joints and a worsening of the autoimmune disease. It would also mean putting a return to paid employment on hold again. He opted, without hesitation, for a vasectomy.

In Shetland, medical abortions are offered, if there are no complications, up to and including ten weeks of gestation. After ten weeks, pregnant women and people seeking an abortion must travel to mainland Scotland for a surgical procedure. Abortion, like giving birth, can be more complicated in island settings.

The turnaround at the Stronsay pier is swift, and soon the ferry is sailing towards Sanday, an island that lies so low in places that, approaching from the sea, it looks part-sunken. On the island's eastern coastline, a tattered ridgeline of storm-breached sand dunes rises out from the sea. To the south, community-owned turbines stand high on a hill and loom over the pier as if guiding the old diesel ferry in. On this day, their blades have been stilled by the absence of wind. The flaccid white remains of a whale cover the rocks of The Swarf like an eiderdown.

The first beach that we visit in Sanday is the wide sweeping bay of Lopness. The tide is in and we must slip our precarious way through the torn kelp that covers the steep bank of pebbles at the back of the beach. Within seconds, my daughter and son have each found a flapper skate egg-case. I am slower to pick them out as their colours blend in so well with the browns of the kelp, but then I find one and begin to see them everywhere. I turn to my husband and grin and see that his hands are already full. We all laugh at this abundance. I swallow a sob.

In the highest of the strandlines, the eggcases are dry, shrunken and shrivelled by desiccation. But lower down the bank of pebbles, some are newly ashore and sleek, still plump with the sea and huge, almost twice the length of my hand. One fresh specimen is intact, heavy and full. I take my small knife and carefully slit one end open. If it contains a young fish that looks close to hatching, we can release it back into the sea, but it is empty except for a clear gloop of liquid that pours from the knife's cut; it is a wind egg of sorts. We keep gathering eggcases until our two bags are full.

Near the parking space, caught by the hollows of a tus-socky sward, there are many small eggcases. Most are the eggcases of spotted rays. They shine like black patent lea-ther, and with their long and sharply pointed horns they look a little sinister. In the Northern Isles, eggcases were once called craw's (crow's) purses. On the other side of the Atlantic Ocean, they are also known as Devil's purses or Devil's pocketbooks.

My heart flips at the sight of a single cuckoo ray eggcase caught in one of the hollows. It has a tiny bulbous capsule and very long and sinuous horns. If the spotted ray egg-case is shaped like a sinister warning, then the eggcase of a cuckoo ray is shaped like a lingering embrace. I have only found a few cuckoo ray eggcases in Shetland; when they are fresh they can shine like bronze. One winter, a report came in from the island of Foula. More than a hundred cuckoo ray eggcases had washed ashore on the tiny beach at the head of Ham Voe. This number seems almost miraculous but I do not know if they were damaged, or intact and spent. Older Shetlanders have told me that eggcases of all kinds were once much more common and that they were considered lucky finds. We have fished our luck away.

The week in Sanday passes in a blur of beautiful white shell-sand beaches. My children revel in the absence of coats and jumpers. I watch the sun rise out from the sea each morning and sink again each evening, under wheeling flocks of waders and many skeins of geese. There are no hills to obscure the first and the last of the light.

It is an astonishing island; few places have made me feel the past and the future collide so neatly. In the heat of February, we hear the first skylark song of the year as we walk along the wide arc of Cata Sand at low tide. Whale bones, excavated by the tides, lie scattered on the slim strip of beach like the waymarkers of a trail. We follow them and find the place where the ribs of a long-buried whale rub against the stone of a Neolithic hearth.

Above the whale graves, the high dunes of Tresness are covered in raven pellets, each packed with the black pupal cases of kelp flies. We watch a hatch of kelp flies stream south along the shore below the sea defences that protect the chambered cairn at Quoyness. In the earth bank at the Bay of Stove, where Neolithic inhumations and cremations are being eaten away by rising seas, my husband finds a flake of bone in a dark layer of ashen soil. At Scar, where the sea has scoured away the shore to reveal a Viking boat burial containing the bones of a pagan woman, man and child, we gather white cobbles of flint left by a glacier.

I feel dizzy at the telescoping of time that this low and soft-edged island allows. I never wish to leave. I would stay here, if I could, and search for eggcases while the seas rise and steal away the land, but I know that the reality of living here would puncture my fantasy. No island can ever live up to the heightened expectations that we always seem to place on them; life catches up with us, sooner or later.

At the end of the week in Orkney, at the airport in Kirkwall, I check in a bag that contains more than two hundred eggcases, but even then, with all of these in my possession, I am not sated. I ask my children what they most enjoyed about the holiday, and both in synchronous unison reply that it was playing Mario Kart on the Nintendo Wii in the Sanday Youth Centre.

Comb Jelly, Amphipod and Salp

Rupert Brooke said the brightest thing in the world was
a leaf with the sun shining on it. God pity his ignorance!
The brightest thing in the world is a Ctenophor in a glass
jar standing in the sun.

W. N. P. Barbellion, *The Journal of a Disappointed Man:*
& A Last Diary

It is rare to experience a heatwave in Shetland, so when the
temperature reaches 21 degrees Celsius for a few days in the
summer of 2019 we all feel a little stunned. My children eye
the shorts I offer them with suspicion. The average max-
imum temperature in Shetland in July is 14.4 degrees Celsius
and we have had little need for a summer wardrobe.

There is no wind to cull the warmth or to brace against. It
is bliss. I cherish the novelty of heat-slackened muscles in
a body that is more often tensed with pain, braced against
the weather, or both.

But my bodily ease is disturbed by images of a burning
world. More than a hundred wildfires are ablaze in the Arctic
Circle and over 75,000 fires burn in the Brazilian Amazon.
There are many photographs of protests too, some led by
Greta Thunberg and others led by Extinction Rebellion.
Even in Shetland, where public displays of dissidence are

rare, over two hundred people will soon take part in the global climate strike, some waving placards that read 'Wir Hame is on Fire'. I will paint a picture of a puffin on a piece of card, as if the climate emergency in Shetland is relevant only to other creatures.

I am unsure what climate breakdown will mean for us here in these islands, how it might be felt in our bodies too. The push and shove of the wind in a storm causes pain to sear in inflamed joints. I feel the wind on my skin and deep within my body. Standing outside during a storm, I can start to believe that this is the beginning of what comes next; an increase in the violence of the wind will disproportionately affect those of us who already understand the weather through our bodies. And while the warmth of a rare heatwave may soften my resistant body, it is still a warning.

We make for the sea, all four of us. The sky is cloudless and a heady shade of blue; the surface of the sea is perfectly still. I leave all thoughts of the unfolding climate emergency with my towel on the shore, but find that the sea is thickly green and uninviting. A cold spring has caused the phyto-plankton to bloom late. The underwater visibility is terrible. In conditions like these, when I cannot see far ahead, my imagination fills the sea with danger. The day before, a group of orcas was seen hunting common seal pups further along the Atlantic coastline of Shetland, and now I imagine them, hidden in the green.

I know that they do not hunt humans but we have watched, from the vantage point of an inter-island ferry, an orca swim by with ragged white seal-flesh in her mouth. On another occasion, a gathering of ravens drew me down to the shore, where I found the stomach of an eviscerated seal bobbing in the swell, intestines strung out and snagged around a rock like a mooring rope. In my dreams, orcas have hunted my children, their fins surfacing through the living room floor.

Even when thoughts of orcas do not enter my mind when I am snorkelling, I am still scared. Panic rises when I lower my head into the sea. My nerve often fails and I pull back with a gasp. I try again, desperate to see under the surface, and as soon as my snorkel mask is submerged my fear lessens. I'm too absorbed to panic. When I return to the shore, I cannot stop thinking about all the strange and beautiful things that I have seen:

> the eye of a fish, a *sillek* or young saithe, holding
>   my gaze
> light pulsing down taut lengths of *lukki lines*
>   (*Chorda filum*)
> a starfish the size of an infant's fingernail
> an ebb-tide procession of pink moon jellyfish
> suspensions of glittering mica, the way it vanishes
>   when a cloud covers the sun
> a tiny hermit crab in the unicorn horn of an augur
>   shell
> kelp falling away into an abyss of the deepest blue
> a curlew that has not marked me as human,
>   landing on a nearby rock.

Beginning to know the sea, from within the sea, is a little like learning another language. With each snorkel, an increment more insight accumulates. Fluency is forever beyond

reach, but small efforts to understand bring disproportion-
ate joy. Bit by bit, snorkelling has made me fear the sea less,
or at least manage my fear better.

The effort may be small but it is not insignificant when phys-
icality, as measured by most norms, is different. In 2017, I
bought a wetsuit because my wish to snorkel, to see under
the surface of the sea, had become all-consuming. Eggcases
had pulled my imagination into the sea but imagination
alone was no longer enough. Years had passed since I last
swam in the sea; brief swimsuit-clad dips, my head always
clear of the surface. The first immersion, in my new wetsuit, flooded me with intense joy. The sea was flat-calm and
terns flew low over my head. I submerged my mask and saw
shoals of tiny fish with silver flanks darting between columns of seaweed. When I returned to the shore, I found
that I had stolen, or perhaps I had been given, some of the
sea's calm.

I began to gain more confidence in my body again and
my mindset changed, from dwelling on what was no longer
possible, to what might still be possible. Cramming an unpli-
able body into tight neoprene is difficult but I am grateful
that it is still possible. The tightness of the wetsuit squeezes
tender joints, and its buoyancy in water can bend the damaged joints of my spine and pelvis to the point of sudden
immobility. I mostly float and drift with the tide and wind,
sculling my way back to shore like an inelegant water beetle. After one cold winter snorkel in crystal-clear water, the
joints in my hands seize up for three days. Even so, snorkelling, more than anything else, restores my confidence in my

physical self. I wait impatiently for each window of opportunity to see below the surface of the sea, when a lull in the wind coincides with a lull in the stormy weather within my body.

Slowly, in the pea-soup sea of the hot July day, my eyes adjust. There are many tiny jellyfish pulsing everywhere; some are no bigger than a fingertip, and they trail tentacles so fine that they slip in and out of sight. Scale is reset and I become monstrous. The bell of each miniature jellyfish is transparent and marked only by a neat trim of little black dots. The shadows that these gelatinous creatures cast are more substantial than their beings.

I am learning that these medusae are the sexual body form of colonial creatures called hydroids. I have never seen a hydroid growing on the seabed, but occasionally a frond of storm-torn kelp washes ashore covered in a white fur of zigzag-stemmed hydroids. My field guide shows images of fern-like creatures covering the sea floor as if it were a forest glade. The sessile forms of hydroids grow asexually and bud new polyps. Some of the polyps are reproductive in function and produce the medusae. I imagine these medusae factories in action, small jellyfish rising like puffs of smoke from fat polyp chimneys.

The sea can sometimes seem full with these miniscule jellyfish forms. Hydroid medusae are released in great numbers, all at once. Some of the medusae shed sperm and others shed eggs, and through sheer chance and excess, free-floating eggs are fertilised by free-floating sperm and develop into planktonic larvae. The larvae drift and find new places to settle on the seabed, and so sexual reproduction enables a hydroid species to spread its range; this is a kind of insurance, should anything happen to the parent colony. My field guide tells me that not all hydroid medusae have been assigned to a hydroid species. The sea still keeps some of its secrets.

I keep my mouth firmly shut and try not to dwell on the thought that I swim through a sea fecund with sperm and eggs. I once saw a vast gelatinous mass of tiny hydroid medusae rim a beach, rising and falling in the gentle swell as if they were jostling to come ashore, sex-spent, weakened and exhausted.

A copepod, a small crustacean, emerges from the green to swim through towering columns of seaweed. It jerks forward, using its long antennae to row through the water. It is feeding on phytoplankton and its presence brings to my attention the unseen. In my mind's eye, the green soup disintegrates into billions of microscopic life forms. Scale is reset again; I become ever more monstrous.

The oval of a gelatinous creature, the length of my thumb, drifts into view. Its flesh is cloudy and it is easier to follow through the water than the hydroid medusae. But my forward momentum is too much; I cannot stop myself in time and batter the creature with the mask of my snorkel. It hangs in the water, motionless and horizontal, like the balloon of a tiny airship. Then it slowly rights itself to a vertical plane and shudders back into life. Fine lines of iridescent light start streaming down its sides.

A comb jelly, a ctenophore!

In my excitement, I try to scoop it up in my hand to show

my husband and children, but my gentle touch is still too rough and I tear its body. It hangs flaccid in the sea and does not pulse with light again. My son catches sight of another comb jelly, my husband too, but my daughter does not and she returns to the shore a little indignant with disappointment.

The next day, we wait for high tide and then return to the sea to try to find her one, or so I tell myself. The sight of the comb jelly's iridescence will not leave my mind. I think of little else. It feels a little like being in the first throes of love, an infatuation of sorts. I want to capture a comb jelly and keep it for a while. And so maybe it is not love that I feel but a need to possess beauty.

A rain cloud, vast and dark, moves in from the Atlantic and dulls the silver of the sea. We launch the paddle board. There is no wind, and we glide along unhindered by waves. My husband paddles and I scan the deeper water for orca fins. Our children perch between us. Peering through the surface, it is as if someone has turned out all the lights. There is no seabed or seaweed, just an unfathomable dark. The ghostlike form of a comb jelly drifts into view. I place a wide-mouthed bottle in its path and it flows in, gently and without tearing. Emboldened by this, I gather another, and a single hydroid medusa too.

I drift along on the paddle board with my children while my husband snorkels. He emerges, suddenly, to exclaim that he has seen one comb jelly engulf another. I am consumed by envy. Comb jellies eat other comb jellies, including those of their own species. Certain types of ctenophore may even extend their seasonal longevity by eating the young of their own species. They eat plankton too, including the copepods that we can see rowing through the dark water. We drift through a simplified diagram of a marine food chain. Copepods eat phytoplankton, comb jellies eat copepods, fish eat comb jellies, seals eat fish and orcas eat seals. And with our feet dangling below the surface, and with the knowledge that orcas are still hunting seals somewhere in Shetland, we do not feel so separate to all this.

Torrential rain begins to fall and we make for the shore in silence. To the east, the islet broch pokes out through the surface like a nipple, and above us, sheep graze on the grassy mound of the chambered cairn. Two standing stones seem to watch our progress. A harbour seal trails our wake and spooks my daughter. At home, we lie on the tarmac and laugh as rainwater floods around our outstretched bodies.

Freed of our wetsuits and warmed by hot showers, we pour the comb jellies and medusa gently into a large glass jar and then sit and watch our captives. One of the comb jellies seems listless. It rests at the bottom, passive, as if it has been compromised by its capture. The other comb jelly pursues the tiny jellyfish but the pulse of the medusa's bell pushes it away. It gives up the chase and switches to rising and falling in the shallow water column of the jar.

Through a magnifying glass, it is possible to see the comb jellies' cilia, the tiny hair-like structures that have fused to form the comb of their name. The cilia propel the jelly through the water, and as these combs move they rake bright colours from the light – neon shades of blue, purple, green, orange, yellow and pink. Light spills down their sides like viscous droplets of oil. My heart contracts. I imagine filling the house with these creatures, a jar in each room. But the limp comb jelly never recovers and this punctures my fantasy. In the evening, guilt makes me return all three gelatinous creatures to the sea, and when the current pulls them away from the shore, I am bereft.

The following January, south-westerly gales rage for weeks. The last time that the wind blew from this direction for such a prolonged time, a friend tells me, the *Braer* oil tanker wrecked on the cliffs of the South Mainland.

When the wind is this persistent, it whittles all energy away. We become a little tense from being cooped up, week after week. The sea is far too wild for snorkelling and even beachcombing has become a miserable occupation. It is also unnervingly warm for January. The grass has greened and the snowdrops have bloomed early only to be shredded by the wind. A conversation with a marine ecologist drifts to the fore of my mind. We were discussing what the climate emergency might mean here in Shetland. He suggested that it might take the form of higher average wind speeds and more frequent and damaging storms. It seems as if the abstract future of this speculative conversation has arrived.

In a relative lull, on a day of fast-moving clouds and low winter light, my husband and I seek out a beach that faces the south-west. We walk down the path to the shore, past the hulks of trees that have drifted across the ocean and then been carried far inland by a storm surge. When the sea comes into view, the swell is wind-torn and mountainous. Fulmars fly through the tumult of the waves as if asking the wind for more. The tide is out but I eye the pebble beach warily; it shelves steeply and I don't trust the sea when it is like this.

This beach is little visited but well tended by someone. There are several *noosts*, small stone enclosures that once cradled boats and kept them safe from the sea and the wind when they were not in use. The first *noost* is brimful with stowed marine litter, fish boxes, plastic gallon drums and many bottles, all weighted down by a heavy trawl net. The next *noost* along is empty except for a fish box filled with cetacean bones, a beachcomber's ossuary of holy relics. The lower jaw of a toothed whale, empty-socketed and green with moss, lies among assorted ribs and a huge scapula that crumbles to dust at my touch.

At the reach of the crashing waves, a freshly wrecked by-the-wind sailor lies on a pile of bladderwrack. I pick it up by its chitinous sail and stick its violet-blue tentacles to the skin of my wrist, eager for its soft sting. I found a mass wreck of these surface-dwelling creatures on the beach nearest to our house years ago. I'd read that they do not sting but found that they did, only a little but enough to diffuse sharp pain. But the wind catches on its sail and rips it away before I can feel anything other than its sticky gloop. I search but don't find it again, and I curse the wind.

But then a wave washes in and leaves the strangest thing. It radiates an icy light and looks carved from crystal, barrel-shaped and smaller than my thumb. It is tough and rubbery to the touch. I pick it up and, inside, a four-eyed creature stares back at me and raises two muscular pincers in defence. Its other limbs splay out and clasp the inside of the jelly, as if braced for another tumbling ride in the surf. It looks like a little lobster made of the clearest glass but has survived the force of the waves without being shattered or dislodged.

Another wave washes in and leaves a second jelly-barrel creature at my feet. The inside of this barrel is speckled with tiny eggs. I drop both barrels into a bottle filled with sea water and take them home, a little puzzled to meet a creature that I do not know how to place.

In the shelter of my kitchen, I learn that the glass lobsters are a type of deep-water amphipod – marine crustaceans and relatives of the sand hoppers that live under rocks and among the seaweed on the shore. Their common name in English is 'pram bug' because they sometimes leave their jelly barrel and push it around the sea. In French they are called *tonneliers de la mer*, 'marine coopers'. They fashion their barrel home from a living creature, a salp, a type of planktonic sea squirt. Less often, pram bugs live in the bodies of comb jellies. I look up from the computer screen and examine the crystal-like barrel. I see the resemblance to a sea squirt, but only just.

Sessile sea squirts sometimes wash up on the shore after being ripped from the seabed, or from seaweed, by strong winds and wave action. When they lie desiccated in the strandline there is nothing that readily identifies them as a creature. They look like a lump of shrivelled flesh, and they feel tough and gristly. But when they are still fresh and full of sea water, they are plump little sacs with two puckered openings. I always feel an urge to squeeze them, and once did. A jet of water shot metres into the air.

The sea squirt diagram in my field guide shows a heart,

brain, testes, ovary and anus. Water enters the larger of the two openings, and as it flows through, food particles within the water stick to the mucus of a net-like chamber. Wastewater is expelled through the smaller of the openings. 'Tunicate' is another name for the sea squirt, after the rubbery tunic that encloses their siphonous bodies. Sea squirt larvae are quite different. They are tadpole-shaped and have a notochord, a skeletal rod – a spine of sorts. It is this larval feature that places these creatures in the Chordata phylum, along with all vertebrates including humans. My field guide remarks how amazing it is that we, as humans, should share a taxonomic group with sea squirts. I am a little amazed to learn this too.

In recent years, molecular analyses have demonstrated that humans are even more closely related to sea squirts than previously thought. In an essay on rethinking the use of metaphors in western and colonial discourses of evolution, Andreas Hejnol, a comparative developmental biologist, explains that judgements of primitiveness have proven to be wrong, misinformed by a long usage of hierarchical metaphors, like ladders and trees, in which humans sit firmly at the top as the most advanced beings.

He suggests that, by moving away from a western anthropocentric perspective that uses hierarchical metaphors, we might pay more attention to the complexity of creatures deemed primitive, like sea squirts and sponges. They have lessons to teach us, and perhaps the first is humility. Though I know that I will remain tempted to squeeze each plump sea squirt that I find washed up on the shore.

*

It is difficult to identify the 'host' salp or comb jelly of a pram bug to species level, stripped as they are of their internal organs. The pram bugs cut holes in each end of their gelatinous prey, and then hollow out the insides to create their shelter. Curiously, the pram bugs' jelly barrels are robust but comb jellies and salps tear easily. It is possible that pram bugs inject chemicals into their hosts to make them more resilient.

The incessant south-westerlies have been worth their trouble for the sight of these strange beings. I send a photo of the pram bugs to a marine ecologist, Rachel Shucksmith, and ask her why these deep-sea creatures may have wrecked on the shore. She tells me that Shetland sits close to the shelf break, the place where the continental shelf falls away into deep oceanic water. Wind-driven currents can bring water inshore from the area of the shelf break. If the pram bugs were spawning at the surface of the ocean, they may have been caught in this movement of water.

I wonder what the pram bugs in the jar on the kitchen table sense – if they are stressed by the harsh electric light. Their two sets of eyes operate independently. The upper eyes watch for the silhouettes of creatures in residual daylight, and the lower eyes detect pulses of light from bioluminescent organisms. My own eyes are distracted by a frantic movement in the jar. The female has left her jelly barrel and is pushing it around the container at speed, as if she is fleeing from impending danger.

The next morning, she is back inside her barrel but the egg mass is smaller. Some of the eggs have hatched, and minuscule pram bugs cling to the inside of the jelly wall.

When I add fresh sea water to the jar, both adults animate. The eggless pram bug fans water through its jelly with its tail. Feeding limbs grab at the water and brush across mouthparts too small and transparent to see.

I check the jar one last time before heading to bed, and find the eggless pram bug trying to push its way into the jelly of the egg-attending pram bug. The empty jelly barrel lies abandoned, gently rocking at the base of the jar. The pram bug with eggs spins furiously in the confines of her jelly and slaps at the intruder with her tail. I watch for as long as my nerve holds and then scoop out the eggless pram bug, place it in a second glass of sea water and drop its jelly barrel in too.

In the morning, both pram bugs are back in their jelly barrels. Both are perfectly transparent but after a while they become speckled with chromatophores, cells containing light-reflecting pigment. The chromatophores are tiny, cross-stitched stars made from the finest of orange threads. When they contract, the pram bug becomes more transparent. The more transparent a creature is in the featureless zone of water, the more able it is to capture prey and to avoid being captured itself.

On the third morning, I find that the pram bug with the eggs has died. She lies curled tightly in her jelly like a foetus in the womb. Her body has been infilled with a creamy yellow. The young have mostly all hatched, the egg mass has disappeared, and clusters of tiny pram bugs sit on the surface of the water like little islands of scum.

The eggless pram bug lasts two more days before it becomes listless even when I add fresh sea water to the jar.

I watch for the moment of its death. I want to preserve the creature, clear and glass-like, in gin. When the pram bug looks entirely lifeless, I use a spoon to try to scoop it up but it is still alive. Clawed limbs shoot out through the hole in the barrel. I drop it into the gin anyway. It struggles for a few seconds and then lies still. The jelly barrel, which had already lost its bright glisten, dulls further in the alcohol.

I take the jar of sea water with its scum of young pram bugs to a beach where the wind blows offshore, and release them into the sea. Maybe this is a futile gesture, or maybe a few will survive and drift their way back to the ocean deep.

Foula

From Old Norse *Fugla-øy*, 'Bird Island'

On the afternoon that we are due to fly to Foula for a short family holiday, on a summer's day in 2019, the sky is overcast. The pilot of the small Islander plane decides that it is still worth a try. The flight is only fifteen minutes long, but once we are airborne we can see that the route ahead is obscured by low cloud. The pilot shakes his head and loops the plane back to the airstrip. The island's ferry will leave the next day but it is a two-hour crossing in a small boat on the open ocean, and none of us are good sailors. We rearrange the trip for September. It is disappointing to miss out on a midsummer visit when the seabird breeding season is in full swing, but Foula is never a place that you can bend to your own schedule.

In September, on the day of our second attempt, the weather is poor again. We wait in the small passenger lounge with an older gentleman who is island bagging and two teenagers who are returning home for the weekend from the secondary school in Lerwick. My children, now six and nine, fidget and complain of boredom and so we stick on a DVD, a black and white movie called *The Edge of the World* that was filmed in Foula in 1937 and tells the story of the abandonment of St Kilda. In the film, a man falls from a very high cliff and dies. My children ask if we can please go home.

When the weather suddenly improves, the ground crew waste no time. The plane flies up over high ground and the route west looks reassuringly clear. The pilot presses on. We have the view of a soaring bird. Below us, water laces through the boglands in intricate threads of silver, and it reminds me of the pale shine of stretchmarks braiding across skin. Two narrow peninsulas mark the place of a sea-drowned valley. Beyond them, a wide *voe* shelters a scattering of small islands and the industrial clutter of many salmon cages. And then we pass over the fractured edge of the land, the red granite cliffs of Westerwick and Silwick, the sharp spire of Erne's Stack and the rocky islet of Giltarump, named by the Norse for its likeness to a pig's arse.

The sight of the ocean's surface, free of the safety net of land, is both mesmerising and unnerving. We fly under the press of cloud but high enough to see the fine imprint of the endless and ever-moving swell. Drifts of grey showers join the ocean to the sky in places, but the route ahead looks clear enough.

Or so I think. Without warning, we fly into a cloud and the view disappears. Seconds pass. My husband begins to watch the plane's instruments a little too intently. My daughter looks up at me to check that everything is okay. My son doesn't seem worried. In the seats behind us, the two teenagers stare out of the window without concern. I vow never to take my children in a small Islander plane again. But this vow is immediately forgotten when, at last, the plane clears the cloud. Foula rises from the ocean, a deity in island form.

*

Most days, I look for Foula from my kitchen window. All that we can see from our house is a sharp ridgeline of high peaks. The rest of the island is hidden behind the low hills of the West Mainland, but even this glimpse is charismatic enough to make it the lodestone in our view. I sometimes head to the cliffs of the West Mainland, just to be able to see Foula in full. The island is small, if dramatic, at 3.5 miles long and 2.5 miles wide. It does have a school but there is no shop. A nurse provides medical care. Through binoculars I can make out a scattering of houses below steep-sided hills. The sheer cliffs of the western coastline are out of sight. Some days, Foula looks distant and impossible to reach. Other days, I can believe that it is close enough to row out to. I am never sure if this is a trick of the light or a trick of the island itself.

My thoughts wander to Foula in the worst of the westerly storms – if it is this bad with us, then how must it be there? In her book *Flora of Foula*, Sheila Gear writes: 'Strong winds are common, gales are frequent and very violent gusts occur when the wind is compressed against the big cliffs on the west side of the island and then suddenly released over the top.' Great *flans* of wind slam down the hillslopes and batter the houses. I wonder how the thirty or so Foula islanders hold their nerve in the face of such capricious weather.

I always imagined that visiting Foula would be uncomfortably intrusive, as if I would be watching the people as much as the birds. But in 2016 I flew to the island for a day and was warmly welcomed by Fran, one of the island's rangers. A young woman with long fair hair, she pushed her older child along in a buggy and carried her baby in a sling on her back. She looked up to the job of living in such a place – capable, and confident in a gentle way that made me feel immediately at ease. It was a magical day spent with all the island's birds, but I was glad when the plane arrived to take me back to the Mainland. I know that I do not have what it must take to live in such a place.

When we first moved to Shetland, I repeatedly borrowed a book from the library in Lerwick called *Foula: Island West of the Sun*. I have my own copy now and return to it often. It was written by Sheila Gear, a Foula islander and naturalist, and was published in 1983. In her book, Sheila describes life in the island over the course of a year. Seasons are defined by crofting activities and through the comings and goings of the island's birds. Tropes of 'remote' island life are directly addressed and firmly rejected: 'We never consider ourselves as being cut off or isolated from the outside world – we feel as much a part of it as anyone else in this country.'

When we booked flights to Foula, I wrote to Sheila to ask if she would be willing to meet. I wanted to ask her about the island's bird life. She is another of Foula's rangers and has monitored the island's bird populations for several decades. I felt nervous that she might detect my outsider's curiosity and be on guard, but I need not have worried. At the airstrip, while waiting for the bags and the bulk of the supplies to be unloaded from the plane, a tall spectacled woman approaches me, her grey hair tied in a neat ponytail. Sheila smiles warmly and introduces herself and tells me that she will call by in the evening, and then we can talk about the seabirds of Foula.

Sheila's nephew, Kenny, grabs our bags – and his wife, Mai, drives us to Ristie, a restored old croft house that is let out for short stays. We pass the school and wave to the children in the playground, and my son and daughter look on enviously at the slide and climbing frame. Small groups of *bonxies*, great skuas, sit by the road, but they seem more intent on chasing one another now that the seabirds that they usually steal from, or kill, have left the breeding cliffs for the year. In another week or so the *bonxies* will leave too, for warmer coastlines in southern Europe and north-west Africa.

Ristie sits under the slope of a hill called Soberlie. From below, the ridgeline of this hill looks like the gently hooked dorsal fin of a *neesick*, a porpoise. The tip of the fin is an overhanging cliff that points north-west. A bird launching from Soberlie and flying in a straight north-west line over the ocean would next meet land in Suðuroy, the southernmost island in the Faroese archipelago. Behind Soberlie the Kame towers even higher still, a sheer cliff of 376 metres. A swirling mass of many hundreds of *maalies*, northern fulmars, circle around its height.

I'm waiting for the kettle to boil and staring out the kitchen window of Ristie when a fulmar falls from the sky and crash-lands in the garden. It soon recovers its composure but seems to know that it is trapped by the garden wall. These birds are ungainly on land, their legs are positioned far back on their bodies, but once they are in the air there is nothing quite like them; they thirst for wind. Fulmars are petrels and belong to an order of birds called Procellariiformes – from *procella*, the Latin for 'squall'. They do not flap so much, like gulls, but glide on outstretched wings, and the stronger the wind the better. On calm days, the sight of a fulmar flapping its wings reminds me of a human treading water.

The garden fulmar uses its wings as paddles to shuffle its way to the closed gate, where it sinks to the ground and sits on its belly. I open the front door slowly and step out into the garden. The fulmar turns to watch me. I dare not approach it directly in case it vomits noxious-smelling oil at me, a defence these birds more usually employ to protect their nests. It rests against the gate which opens inwards, into the garden. I will have to climb over the wall and out of the garden to free the bird. My husband and children watch gleefully through the window, eager to see if I will be sprayed with fulmar oil.

Fulmars are very beautiful and I sometimes overlook this beauty. They are so numerous, out on the cliffs, that I take them for granted. But if I am walking a line of cliffs that I do not know so well, then I watch for them intently. When they seem to rise out of the very ground itself, it is a warning that a geo lies unseen ahead. They are guardian angels in avian form, gently reminding me that I am constrained by land and that the land is about to fall away.

The head, belly and tail of the garden fulmar are white; the wings are a soft grey. The eyes are black and watchful. There is a smudge of dark plumage next to each eye, and this, and the deep indent of the brow, makes each fulmar look fierce or gentle, depending on the context of the observer and the observed. The head is domed, and the bill is segmented like plated armour and sharply hooked in a downwards curve. All petrels, including the fulmar, have external nostrils enclosed in a tube-like structure that sits heavily on the top of the bill, like the double exhaust of a fast car. Through these tubes, ingested salt is excreted. This nasal structure may also enhance scent detection and help them to forage. I can smell the fulmar from where I stand, musty and not altogether unpleasant, and no doubt it smells me too – perhaps the fear from the Foula flight still lingers as a scent on my skin.

From behind the safety of the wall, I undo the latch and slowly push the gate open but the bird stays put. Pink webbed feet appear under the gate. One more gentle push and the bird falls backwards and then bursts forwards and out of the garden. It rushes to freedom with a clatter of wings, sits back down on its belly and faces out to sea. When I check a few moments later with a mug of hot tea in my hand, it is nowhere to be seen but its musty smell remains – not acrid like a raven, nor as sweet as its much smaller relative, the storm petrel.

After the excitement of the fulmar, we make for the shore, where I begin to feel more myself again. The high ground of Foula, with all its steep slopes and summits, displaces me back to the time when I hillwalked, but now there is no escaping the fact that my body is mostly tethered to low ground. I long to sit at the height of the Kame to experience what Sheila describes in *Foula: Island West of the Sun*:

> Poised on the top of a high cliff there is a peace not found anywhere else: a vast space, an eternity of sea and sky, a free-dom. Sit here and scan the distant horizon where sea and

sky meet in a far silver line, let your mind roam free; here you will find a glimpse of understanding of life, of its eternity, formed from a million myriads of mortal fragments, a million upon million of livings and dyings, creatings and destroyings, buildings up and wearings down – a grain of sand, a wave, a bird, a man, an island, all add their small part to the eternity of the universe.

But it is not to be. I tear my gaze away from the high ground and return it to the shore, where I fall into the comforting familiarity of beachcombing.

The boulder beach near Ristie has pockets of fine shingle where there are small pieces of perfectly smooth sea glass. The glass has been worked hard by the sea. The coast of Foula is steeply shelving. There are no natural harbours, and in the winter the island's diminutive ferry sits in a boat lift, like a cradle, high on the pier as if taunting the waves. If it were left moored in the water, it would be smashed to smithereens.

To the east, the Mainland of Shetland looks slight and insubstantial, a thin slither of low-lying land in the vastness of the ocean. Our home island looks vulnerable and Foula feels solid. It is good to invert a Mainland perspective for a while, but the weather is fair.

Part way along the beach I crouch to pee in the cover of a *planticrub*, a small circular drystone enclosure which would once have sheltered cabbage seedlings. When I stand back up, I notice a fulmar sitting two metres away, watching me with a look that seems wholly disapproving.

*

When dark falls, the shelter of Ristie intensifies with the thought of being in a small island surrounded by deep ocean. I'm sat reading when the door opens and Sheila enters, switches off her torch and shrugs off her raincoat. A blast of cool air follows her in. We sit at the table and talk in dim light and hushed voices while my children sleep on bench beds. When I mention the fulmar that crashed into the garden, Sheila tells me that the first three fulmars to colonise Foula are said to have sailed in on the carcass of a whale.

Before the late 1800s, fulmars were only ever seen in Shetland by men out at the *haaf*, the deep-sea fishing grounds. The first fulmar nest in Foula was recorded in 1878. The island is now home to more than 20,000 of these birds when, not so long ago, it was home to none.

Fulmars may, in part, have been lured south from the Arctic by returning whaling ships and all their flesh and offal waste. Shetland whalers came home with the name *malliemawk*, from the Dutch seamen's nickname for this bird, *mollymawk* or *mallemuck* (from *mal-mok*, 'foolish gull'). *Maalie*, a word as soft as down, is the name used in Shetland now. I prefer it to *fulmar*, which comes from Old Norse and means 'foul gull'.

We leave discussion of fulmars, and turn our thoughts to the seabirds of Foula that are disappearing. The word 'catastrophic', in relation to the decline of certain species of seabirds in Shetland, is not hyperbole. But data, however stark, can still seem cold. I have only ever seen the seabird cliffs as they are now, much depleted in certain species. As I listen to Sheila, data begins to lose its distance. In my mind,

I can start to imagine what I have never seen – great cacophonies of seabirds thronging the island's cliffs. I start to *feel* the loss of seabirds.

Sheila is in her seventies and has monitored Foula's seabirds for many decades. Her connections to the bird life of her island run deep, and she can map the declines of certain seabird species against the different phases of her own life. Though, she is quick to add, even when she was young the older folk of Foula would tell her that seabird numbers were much higher before the advent of industrial fishing. Tourists come to Foula now and marvel at the few puffins that are left, when once 'myriads and myriads of *nories* could be seen flying like clouds of midges off the Nort Banks'. I am guilty of this too.

Sheila first came to Foula as a child, to visit relatives. She would walk with her sister to a freshwater loch where they would each cut three *fells*, strips of turf the size of a foot. The buoyancy of the *fells* would stop them becoming stuck in the thick peaty gloop lying at the bottom of the loch. Each *fell* would sink with the weight of a foot; the third would be placed ahead for the next step. The first *fell*, released, would bob back to the surface, and in this way Sheila and her sister would reach a small island where they would lie and watch the kittiwakes that had come to the fresh water to bathe and fetch the *slie*, the weed that these birds gather when they are building their nests.

She would lie in the sun and stare at these delicate white gulls, with their ink-dipped wings, rising from the loch's surface. Droplets of water, peaty and golden in the sunlight, would fall from their white feathers. In *The Atlantic*

Islands, a book on the Faroe Islands published in 1948, the author Kenneth Williamson describes seeing a freshwater loch thickly rimmed with white feathers cast from bathing kittiwakes. When a bird is lost from a place, we lose the raw sight, sound and smell of them, but we lose these finer intricacies of their presence too.

During visits to Foula as teenagers, Sheila and her sister would wait until dark before climbing out of their bedroom window. Then they would make for the height of the Noup, the southernmost of Foula's peaks, which towers 248 metres above the ocean's surface. On the cliffs of the Noup, there are steep and grassy places, some of which are covered in boulders. This is where Manx shearwaters once nested. Their Shetland name, *leeries*, comes from the Old Norse name, and they belong, like fulmars and storm petrels, to the petrel family. Manx shearwaters return to their burrows under the cover of darkness, to avoid being preyed upon by skuas and great black-backed gulls. Sheila and her sister would scramble down precipitous cliffs, in the dark, to seek out the 'strange wild laughter' of these birds. I ask Sheila if she ever told her parents about these precarious night-time adventures. She laughs at the open-mouthed expression of shock on my face. No, she replies, she did not tell her parents.

Sheila completed a degree in zoology at Aberdeen University, and in the 1960s she married a Foula man, Jim Gear. When newly married, they would visit the Manx shearwater colony together, to listen to the *leeries*. Then came the busy years of three young children. By the 1980s, when the children were old enough to accompany them up to the Noup at night, Sheila and Jim found that the boulder fields had fallen silent. This species, like the storm petrel, is particularly vulnerable to the predations of feral cats and rats. There are no rats in Foula but there are feral cats. And, no doubt, the *bonxies* contributed to their demise too. Manx shearwaters gather on the surface of the sea at night before flying into their colony, and they would have been easy prey.

I picture the last of the *leeries* flying up from the waves to the height of the Noup in the dark of night to find it silent, their cold eggs lying in the burrows. No one knows if there are any Manx shearwaters still breeding in Shetland now. The inaccessibility of many cliffs in Foula, and elsewhere in Shetland, gives hope that there may still be some hidden away, but the absence of rafts of these birds on the surface of the sea on summer nights suggests otherwise. The word *leerie* and its variants, *lyra* and *leera*, now mark the maps of these islands like memorials.

Kittiwakes still nest in Foula, but only just. In 1975, Sheila counted 7,750 well-built, meaning probably occupied, kittiwake nests. In 2019, she counted just 223. At the kittiwake sample plot that she checks each year – a single colony at a place called In Under da Stee – she counted 145 nests in 1989 and just 4 in 2019. Sheila juxtaposes these figures with a Foula kittiwake story.

In the 1950s, an unbroken flight line of kittiwakes commuted between the cliffs and the fresh water of Mill Loch. They flew straight over the croft called Leraback. The Isbisters, who lived at Leraback, could not hear themselves speak over the noise of these birds, a sound which they described as *lightsome*. This family must have had a fondness for birds, because they also fed a tame Arctic skua the remains of their morning porridge.

Now that I have seen Leraback, I can imagine this. Early morning, thousands of kittiwakes passing over the house, and the door opens and a woman comes out and empties the porridge scrapings onto the ground. A dark-coloured Arctic skua neatly steps in for a feed. And when I imagine this, a hollow and heavy feeling of loss, the opposite of *lightsome*, settles over me.

Sometimes when I visit Lerwick, if the tide is out, I leave the main shopping street and take some dank stone steps down to a beach of rich yellow sand, where there is often a scattering of sea glass and sea pottery. It is a sheltered spot, nestled between the Lodberries – the stone buildings that jut out into the sea where goods were once unloaded from boats.

When I searched for sea glass there once, I found sandeels swimming close to shore, their camouflage so complete that the shoal was made entirely from the thin dark ribbons of their shadows. Now and then, the sun would catch on their scales and the sandeels would shimmer with silver and many iridescent shades of pale greens, blues and pinks. I lost myself in this watching, forgetting that I was there to seek out sea glass. Another time, on a beach of red sand, a wave flung a sandeel ashore. It landed by my feet, wriggled for a moment and then buried down into the sand as gracefully as an auk folds itself through the surface of the sea.

Sandeels are not entirely lost from the seas around Shetland but there is little chance now of witnessing a fuglicaa. The late Bobby Tulloch, a renowned Shetland naturalist, explains this dialect word in *Migrations: Travels of a Naturalist*, a book published in 1991. He describes how it was once possible to sit on a cliff top in Shetland and watch seabirds 'herding' sandeels into a seething sphere-shaped mass. *Fuglicaa*, he explains, 'is derived from Old Norse "fugl" meaning bird and "caa" to drive (as in sheep) – literally a "bird-drive"'. When I first met this word, it reminded me of a conversation with the writer and broadcaster Mary Blance. We had been talking about Arctic terns – how she had visited a colony once to see how they were faring and had found that all the nests lay abandoned. She taught me the old Shaetlan word *brimbortend*, used to describe a fishing ground quite stripped of fish.

Sandeels are lipid-rich and they were once the staple diet of many kinds of seabirds, larger fish and certain marine mammals. They formed a critical component of the marine food web. In the 1970s, fishing boats local to Shetland began to fish for sandeels. Before this time, only Danish trawlers caught sandeels in these waters, to be processed into fish meal and fed to factory-farmed pigs. In one example of extreme profligacy, sandeels were also used to fuel Danish power stations. The sandeels caught by Shetland boats mostly ended up as feed for industrially farmed salmon.

In 1982, at the height of the Shetland sandeel fishery, 52,000 tonnes of sandeels were hauled out of the sea. In 1987, counts at 120 monitored Arctic tern colonies revealed that only a single chick had fledged. Kittiwake chicks fared little better, with most dying before they fledged. Both species had been unable to find enough suitably sized sandeels. In 1988, the Shetland Bird Club met with seabird and fisheries scientists, as well as fishing industry representatives, to try to understand the decline in sandeel numbers. The 1989 breeding season was again disastrous for many types of seabirds, with Arctic terns, Arctic skuas, kittiwakes and puffins the worst affected. Though the exact cause of the sandeel decline remained uncertain, in 1989 the Shetland Bird Club handed in a petition of 4,500 signatures to 10 Downing Street, calling for the closure of the Shetland sandeel fishery as a precautionary measure.

In his book *A Naturalist's Shetland*, J. Laughton Johnson examines this mid-1980s collapse of sandeel populations and suggests that overfishing was not the sole cause. Shetland sandeels, he writes, are not a discrete 'stock'. Planktonic sandeel larvae drift to Shetland from Orkney but, for some reason, this influx failed to appear in the 1980s. This may or may not have been an early warning of what is now understood to be happening in many places, including the Faroe Islands. The sea has warmed, and the species of plankton that the sandeels prey upon have been displaced to colder waters. I think again of this old Shetland word, *brimbortend*, and that there is more than one way to strip a sea of fish.

As a child, Sheila noticed that there was often a pretty white line on the surface of the sea near the Kittiwake Haa – the Kittiwake House – at a place along the cliffs called the Est Hoevdi. The line mirrored the contours of the cliff and she thought that it was made of sea foam. When she was old enough, she would go off round the island in a boat with her father. To her distress, she found the line was made from the floating wings of countless kittiwake corpses – the bodies of the birds had been eaten in part. She remembers crying inconsolably as they rowed back home, past the place called the Stacks.

Bonxies are known for their habit of stealing fish from other seabirds. It is fun to sit on a cliff top and watch these large brown birds gliding along, patrolling for incoming puffins or gannets returning with fish for their chicks. The drama of the *bonxie*'s swoop and attack, fish falling from a bill, a *bonxie* plummeting to the sea's surface before another of its kind gets to the stolen fish first. But, as Sheila learnt as a child, they kill seabirds too. I've watched a *bonxie* drown a puffin. It took a while to die. To speed things up, the *bonxie* would flare its wings skywards to push the puffin further underwater. Other *bonxies* gathered in, as if priming for a fight.

On my first trip to Foula in July 2016, I could not believe my eyes. The sky was filled with hundreds of *bonxies*, riding on thermals and circling the island's peaks like a vast flock of vultures. There were many more on the ground, single *bonxies* sat or stood on grassy mounds, guarding their young at the nest. It was disconcerting to see.

Foula now hosts one of the largest colonies of great skuas in the world, with more than 2,000 breeding pairs and several hundred non-breeding individuals. But, like the fulmar, they are relative newcomers. There are no traces of *bonxies*, locally, in the archaeological record. The origin of the great skua is still being debated by ornithologists, and it may be that their closest relative flies over the Southern Ocean. The first records of great skuas in Shetland come from the Orcadian naturalist George Low. In 1774 he found *bonxies* breeding in Unst, and recorded six or seven pairs on the hill of Hamnafield in Foula, but Sheila believes that more were probably nesting on the island's high ground at this time.

It is said that the Foula islanders welcomed the presence of the *bonxies* because they kept the white-tailed sea eagles away. These eagles had a reputation for stealing chickens and lambs. Foula fishermen saw *bonxies* as lucky omens and fed them with fish. But *bonxies* were not sacred per se. By the early 1800s, naturalist collectors were travelling to Shetland with their guns to take dead specimens of these then-rare birds. By the late 1800s, Foula islanders were selling blown *bonxie* eggs to egg collectors. Sheila recalls that her husband's grandmother and grandfather would gather six-score *bonxie* eggs from the south side of Hamnafield, to sell to the baker in Scalloway in the Shetland Mainland.

Foula is now a Special Protection Area, in part for its population of breeding *bonxies*. Sheila tells me how the increase in the number of *bonxies* here has changed the island in her lifetime. The fresh water of Mill Loch has become nutrient-rich and choked with algae. Hundreds of *bonxies* bathe in the loch and gather by the shore. The soil of the island has been enriched by their faeces, noticeably changing the vegetation to a brighter green.

My first visit to Foula was for the purpose of gathering *bonxie* pellets – the bone, feathers and now plastic that they cannot digest and regurgitate – for an ecologist, Lucy Gilbert, and her student colleague Susanna Quer. Lucy and Susanna are gathering these pellets to understand how the diet of *bonxies* is changing in Shetland. It is painstaking work.

They must dissect each pellet and identify fish remains by the unique anatomy of otoliths (ear bones).

Until recently, fish were discarded over the side of a fishing boat if they fell below the minimum size allowed for landing, or if they were bycatch and not the target species. Sometimes the target species would be discarded too, if the boat had already met its quota. A wasteful practice but also a time of plenty for many kinds of seabirds, including *bonxies*.

The EU started phasing in a ban on discards in 2015, and from 1 January 2019 all fish, for which there is a quota, had to be landed. It became illegal to discard them at sea. But the quantity of landed fish was lower than expected, suggesting the continued discarding of quota species. Even so, ecologists have found that *bonxies* are increasingly preying on seabirds now that discards have decreased, and small shoaling fish like sandeels have become scarce. This trend is reflected in the Shetland data too, as analysed by Lucy and Susanna, and it does not bode well for the remaining populations of puffins and kittiwakes.

I had gathered *bonxie* pellets once before, from the island of Fetlar, and was nervous from the memory of being dived at by these huge hook-billed and sharp-clawed birds. They swoop at human intruders from height and only swerve away at the very last moment, leaving a rush of air washing over bare skin. On that warm July day, a man from the Council had flown to Foula to inspect the island's roads. The inspection did not take long and so he went for a walk up a hill to see the view, and when he returned his scalp was bleeding. Sheila assures me that they rarely draw blood and they do not aim with their claws or beak – but, she adds, a diving *bonxie* did once knock a Foula man unconscious.

My family and I gather more pellets for Lucy and Susanna during our September visit to Foula in 2019 but it is uneventful; the breeding season has passed and the remaining *bonxies* are uninterested in our presence. My children run about the loch's shore shouting 'Got one!' and stand and mark the spot until my husband or I arrive to scoop the pellet into a plastic bag. Most are formed of fish bones or dark feathers, or light feathers. Two pellets contain plastic, and one the translucent shells of goose barnacles. In another, I find a small, hooked beak which I cannot identify. A wishful thought crosses my mind: that it might be the beak of a Manx shearwater chick. I show it to Sheila and she guesses that it is from a juvenile bird. Lucy later confirms that it is the beak of a *bonxie* chick. They eat their own too.

Sitting in the warmth of Ristie, with one eye on the gentle rise and fall of my children's sleeping bodies, I ask Sheila what it feels like to have witnessed and recorded the loss of many of Foula's seabirds. She tells me that it is a relief now, when each seabird monitoring season is over. An activity that was once joyful has become depressing. She suggests, without emotion, that more attention should be given to the psychological impact of witnessing the loss of species. There is a quiet power in her voice and her words are measured, but she holds my gaze long enough for me to think that she is not only speaking in general terms.

We discuss the notion of solastalgia, a term introduced by the environmental philosopher Glenn Albrecht that broadly concerns a sort of homesickness when the place in which you live is adversely impacted by environmental change. When I think of this term I think about my neighbour Michael. In the summers of his childhood, Michael would leave Lerwick to stay with an aunt in the island of Whalsay. She lived next to the beach at Vevoe, where a large colony of Arctic terns would nest in the shingle each summer. The noise of the birds was so great that he could not sleep at night.

Once, when Michael and I were both working in our respective gardens, two *rain geese*, red-throated divers, flew overhead, calling wildly, followed by their two young. All summer we had watched the adults commuting back and forth between their nest at the hill loch and the sea where they fished. They always flew low over the house, and the fish in their beaks were not sandeels. But somehow they had caught enough fish to raise two young. We both stopped what we were doing to watch the adult birds leading their fledglings out to sea for the first time. When all four of them landed safely on the surface, we both spontaneously lifted our arms in celebration of their success. The presence of red-throated divers in these islands, like the kittiwakes, is uncertain. In some years they raise few young.

I think of my friend Oliver Cheyne too, who can point to the exact places in the heather where Arctic skuas, *scooty alans*, used to nest in the hill ground, year after year. Arctic skuas are more elegant versions of great skuas; their wings are sharply angled and their tails are narrow and sting-like. Their manoeuvrability in the air, when stealing fish from the beaks of Arctic terns, is astonishing. But the chicks of

Arctic skuas have also fallen victim to the decrease in sand-eels and the increased predations of *bonxies*. There are no Arctic skuas nesting on our local hill ground now, but Olly and I have both watched the same pale-coloured bird, buff-bellied and dark-winged, sitting listlessly next to one of the small lochs each summer, as if it knows that it has flown all this way for nothing. With each loss, an emotional pain accretes for those who have paid attention. My experience of these losses in Shetland is mostly second-hand, but even with this distance it is painful enough.

Before she leaves Ristie and heads back out into the dark, Sheila also speaks of the joy that can still be found. There are other birds to count too, the summer breeding species that are still abundant enough in Shetland: waders like *whaups* (curlews), and passerines such as *laevereks* (skylarks) and *sten-shakkers* (wheatears). In April, *tysties* (black guille-mots) come to the low cliff tops to lek – to hold courtship gatherings – and in later summer there is the fun of ringing Arctic skua chicks, if there are any, and *bonxie* chicks. The adults of both species, she explains, become quite docile when you handle their chicks, as if they have accepted that their young are lost. She adds that she only wears metal-framed glasses now. Nest-defending *bonxies* have broken those made from plastic.

I ask Sheila if she will write a book that will follow on from *Foula: Island West of the Sun*. She smiles and explains that she always said that she would write another when she reached the age of eighty, but it takes time and she is busy. It would be a difficult book to write. Foula is still the island of the birds, but some, like the kittiwakes, seem as good as gone, and the strange wild laughter of Foula's *leeries* now exists in memory alone. Sheila gathers her torch, wraps herself in her waterproof and returns up the track in the dark. I am left with memories that are not mine. I am both a little more sad and immensely grateful.

On our last day in Foula, we wake to a deep blue sky and a sea of the same colour. A brisk breeze steals the heat from the sun and caps the waves in white. My daughter asks if we can walk up and along the ridgeline of Soberlie. I am doubtful of this plan but my family slow their pace to mine and, steadily, we gain height on a slope scattered with the soft grey feathers of fulmars. A single large puffin egg, the contents long drained, lies within a hollow of grass, and nearby there is a raven pellet, stuck through with tiny white bones and shining with the violet iridescence of a beetle's wing. A small herd of Shetland ponies watches our progress.

It is a kind of ecstasy to reach the height of Soberlie. I catch my husband's eye and we embrace. At a safe distance from the edge of the cliff we sit and eat a picnic lunch. We are riding through the Atlantic Ocean on this porpoise-shaped fin of a hill. To the north, the lighthouse on the low-lying Vee Skerries aligns with the bare rock dome of Muckle Ossa. To the north-west, the faint shadow of an oil platform interrupts the otherwise-clear horizon. It is the Clair, or maybe the new Clair Ridge. The *Island Constructor*, a ship so large that it dwarfs the Mainland's coastline, moves out towards the oilfield; and high above, a jet flies towards Canada, trailing white through the bright blue sky.

My children sit and stare in quiet contemplation at the

island laid out below them. My son breaks the silence and points to the school with its slide and its playground poly-tunnel, a small oasis of shelter from the wind that is filled with flowers and fruit trees heavily laden with plump apples and pears. We locate the suntrap where we sat yesterday, a stone bench sheltered by the high wall of Sheila's kale yard, a beautiful sanctuary-like walled garden. The air had been filled with the scent of honeysuckle and mint. A migrant chiffchaff had flitted around the wall, neatly marking the shift from summer to autumn.

High on Soberlie, a painted lady – a migrant butterfly – lands on the grass and then launches out over the cliff's edge to become a tiny speck of summer flying north over a vast expanse of ocean. Moments later, as if in exchange, a single swallow appears, and we speculate where in Norway it may have nested and where in Africa it will winter, though Sheila later tells me that it could have been one of the swallows that nests in the old house near Ristie. The swallow crests the cliff in near-vertical flight, slows and then levels out to skim low over the grass, all the way down the steep slope to the sea. And all the while, above us and below us, fulmars circle and circle.

Maalie

Northern Fulmar

Two weeks after visiting Foula, I drive down to the airport at Sumburgh to catch an early morning flight to Orkney. I'm travelling with a suitcase of frozen fulmars, each destined to become a data set in a research project that analyses the plastic content of their stomachs. Nine fulmars in total, all found dead on Shetland beaches or roads during 2018 and 2019.

The sky is pale pink and cloudless, but a thick bank of white haar sits on the sea to the east of Shetland and threatens to roll in and delay the flight. I fret that the fulmars will defrost and smell, leaving me to explain my unusual cargo. But the plane slips out before the haar reaches in, and banks low over the lighthouse and seabird cliffs of Sumburgh Head. The breeding season is over and the cliffs are bare and melancholy in the absence of all the guillemots, puffins and razorbills. I am glad of the company of fulmars in winter. They soften the desolation of cliff-bound places. Through the window of the plane, Fair Isle rises green and jewel-like from a pale-blue ocean. Minutes pass and then the Orcadian island of Sanday comes into view, its scalloped outline bright with shell sand.

This opportunity to be trained in the measurement and

dissection of fulmars has arisen because I volunteer for the beached bird survey. I had asked Will Miles if I might watch a fulmar dissection. But he generously suggested that I undergo the training myself. I hesitated to say yes. I'm not sure how I will cope, cutting a bird open. It is also a long time since I've been on a training course of any kind. But I did say yes; the chance to know these birds more fully, both inside and out, is intriguing. Inside me, palindromic rheumatism is still quiet after the course of immunosuppression. I will not have to worry about my hands. They will function well enough to wield a scalpel with accuracy.

At the airport in Kirkwall, Jenni Kakkonen, a young Finnish woman and marine biologist who lives and works in the Orkney Mainland, greets me with a warm smile. She is much taller than me and slows her pace to mine as we walk to her car. She slings the bag of Shetland fulmars into the boot, where they sit alongside a bag of fulmars gathered dead from the beaches of Orkney. We set off to a veterinary shed in Harray, where the seabird ecologist and fulmar specialist Jan Andries van Franeker and his wife, Yvonne, have come from the Dutch island of Texel to train us both in fulmar dissection. Jan has devoted most of his working life to studying the plastic content of fulmar stomachs. His data set is already, for some places, more than thirty years long, but ridding the oceans of plastic will take much longer than this. He is due to retire soon but his work will continue, led by his colleague Susanne Kühn. Jan has already trained many people from all along the North Sea seaboard to carry out this work, and Jens-Kjeld Jensen in the Faroe Islands too.

We drive past the Neolithic chambered cairn at Maes-howe and fields of cattle, and under big skies filled with ragged skeins of geese and rolling flocks of swallows. Ork-ney appears a gentler place to live than Shetland. There is the same close play between land and water but the soil is more fertile and the coastline is less obviously sea-torn. The islands of Orkney appear more at peace with the sea somehow. Only the island of Hoy looms tall, like a shep-herd tending to a flock of sheep. A ferry connects Orkney with the Scottish mainland in a journey that takes only an hour, and this alone sometimes makes me wish I lived in this archipelago. It seems an island place that is easier to leave and to come home to. The mainland of Scotland is often in sight, and in the summer both swallows and Arctic terns can be seen. Swallows nest in the airport buildings at Sum-burgh, and a single pair sometimes nests in Unst and in Foula too, but otherwise we only see these birds of summer as they pass through Shetland on migration. One here, two there, and many of these encounters are so brief that they are over before they have begun.

But on each visit to Orkney, I have found it difficult to reach the shore at times. There is more arable land, more barbed-wire fencing containing cattle. It is easier to roam freely in Shetland.

Jenni and I confess to each other that we are a little ner-vous at the prospect of learning how to navigate the bodies of fulmars. I am, by now, used to handling dead seabirds, but I have never taken a knife and cut one open. But Jenni's company puts me at ease. She is warm and thoughtful. I ask her about her work as a marine biologist. She monitors the tiny invertebrates – creatures like marine worms – that live in the sand along the shores of Scapa Flow. This monitoring work began in 1974, when the oil terminal was constructed in the small island of Flotta. Jenni has analysed forty years of data, and has found that populations of marine invertebrates have not significantly changed despite all the oil- and gas-industry activity in the sheltered water of Scapa Flow. This is good news, but I sit in subdued silence and contemplate the next forty years and the unfolding climate emergency. I sometimes question if the time that I spent working in conservation was time spent in vain. I don't think so, but sometimes it can seem that way.

At Northvet in Harray, a herd of cows gather at a barbed-wire fence to watch Jenni and me unload the bags of dead fulmars from the boot of the car. Jan and Yvonne welcome us into the small autopsy shed – the kind that is used for cattle. The ceiling of the shed is rigged with chains and hoists and there is a poster on the wall illustrating vast and cavernous hearts, some healthy, some not. A neat row of fulmars, from the north-east of England and the east of Scotland, have been set out on a metal table that drains centrally into a bucket. There is a single fulmar on a workbench between a metal rule, callipers and a scalpel. It looks like a meal set out on a table. Jan is impatient to begin, and so Jenni and I put on our lab coats and Yvonne readies a data recording sheet. I am already a little queasy from the early morning start and not sure that I will be able to stomach the sight and smell of a dissected bird.

Some of the corpses smell truly rank. Some smell only of their usual musty scent. Jan warns us that we will smell of fulmar by the end of each day and that this scent is hard to remove. He laughs when I say that I am staying in a hostel and sharing communal spaces. He is softly spoken and looks a little like Father Christmas, white-bearded and with twinkling eyes. His dedication to the accuracy of his work is absolute but he is also a patient and encouraging instructor. Yvonne is a plant scientist by training and is similarly rigorous in her recording of data, gently correcting Jan if a measurement is missed. She is kindly attentive and makes sure that Jenni and I have all that we need. I begin to feel enough at ease to settle into the work, and find that I am able to ignore the pungent smells.

For all my accumulated hours of watching, I know little about the internal anatomy of birds. Jan makes it all look so easy, with the muscle memory of more than a thousand such dissections. I baulk at first, watching him remove a fulmar's stomach, but curiosity soon takes over. He reaches up into the cavity of the bird's chest, past the glistening liver and the dull muscle of the heart, and pulls away the connective tissue to release the oesophagus. When he yanks the oesophagus down, the bird's head animates, jerking backwards and into its body. One clean cut of the oesophagus and one clean cut of the intestine, and both stomachs are free – the soft-walled proventriculus, where the fulmar's foul-smelling and lipid-rich oil is stored, and the tough gizzard where plastic is ground down. Both are carefully bagged in a sealable and coded plastic bag, and when all the notations are complete, the gaping remains of the excavated fulmar are placed in a bin.

Jenni and I watch as Jan cuts open a stomach and shows

us how to wash the contents out over a very fine-meshed sieve. Slowly, and peering closely through his glasses, he uses tweezers to extract items from the mess of gloop. Each find is placed in a plastic Petri dish:

> the lens of a fish's eye, a perfect sphere
> a squid's beak, black and hooked
> the tiny seeds of a plant
> the sodden feathers of a migrant songbird that
>   has succumbed to exhaustion
> a nurdle, a pellet of industrial plastic
> a sharp fragment of a plastic container.

It is a little like beachcombing. I am hooked. I ask Jan if he has found drift-seeds from the tropics in fulmar stomachs and he shakes his head to say no. I mention a record of them being found in the stomachs of fulmars by the islanders of St Kilda in the mid-nineteenth century, and he nods.

Jan focuses his work on fulmars because gulls and skuas regurgitate indigestible material – bone, feather, shell and plastic. Fulmars break these tough materials down in their muscular gizzards. More than any other seabird in the northern hemisphere, fulmars eat the small fragments of plastic that float at the surface of the ocean. Some scientists suggest that the algae that accumulates on the plastic's surface makes the litter smell like food, but this hypothesis is contested. The reasons why fulmars ingest plastic remain unclear, but we do know that they do not forage on land or close inshore – and so the plastic in their stomachs has come from the open ocean.

Every intact fulmar found on the shore, or by the side of

the road, is a potential source of data. The northern fulmar, as a species, has become an unwitting ecological monitor of marine litter, the maritime equivalent of a canary in a coal mine. Thanks to Jan's work, we now know that 93 per cent of northern fulmars have plastic in their stomach, and that the average number of plastic pieces in a northern fulmar's stomach is twenty. The average cumulative weight of plastic in a northern fulmar's stomach is 0.2 grams. On a human scale, this would equate to a lunchbox full of plastic.

In almost all the birds that we open up, we find that there is no subcutaneous or intestinal fat; the breast muscle is concave, not convex. All have starved. In several birds, the down is missing too – there is no dark fluff covering their skin. It is possible that the plastic load in their stomachs made them feel full. It is also possible that the plastic in their stomach reduced the space that could have been occupied by food. Shards of plastic can damage the stomach wall and plastic can become a surface on which toxic pollutants concentrate. Microplastics can penetrate organs. It is a coalescence of several sickening factors. Plastic may not kill fulmars directly, but it decreases their fitness and ability to reproduce. It edges them towards an early death, before which they will hunger and sense cold.

Jan's research has shown that the levels of plastic in the North Sea are decreasing, albeit very slowly, but still, this is a kernel of optimism to hold on to when faced with a strandline of plastic. The OSPAR Commission, who oversee the (Oslo Paris) Convention for the Protection of the Marine Environment of the North-East Atlantic, has set the target that less than 10 per cent of fulmars should have 0.1 grams or more of plastic in their stomachs, a target that is unlikely to be reached before 2049.

It is rare to find an intact dead fulmar on the shore. Gulls, ravens and crows usually reach the corpse first and open the body, or the sea strips the corpse and washes ashore a pair of wings still joined to the sharp jut of the bird's keel bone. But one day I did find an intact fulmar lying on its belly, where the ebb tide had left it. Its plumage was a mess of sodden feathers. I gathered it up and gave it to Martin Heubeck, who passed it on to Jan. A few months later I received an email with a report of the plastic found in this fulmar's stomach: thirty-seven particles with a total mass of 0.2369 grams. There was a photograph of this plastic. I could make out a cluster of dirty polystyrene, a few shards of sharp-edged rigid plastic, the fragment of what looked to be a plastic bag, and a single yellow sphere, the soft pellet of an airgun. An accompanying note explained that airgun pellets are regularly found in the stomachs of fulmars. The report detailed the stomach contents of ten more Shetland-found fulmars. One had been oiled. Five had starved. One of the starved birds, an adult female, had almost five grams of plastic in her belly, including the jagged yellow fragment of a Nestlé coffee jar lid.

While we work, Jan tells Jenni and me about a grim incident in the Orcadian island of Papa Westray. In the spring of 2016, more than 460 fulmars became trapped, and then died, in a partly renovated croft house. Jan was able to work out that most of these fulmars were young. They had probably been prospecting for nest sites. A few must have become trapped and then lured the rest in. From the heap of corpses, Jan salvaged 117 stomachs and found lower than expected quantities of plastic. He thinks that the birds sat and starved, and all the while their muscular gizzards broke down the plastic. It would have passed through their intestines, out onto the mess of the corpse-strewn floor.

By the third morning of sitting in the cold veterinary shed, with its sliding door that bangs in the wind, I'm at ease with the work and find a steady rhythm. My fulmar 'manual' is splattered with yellow oil and bloody thumbprints, and Jan remarks that this is good, it is there to be well used. Despite the gore and the maggots, it has been a pleasant few days listening to Finnish and Dutch accents. We make a merry team.

I find that I can cope better with birds that have decomposed a little. The freshness and the brightness of the blood of some of the birds is disconcerting; they smell almost alive. I recognise the smell of my own blood. At times, my hands are covered in a mix of abrasive sand that glitters with mica, blood and the yellow sludge of intestinal fluids. Dead lice fall from feathers, dead maggots emerge from skin and organs, immobilised at the point of freezing. I do not wear disposable medical gloves. Jan never does, he says they make him clumsy, and after one butter-fingered attempt I abandon them too. Jenni prefers to keep hers on, to put a more comfortable distance between her skin and the dead bird. In the 1930s, in the Faroe Islands, there was an outbreak of a disease called psittacosis that passed from fulmars to humans, and pregnant women died. More women than men were infected, possibly because it was the women who processed the fulmar chicks for consumption.

We see birds of all ages. Young males with dark testes the size of mouse droppings. Breeding males with large white testes brimful with sperm. Females with ovaries bursting with follicles and a lace-like oviduct that has been stretched by the passage of an egg. Jan points out lungs that have been damaged by drowning. Fulmars drown in trawl nets and on longlines. Longline fishing is not practised by Shetland boats but I have found lethal tangles of nylon line washed up on the shore – long lengths of it, covered in regularly spaced hooks. When these lines are reeled out, the baited hooks sit at the surface for a while and ensnare birds. As more line is reeled out these baited hooks begin to sink and the ensnared birds drown.

We check each lower mandible for hook injuries by pushing our finger up to stretch the skin taut. We find no tears but Jan confirms that one of the Shetland birds also has damaged lungs and probably died by drowning. The Atlantic beach where it was found is a favourite of mine. It is also a place where longline fishing litter washes up. On one visit, a gannet lay above the strandline, fresh and pristine except for the fishing hook deep in the shoulder of its wing. A few weeks later, the corpse of a young minke whale washed ashore there. The damage to its fluke suggested that it too had been entangled in fishing gear.

When Jan places another fulmar found in Shetland on the workbench, grains of mica-rich sand and tiny fragments of plastic fall from its feathers. Its wings are flecked with sticky balls of dark oil. Even in death, the body of this bird became a gathering place for marine pollution.

Towards the end of the workshop, I begin to imagine the

life of each bird that we dissect. I find it difficult to imagine the places where they fly, far out at sea. But I can see them alive, binding the dark to the light as they loop in and out of the deep confines of a shadowy geo. The RSPB in Shetland has collaborated with doctors to develop a set of nature prescriptions to improve our well-being. One prescription, or suggestion, is to watch *maalies* in flight – to be lost in the beauty of their looping, gliding movement. But it is not always easy to forget the plastic that fulmars hold in their stomachs once you know that it is there, however mesmerising these birds can be. Sat in the shed at Harray, I wonder if I will ever be able to watch fulmars again without thinking of their insides.

Two of the birds that we dissect are 'blue' fulmars, or dark-colour morphs, visitors from the Arctic. I have yet to see an Arctic fulmar alive. I strongly wish to travel to the Arctic to see them at their breeding grounds – but now there is no escaping the fact that we are within a climate emergency, I will have to content myself with sitting on a Shetland cliff in winter, and maybe, just maybe, one will fly within the range of my telescope.

Jan shows us a picture of a decomposing fulmar lying on the sand of a beach. A single white egg lies encased in a fragile cage of tattered feathers and exposed bone. Just one of many fulmars that washed ashore in a wreck of this species in the North Sea in 2004. All the dead fulmars were missing down, or had very little, and almost all were mature females. Jan explains to us that fulmars do not normally reproduce if they are in poor condition. It is strange to see an egg like this. He thinks that a pollutant might have disrupted the endocrine system, the hormones that trigger reproduction.

This photo brings to mind another image of a stricken fulmar. In the winter of 2019, in Shetland, a fulmar was found lying dead in the snow on a beach, entirely smothered in thick black fuel oil. A sample of the oil was analysed. A ship had illegally cleaned its bilge tanks at sea. One spring day, I met a guillemot standing on a sea-bound rock, just a few metres from the shore below our house. Guillemots never come ashore at this place and it was strange to see, but as I walked closer it turned to face me. The feathers of one wing were slicked in oil. Its white belly was smeared brown. Yet it had survived all the storms of winter and looked so full of life.

These auks spend much of their time swimming on the surface of the sea and so are vulnerable to oil spills. Just as fulmars are used to monitor marine litter, guillemots are used to monitor the amount of oil pollution in the sea. OSPAR has set a target: 'The average proportion of oiled Common Guillemots in all winter months (November to April) should be 10% or less of the total found dead or dying in each of 15 areas of the North Sea over a period of at least 5 years.' The seabirds that have been found dead and oiled on Shetland's shores can map the world in oil: fuel oil made from Nigerian or Russian crude; unrefined crude oil from the Middle East or the East Shetland Basin. Incidences of oiling have remained low since the late 1990s, but they do still happen.

Sometimes, in the veterinary shed in Harray, small white feathers swirl around the tabletop and cling to our gut-wet fingers or stick to the polyester of our lab coats. I think of the women of St Kilda, the endless plucking of fulmars and all the feathers that must have clung to their clothes, skin and hair. The St Kildan birds were eaten by the islanders; the feathers that did not escape were sold to pay the rent, and were used to stuff pillows and bedding. We place one bird on the dissection table and yellow oil gushes out from its open beak. I've read that the St Kilda islanders used this oil as a salve for rheumatic joints. I am not at all tempted to smear it all over my fingers and wrists, but maybe I would be if it was a day of pain.

I part the breast feathers of my last bird, find the sharp ridge of the breastbone and slide the scalpel down, stopping where the breastbone stops. I peel the skin apart with my hands. Under the skin, the soft white shafts of moulted feathers lie flaccid. The flight muscle is a deep red and a sheet of filmy connective tissue hides the organs. I pinch the connective tissue up and away from the stomach, nick it with the scalpel and widen the small tear with my fingers to reveal the stomach and the intestines. I move these to one side and gently pull away connective tissue that is moist with blood.

It is a female. Her ovaries had been producing follicles and the oviduct has been stretched wide by an egg. The absence of fat on her body tells us that she too had starved. Jan places her stomach in a labelled bag to wash out later. He will send us a full report in due course, and I cannot wait. I wake in the night thinking of this fulmar, and though I scrubbed my skin and my hair before going to bed, I remain enveloped in her smell.

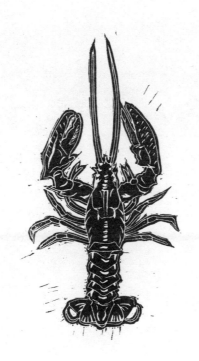

Netukulimk

On my last evening in Orkney, Jan gives a talk on his work on fulmars and plastic pollution to the Orkney Natural History Society. I sit beside Jenni and Yvonne in the spacious hall of the St Magnus Centre. Jan's talk is more of a story-telling than a lecture, and his engaging style makes the grim facts of marine litter all the more compelling.

Plastic objects washed up on a shore can sometimes tell a story, Jan explains. Most often, these stories are mundane. He talks us through a day in the life of a human, using photographs of objects he has found on the Texel shore: a coffee jar lid, a UHT milk carton, a toothbrush, a bottle of toilet cleaner and a toilet brush, and so on. We laugh, but uneasily.

Once you begin to take notice of plastic on a beach, or coming in on the flood tide, Jan observes, then you will never not see it again. It took me a while to learn this but I have found it to be true. At first, it was a shock to realise how much plastic must be held in the sea. But years later, I do not completely recoil from the sight of plastic in a strandline. I am not inured to plastic litter and its harms, but my revulsion is now tempered by desire. There are plastic objects that I am thrilled to find: toys or parts of toys, oil- and gas-industry safety checklists and valve-maintenance-procedure labels, the bright orange bait pots and many-coloured fish boxes that I grow herbs and flowers in. But most of all, I like to search for plastic lobster trap tags from North America.

In six years of searching, I have collected more than one hundred of these lobster trap tags. My eyes are so attuned to their exact form – these thin strips of curved plastic – that I risk walking past sea beans. Almost half the tags in my collection are from Newfoundland or Labrador and the rest are from Nova Scotia and Maine. I have four from Massachusetts, three from Rhode Island, two from New Hampshire and one from New York. New York!

A hundred or so tags seems like an abundance, but more than 3 million lobster traps are set each year in Maine alone. And each year, lobster fishers in the USA and Canada must secure a new tag to each of their traps. A licence number, licencing year and a state or province code is imprinted onto the plastic. The tags are often colour-coded by year too. Inevitably, many are lost to the sea. Sometimes a bundle of tags wash up, looped through one another, and I imagine these to have fallen from someone's hand. Once adrift, the ocean shuffles their years, and so a tag from 2008 can arrive in Shetland before a tag from 1998.

I keep them jam-packed in a large glass container and they make a bright and attractive display that conjures up a 'vacation land' scene in my mind: a wooded shore with rustic clapboard houses, a picturesque harbour with small creel boats moored up, a restaurant where you can sit outside on picnic benches and eat lobsters with a side of fries. Except for the single tag from New York, which suggests a tiny lobster boat puttering past a backdrop of towering skyscrapers.

Sometimes I dip into the Internet and explore the locations of the tags. On one such search I find a newspaper article on lobsters and climate change. Since 2008, few lobster have been brought ashore south of New York, and more are now being landed in an area north of Boston. The warming of the ocean is moving lobsters north, or further offshore where the water is deeper and colder. But the Gulf of Maine is warming rapidly too. The lobster industry in Maine has experienced a boom but there are warnings of an imminent crash.

Meanwhile, the acidification of the ocean is corroding the calcium carbonate that forms the basis of a lobster's shell, and warmer ocean temperatures make lobsters more susceptible to the bacterial infections that cause shell disease. In Maine, people are advised not to eat lobster tomalley, the creature's liver, which turns green upon cooling and is said to be a delicacy. It contains high levels of dioxins – toxins from industrial effluent.

At a certain point in my Internet explorations, I realise that I know more about the lobsters on the other side of the Atlantic than I do about the lobsters that are caught in the creels in the *voe* below my house. I steer the Internet search engine back towards home and read a 2017 report that details how the seas around Scotland have been contaminated by the pesticides used by the salmon farming industry. Caged salmon are vulnerable to infestations of sea lice. These lice are a type of marine copepod that has evolved to feed on salmon skin and blood. Caging wild fish has meant that populations of sea lice have exploded. On the website of Salmon & Trout Conservation Scotland, there are nightmarish photos of live fish in the confines of a cage in the sea off Skye. Large patches of skin have been completed stripped away and their flesh is exposed.

The salmon farming industry in Scotland uses different methods to rid the fish of lice, including a neurotoxic pesticide called emamectin benzoate. This pesticide harms lobsters too. The beach that we snorkel from looks out through a sound called Swarbacks Minn. In the 2017 report, Swarbacks Minn is listed as being contaminated by these neurotoxic pesticides. I turn my attention back to the other side of the ocean. It is easier to contemplate the pollution of a distant place than the pollution of the sea in which my children swim.

Three of the lobster trap tags in my collection are of an earlier kind – bright orange nameplates imprinted with information that is not standardised. These came into use in the mid-to-late 1980s. They read:

> Jim Muise (found Mainland, Shetland)
> FV [Fishing Vessel] Elsha, J Henderson (found Mainland, Shetland)
> Travis Smith Cedar Island NC [North Carolina] (found Sanday, Orkney).

I post a picture of these orange nameplate tags on the 'All Things Lobstering' Facebook page, and a woman responds to say that she is the daughter of Jim Muise. Soon I am exchanging emails with Jim, who lives in Massachusetts. He was always drawn to the ocean, he explains, and started working as a lobster fisherman straight out of school. He is retired now but used to live and fish from Saugus, and he set his traps in Massachusetts Bay or along the coastline. In the Perfect Storm of 1991, Jim had eight hundred traps out and it took five divers seven days to retrieve 240 of them. The storm changed the map by which lobsters and fish migrate, he tells me, and the fishing was never the same again.

I ask Jim about the wildlife that he would see from his boat. The porpoises and pilot and humpback whales are familiar, but the right whales, great white sharks, thresher sharks, turtles and flying fish are excitingly strange. I ask about fishing superstitions too, and explain that many boats in Shetland still leave their moorings in a *sungaets* direction – clockwise, or following the path of the sun. It is seen as bad luck to do otherwise. There are plenty, Jim replies; never whistle on a boat in autumn because of the west wind, and always pull your boat up to the dock on the starboard side.

I look at Saugus on Google Maps, and my mental image of a vacation land is replaced by the reality of an industrialised area between Boston and Salem. A cursory search on the Internet reveals that the river is heavily polluted, and the toxicity of a coastal landfill incinerator – the oldest of its kind in the USA – is causing nearby residents to raise questions about local incidences of cancer. Still, this named tag has, with the help of the Internet, connected me with a person on the other side of the Atlantic, and I have gained a glimpse of life on a distant shore.

I search for the area code of the phone number from the Elsha tag, and it leads me to Portsmouth in New Hampshire, where the Piscataqua River forms the border with Maine – an area that also looks semi-industrial. But the

North Carolina Cedar Island tag gives me a place in which
to situate my beachcombing-the-western-Atlantic fantasy.
Cedar Island lies at the terminus of a long peninsula, much
of which falls within a National Wildlife Refuge and is sheltered from the open Atlantic by the Outer Banks, a delicate
string of sandy barrier islands that arc north and into the
state of Virginia.

A ferry connects Cedar Island with Ocracoke, the southernmost of the islands. Travelling north, up the Outer
Banks, brings you to Hatteras Island. North of Cape Hatteras, the Gulf Stream peels away from the coast and begins
to cross the Atlantic. I imagine the thrill of casting a message in a bottle adrift from Cape Hatteras, in the wild hope
that it would be carried across the ocean to Shetland. The
wind would be offshore and capping the waves in white,
and I would stand out on the sandy spit and watch for black
skimmers, the Rynchops of Rachel Carson's *Under the Sea
Wind*. Perhaps one would fly past, low over the water, its
huge red and black bill open, skimming the surface for food.
On the Audubon website I read that these birds sometimes
lie prone on the sand, resting like exhausted dogs.

For a while, I read everything I can about the Outer
Banks islands. I order a tourist brochure, compile a mental
list of what I would search for on the beach: a sand dol-
lar and a baby's ear moonsnail. I buy a second-hand book
online, *How to Read a North Carolina Beach*, knowing that I
will probably never set foot on a North Carolina beach.
I track the paths of hurricanes as they bear down on the
Outer Banks, and refresh newsfeeds to follow the progress
of island evacuations. The climate emergency is making life

in these islands increasingly difficult. These lobster trap tags make me wish to fly across the Atlantic, and they remind me that it is no longer responsible to do so.

I am slow, at first, to realise why some lobster trap tags do not have a state or province code. Three are imprinted with 'NCC', which stands for NunatuKavut Community Council, the governing body that represents the Inuit of south and central Labrador. A fourth tag, faded red and issued in 2014, can be traced to Nova Scotia by the familiarity of the code NCNS. The word 'Netukulimk' is imprinted on the plastic.

I find this tag in December 2018, after an Atlantic storm. The wind is still strong when I arrive at the beach. An otter fishes close to shore, in a churn of white water. It clambers out onto a rock to eat a fish but a wave sweeps it straight back into the sea. Out in the Atlantic, Foula floats on a dense layer of spindrift. I am very happy to see two pineapples, lying side by side, I have been waiting for them. In October 2017, a ship called the *Lombok Strait* lost two containers of pineapples while sailing through storm-driven seas. Oceanographers modelled the probable course of the drifting fruit and predicted their arrival in Shetland. The insides of both have turned to mush but the tough skin remains intact.

I pluck eleven starry skate eggcases from sea foam and find a cigarette lighter from Maniitsoq in southern Greenland. A rubber duck in a top hat lies near the remains of a weather balloon. I find seven lobster trap tags in total, including the tag stamped Netukulimk.

Back home, I learn that the Netukulimk tag was issued by

Mime'j Seafoods Limited, a Native Council of Nova Scotia company. The purpose of Mime'j Seafoods is to facilitate Indigenous access to permits, licences and fishing gear. It is notable that out of the one hundred or so tags in my collection, only four can be traced back to Indigenous communities.

I research more, and read that the Netukulimkewe'l Commission has several roles, one of which is to promote a better understanding of the Mi'kmaq access to, and use of, natural resources. I email the person listed as a contact, Tim Martin, who is also the president of Mime'j Seafoods. Tim is generous in his response, and when I ask about Netukulimk, he sends me a document, *Mi'kmaq Fisheries, Netukulimk: Towards a Better Understanding.*

Netukulimk is defined as: 'A Mi'kmawey concept which includes the use of the natural bounty provided by the Creator for the self-support and well-being of the individual and the community at large.' The Creator, Niscaminou, is the sun and the giver of life, and the Mi'kmaq world view 'encompasses all living things. Knowing that all animate and many inanimate beings are alive and embraced with spirit, we are obligated to respect and honour them.' In the document, a quote explains that a tree is animate until it dies. If its wood is made into an object, it becomes animate again, imbued with its maker's power and by the significance of its new function, as a bow or bowl, for example.

Mi'kma'ki, the ancestral homelands of the Mi'kmaq, the document explains, is the world of the eastern rim of Canada, the place of the rising sun. The Mi'kmaq are caretakers of Mi'kma'ki, a territory which extends over five provinces.

'For the Mi'kmaq, our land and its life is not a commodity but the heritage of our community. The Mi'kmaq world view is to live in harmony with the earth and its resources whereas the British held they had the right to exploit and use the land as their property.'

From the document I learn how British colonists severed the Mi'kmaq from their land. The Mime'j Seafood Company must exist because this access has not yet been fully restored. Nine full pages detail the legal and constitutional rights of the Mi'kmaq to hunt, fish, fowl and gather, as granted in various treaties – and in particular those dating from 1725 and 1752. Test cases are listed too, in a long cataloguing of examples of Indigenous people defending their legal right to fish or hunt in the face of frequent prosecution.

In October 2020, a newspaper article reports that hundreds of commercial lobster fishermen, all settlers, surrounded a warehouse near Yarmouth, Nova Scotia, trapping two Indigenous lobster fishermen and four settler men inside. They cut the power, smashed windows, urinated on a vehicle and slashed its tyres, and threatened to burn the warehouse down. Mi'kmaq lobster fishers have the right to earn a moderate livelihood and to fish all year round. Commercial fishers have objected to this out-of-season trapping, claiming that it will deplete lobster numbers – a claim that is dismissed by fisheries scientists. The number of traps worked by Indigenous fishers is a drop in the ocean compared to the number of traps deployed by commercial outfits.

*

If hope is a hierarchy of wishes then I am happy enough, each time that I beachcomb, to find fragments of the bark of paper birch, *Betula papyrifera*, a tree that grows in Canada and the northern states of the USA. It arrives here looking so vibrant, almost aglow, and emanating the life force of a growing tree. Sometimes it comes in the form of neat scrolls; other times it is a mess of dishevelled ringlets. I treasure the rare pieces that are flat and rigid and surround a knot in the bark, because these knots look uncannily like a human navel.

One of the Shetland names for this washed-up birch bark is *neverspel*, from the Old Norse *næfr*, meaning 'birch bark', and *spila*, a thin narrow strip or fragment of wood. There are many other names, and some tell of light: Loki's Candle, Gooniman's Candle and Willie Gun's Candle. *Neverspel* is still gathered in Shetland to light fires with, but I mostly hoard these precious fragments of distant wooded places. I long to visit Canada and spend time wandering through groves of paper birch trees. I'd search their trunks for neat cascades of holes made by the bills of yellow-bellied sapsuckers, a type of woodpecker, and just maybe there would be a ruby-throated hummingbird probing one of these sap wells with the tiny curve of its beak.

A curiosity for *neverspel* led me to the story of the Beothuk, who lived in the place that is now called Newfoundland and whose culture was intimately connected to the use of birch bark. Displaced by European settlers and reluctant to make contact, they retreated to the interior where, without access to the sea, they could not survive. Their last known representative, Shanawdithit, died a young woman in 1829 after succumbing to tuberculosis.

In 2019, the National Museum of Scotland finally agreed to return the skulls of two Beothuk people, Demasduit and Nonosabasut. I try to follow the story of this repatriation but the Scottish press frames the return of these skulls in articles that are devoid of any context, as if it is simply an act of benevolent generosity. I turn to the Internet instead. Demasduit was kidnapped by a European fur trapper, John Peyton Jr. Her husband, Nonosabasut, was killed by this man, or one of his men, when he tried to rescue his wife. She is said to have supplicated herself before her captors, kneeling on the ground and baring her breast to indicate that she was nursing an infant.

A Canadian Broadcasting Corporation report on the return of the skulls simply details that she then 'lived with her captor'. This neutral phrase must undoubtedly hide multiple levels of abuse and trauma. Her skull and her husband's skull were stolen from their burial ground by a white and Scottish-educated settler, and this is how they came to be in the possession of the National Museum of Scotland. The return of the skulls took five years of campaigning by Chief Mi'sel Joe of the Miawpukek First Nation, a detail that is also missing from most of the Scottish media reports.

In my jar of beachcombed plastic toys, I have the remains of a few dolls. The skin colour of each leg and arm, and one full-breasted and narrow-waisted torso, is white. One day, on the home beach, I found a blue plastic figurine moulded into the shape of a young girl with two long braids and a headband – a 'Red Indian' caricature. 'BONUX' is stamped in capital letters on her back, and a search on the Internet reveals that she is a Monchhichi collectable toy that would have been given away free in packets of French laundry detergent powder in the 1970s. The sea has plucked the feather from her headband and snatched the spear from her hand.

It is thought that 6,000 Indigenous children died in Canadian residential schools, the last of which closed in the 1990s. These church-run and government-funded institutions tore children from their families in a deliberate attempt to sever them from their culture in the name of assimilation. In *All Our Relations: Indigenous Trauma in the Shadow of Colonialism* by Tanya Talaga, I learn that the suicide rate in Inuit communities is now ten times the Canadian national average. One Inuit woman recalled how her parents were faced with choosing between sending her away voluntarily or waiting for the police to enforce this edict. Of her own seven children, three died by suicide.

It has been estimated that more than 4,000 Indigenous women and girls in Canada remain missing or have been murdered in the last thirty years. In 2019, the National Inquiry into Missing and Murdered Indigenous Women and Girls concluded that this amounts to a genocide. In 2020, an Indigenous journalist, Brandi Morin, reported that an action plan to address the inquiry's findings had been delayed, ostensibly because of the Covid pandemic. Resources to tackle the issue have not been forthcoming. Yet, as Morin highlights, billions of dollars have been made available to fund the extension of the Trans Mountain oil pipeline, the construction of which will mean all-male work camps of mostly settler men – which will also mean an increased risk of Indigenous women being harmed.

*

In *Mi'kmaq Fisheries, Netukulimk: Towards a Better Understanding*, I learn that the word for lobster is *jakej* and I highlight a paragraph that makes me think of both *neverspel* and sea beans:

> Objects found through one's personal spiritual journey in life are known to hold power. When given as gifts, or kept as personal medicine, by being sewn onto clothing or made into amulets, the objects pacify, honour or invoke assistance from the spirit-world.

In the absence of a sea bean, I do always keep a piece of *neverspel* close. The Mi'kmaq Netukulimk lobster trap tag now sits on the windowsill above my desk, next to a particularly fine piece of *neverspel*. The small blue figurine stares out from my glass jar of beachcombed toys. I've come to think of the ocean as an archive of sorts. Every now and then, it offers up an object that makes me see something that I might have otherwise ignored.

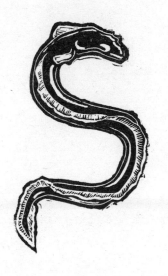

Strandjutter

Beachcomber

Meanwhile, on the shores of Ardnamurchan as on the
Aegean, the tide rises and falls and the amoral sea delivers
itself of its burden.

Alasdair Maclean, *Night Falls on Ardnamurchan*

When the four of us arrive at the Hotel de Waal in the
Dutch island of Texel, one February evening in 2020, it is
dark and the rain is lashing down. Strings of fairy lights hang
from the eaves of a nearby house and flail like a whip in the
wind. We flew to the Netherlands in the wake of Storm
Dennis and the landing at Schiphol airport was frightening.
The wind shook the plane like a toy. I felt rebuked for making such an unnecessary journey but my heart had long been
set on visiting Texel in winter. This island still has a vibrant
beachcombing culture.

Inside the airport, and less than a month since Brexit, we
were courteously ushered into the passport-control lane for
citizens of the European Union. A smartly dressed woman
ahead of us in the queue turned and remarked how kind
this was, all things considering. I was more distracted by
the number of people wearing face masks and news of the

continuing spread of Covid – that a pandemic might soon be declared.

The delayed train from Schiphol to the oil and gas port of Den Helder was a crush of bodies at first, but most people left the train in the city's suburbs. It rushed us through a landscape regimented by industrial crop-growing, each neat parcel of cultivated land enclosed within a grid of waterways. It was bleaker, in a way, than Shetland, though it was a thrill to see so many waterbirds – coots, moorhens, grebes, ducks, herons and egrets. In Den Helder, a bus took us from the train station to the Texel ferry terminal in one effortless connection. We followed a stream of cyclists on board and made our way to the palatial passenger lounge, where we sat among fake plastic trees and ate steaming bowls of pea and smoked sausage soup. The Wadden Sea was calm despite the weather, and a strange milky brown in colour. The familiarity of the slow and steady pace of a ferry was a comfort after the wild ride of the flight and the speed of the train.

Maarten and Belinda, the owners of the Hotel de Waal, usher us into a cosy lounge, and we sit at a table made from driftwood. They make a handsome couple, and a striking pair too. Maarten has the distinction of being the tallest person in the island, and like me, Belinda is short.

I'm thrilled to meet someone who is a lifelong beachcomber. I admire the driftwood table and Maarten explains that most of the wooden furniture in the hotel is made from driftwood that he himself, a carpenter, gathered from Texel's beaches.

Maarten is also a beachcombing guide. Now that the

stress of the storm-delayed journey is over, I'm hit by a rush of excitement at the thought of going beachcombing along the Texel shore. When I explain this to Maarten, he smiles and briefly disappears to fetch a large wooden treasure chest. Belinda returns from the kitchen with mugs of hot chocolate and cake, and laughs at the sight of us all huddled around her grinning husband.

Maarten reaches in and passes a rubber duck, lost during a Cornish river race, to my daughter and a huge mammoth bone to my husband. He explains that part of a Neanderthal skull has been found on a Texel beach, and I watch my tired husband perk up with interest. To my son, Maarten passes a jar of Lego spilt into the sea when a container ship, the *Tokio Express*, was hit by a freak wave twenty miles off Land's End in 1997. I am offered a pine cone the size and shape of a hedgehog, fallen from a Monterey pine that may still grow somewhere in a garden on the south coast of England. There is a hairy coconut in the chest which washed ashore covered in marine growth, proof of sorts that it is a bona fide drift-seed and not rubbish cast over the side of a ship.

The chest also contains two ring binders bulging with all the messages that Maarten has found in bottles. I ask if he sends sea post too. He nods. It is littering, we agree, but we are both under the spell of casting messages adrift. We know of puriot beachcombers who hold the line that littering is littering. I am glad that I am not one of them.

Maarten leaves to attend to other guests and I flick through the folders of found messages. There is a cutting from an English newspaper. In the accompanying photograph, Maarten poses with a bottle which, the caption explains, contains the ashes of a postman from Dorset. The bottle was set adrift by the man's son, in honour of a life spent travelling. With the agreement of the son, Maarten gave the bottle to a Texel fisherman, who took it out on his boat and returned it to the North Sea.

Most of the messages found by Maarten were cast into the sea by enthusiastic children, or adults who have not lost a childlike enthusiasm. They are perfunctory and include a name and address and a polite and hopeful greeting. Others are less anodyne. One young woman reports that she is stuck in an island, somewhere off the English coastline, with her friends and 'some complete wankers'.

The next morning, we wander through the narrow streets of De Waal, between rows of old brick houses with their steeply angled and red-tiled roofs. A bitterly cold wind blows in from the North Sea and delights the cackling jackdaws that swirl through the moving branches of a tall tree. A cormorant flies fast in a tailwind overhead, crossing the island from one sea to another. From the church we walk down a lane that stretches like a causeway through sunken fields.

Texel is a young island, just as the Wadden Sea is a young sea. In the All Saints' Flood of 1170, an exceptional North Sea storm surge claimed Texel from the mainland. It is almost within grasp, this human timescale of island creation and sea formation. Eierland (Eggland) in the north of the island of Texel was once a separate island where gulls' eggs were gathered. English mariners nicknamed it Damn Egg Island because so many of their ships wrecked on its shores, and the Eierland lighthouse marks the place where many English mariners lie buried. In the sixteenth century, a dyke was built on the sandbank between Texel and Eierland, and the channel between them silted up. The Great Storm of 1697 breached this dyke, and many other dykes, and the northern third of Texel flooded.

The island is large, at 463 square kilometres, and is inhabited by over 13,000 people. But for all its tamed land, busy roads and air of timeless permanence, Texel's vulnerability to storms is palpable. The sea is hidden from sight but can be sensed. Dunes form a fragile barrier along the North Sea coastline. The Wadden Sea is held at bay by 26 kilometres of levees and several hydraulic stations. A satellite map of the topography of Texel is mostly coloured different shades of blue, the darkest of which denote depths below sea level. It reads as if the island has already been lost to rising seas or as borrowed time mapped. The highest point is De Hoge Berg, the High Mountain, a hill of glacial boulder clay that rises to 15.3 metres. Texel is an island in which there is no high ground to escape to. The cliffs of Foula and Nólsoy unsettled me, but this island is far too low for comfort.

Later in the day, Maarten drives all four of us to the North Sea shoreline of the island. My son reads a Lego magazine that Maarten's daughter left on the back seat. Strapped to a rack on the boot of the Volvo is a classic Dutch bicycle. My husband looks stoic, as he always does when my beachcombing obsession takes us to beaches in bitterly cold weather, though I sense that he too is excited by the thought of washed-up mammoth bones.

On the way, Maarten explains the intricacies of beach-combing in Texel. There are many rules and it is very structured. The island has an official beachcombing body, the *strandvonderij*. There is a head beachcomber and six assistant beachcombers, all called *strandvonders*. All are men, though one is nearing retirement and it is possible that his daughter may take his post. Each *strandvonder* is designated a stretch of the coastline to patrol.

If anything of value washes ashore, the *strandvonder* will attempt to trace the owner. If the owner cannot be found, the finds are then sold by Texel's council. A *strandvonder* is allowed to drive a car or tractor onto the beach, but no one else can. As an unofficial beachcomber, a *strandjutter*, Maarten is only allowed to wheel his bicycle along the beach and can only collect non-valuable items. Maarten describes how, in the past, *strandjutters* would hide the larger pieces of driftwood in the dunes. They would fetch them home under the cover of darkness, unseen by the *strandvonders*.

In an article on beachcombing in Shetland during the First World War, Ian Tait, curator at the Shetland Museum, writes: 'I've heard of men burying large timbers in peat banks, and I've seen hatches in gables to admit boards, which were built-up with rocks once the wood was in.'

Sometimes, when I return to my house carrying a piece of wood, or some object gleaned from the shore, my neighbour Michael will ask if I have found some good *scran*, though his interest is purely humouring and not one of envy. Ian defines *scran* as 'odds and ends procured free, partly by chance, especially from marine salvage' – the point being, he emphasises, that the finds are both useful and free. Much of what I carry home is not *scran* but *bruck*, rubbish destined only for disposal.

In the early 1900s in Shetland, there were fourteen local and part-time District Deputy Receivers working for the Receiver of Wreck section of His Majesty's Customs and Excise. A beachcomber, at this time, would have been obliged by law to report a find to the relevant Deputy Receiver who would then estimate its value before putting it up for sale. The finder would often be given first refusal to buy. But as Ian explains: 'Of course, most of the timber and other discoveries did have some owner in theory, but losses at sea were an accepted part of merchant shipping. Establishing the ownership of this or that plank was usually impossible and islanders found all of this timber genuinely useful. Bureaucratic rules didn't sit square with Shetlanders' traditional rights, and they didn't adhere to regulations unless they could do no better.'

How would we, in Shetland, behave today, if valuable cargo washed ashore? Would we hide it away from the eyes of our neighbours, and from the eyes of the law? I used to have total faith in the Shetland rule that anything hauled above the high-tide mark is already claimed. But then one day I went down to the shore and found that my small pile of driftwood had been taken. The affront I felt at this transgression lasted for many days. Although this unwritten rule does, for the most part, seem to be respected. So much so that it is possible to find grass growing over piles of abandoned driftwood. In some cases, the finder is probably long dead, but still these heaps lie untouched by others.

I have not found anything on a Shetland beach of any monetary value, but a beachcomber in Yell once found a diamond engagement ring in a Manhattan jeweller's box in the strandline of Otterswick beach. In *Night Falls on Ard-namurchan*, a poignant memoir of growing up in a crofting community, of hay-making by hand and 'going round the shore', Alasdair Maclean writes:

> Coming across something of value on the beach is not at all like finding money in the street, or one can readily per-suade oneself that it isn't. The moral link binding finder to user is less obvious and more tenuous. Furthermore, the loser is likely to be a corporation of some kind rather than an individual and so less attractive as an object of sym-pathy, tending as we do to adjust our honesty to suit our estimate of the loser's need.

Social media now makes it easier to potentially trace the owners of valuable lost property, and perhaps this has shifted, a little, a beachcomber's conscience. If I had found the diamond ring, would I have tried to find the person who had lost it? Maybe, maybe not.

We arrive at the beach a little after high tide. The wind is onshore and very strong. The sky is bright blue but the sea is muddy-looking, rich in sediment, and its surface is wind-torn and white. A cloud of herring gulls billows over the waves. Clumps of sea foam scud across the yellow sand, past oystercatchers that face the cold wind with hunched and motionless bodies. A few sanderlings run back and forth as if daring each wave, and my children do the same.

I can sense Maarten's anticipation. I am prickling with it too. I'm burning to find something new and strange to me.

The beach seems never-ending and, in a way, it is. It would stretch in a straight line for nearly thirty kilometres were it not interrupted by the salt marshes of De Slufter. We have not been walking long before I become disorientated and can no longer see the place where we cut through the dunes. It all looks the same to me. Each kilometre is marked by a *strandpalen*, a large upright and numbered post, a waymarker, but I did not take note of the first post that we passed. I am glad that we are being guided by Maarten. I relish each cold moment but I think that I would not find it so easy to be a beachcomber here. The give of the sand pulls on sore joints. And when would you ever know to stop? Maarten confesses that he sometimes calls Belinda to tell her that he will not be home for a while. I cannot judge, I do the same.

In common with the beaches of home, there is quite a bit of litter. We pick it up and drop it into the panniers on Maarten's bicycle. Many beachcombers have now become beach cleaners. In 2005, six hundred children cleaned thirty tonnes of marine litter from the North Sea beaches of Texel. It seems unfair that children were tasked with clearing up the mess of adults, but anyway, 42 per cent of the rubbish was local to the Netherlands and 14 per cent had drifted across from the UK. In spring each year, many Shetlanders join together for Da Voar Redd Up, the spring clean-up, to remove the litter that washes up on more accessible beaches. In 2019, the last Redd Up before the Covid pandemic struck, 4,500 volunteers collected more than forty-eight tonnes of rubbish. This figure is impressive but the litter is more than replenished each winter, and large stretches of Shetland's shoreline are difficult, if not impossible, to reach and clean.

For a while I saw the plastic litter on the home beach as part of the beach and not separate to it. But one spring day, I moved a bright orange plastic fish basket that dammed a small stream. An eel was lying beneath, its body wet and shining and snaked in the perfect shape of an 's'. I reached for it to show my children but it slipped through my hands and muscled its way down through the pebbles.

The life of this eel began in the Sargasso Sea, a sea which has another name now too: the North Atlantic Garbage Patch. It hatched from an egg among this gyre of plastic, and the Gulf Stream and the North Atlantic Drift carried it north in larval form. Once it reached the European continental shelf, it metamorphosed into a tiny glass eel, and in this small and beautifully transparent form it migrated towards land. In brackish water, it clouded with pigment and became an elver, a juvenile eel, and migrated upstream. In fresh water, it changed again, into a yellow eel.

The eel on the beach was of the freshwater kind. I like to think that it was on the brink of becoming sexually mature and transforming into a silver eel. That it was readying itself for salt water and the migration journey back to the Sargasso Sea, where it would mate and then die, if it did not perish on the way. The sight of it among all the plastic was galvanising. With the help of Robbie and Kath, who work the croft along this stretch of shore, we cleared all the plastic from the small beach. It filled several large black bin bags, and all the five-gallon containers, fish boxes and baskets formed a high heap. We kept a plastic toy soldier.

Between the autumn and vernal equinoxes of 2018 and 2019, I tallied each piece of litter that I found washed ashore on this little beach. It was not an accurate measure. The sea can reclaim the plastic left by an earlier tide and I did not visit the beach every day. But still, from a beach that is only thirty paces wide, I ferried home 627 pieces of litter. Most of this, 98 per cent, was plastic. Just under half, or 41 per cent, could be attributed with certainty to the fishing and aquaculture industries.

I overlooked some pieces of plastic at first because they looked too much like pebbles. Plastiglomerates form when molten plastic binds with lithic material. All the plastic that I took from the beach could be categorised as macroplastics. I didn't attempt to collect microplastics because this would have driven me mad. We fertilise our vegetable beds with seaweed and I am forever picking the fine fibres of plastic from the soil – strands of deteriorated polypropylene fishing-industry rope. I pity the eel that swims through a plastic-filled sea, while ignoring the plastic that may now swim through me.

On the beach in Texel, Maarten is mostly seeking driftwood but there is not much to be found. He picks up a short length of it and explains that he would never have gathered such small and scrappy pieces in the past. Until recently, timber was transported by sea on open decks, where it could become saturated and heavy with water. In rough seas, this extra weight risked destabilising and capsizing the ship, and so the wood was often jettisoned. Now that timber is safely stowed in cargo holds, Maarten struggles to find enough for his carpentry business.

Maarten takes great pride in his beachcombing identity. In the Hotel de Waal's lounge there is a large coffee-table book which celebrates beachcombing culture in Texel and profiles the island's many beachcombers, including Maarten and his late father. But there was a time, in some communities, when beachcombing incurred more stigma than respect. In the 1972 Orcadian novel *Greenvoe* by George Mackay Brown, the character Timmy Folster is a beachcomber and a drinker of methylated spirits, while in the Faroese novel *The Old Man and His Sons* by Heðin Brú, also first published in the 1970s, the word 'beachcomber' is shouted as an insult. Beachcombing, in this novel, becomes synonymous with being left behind by a society that is moving away from subsistence livelihoods eked out from the land and the sea and towards the borrowing of money and increasing consumerism.

I've not heard of beachcombing being stigmatised in Shetland but there are many indications of its former importance. In *The Coastal Names of Fair Isle*, Jerry Eunson notes the geos where driftwood gathers. Sompal Geo gathers driftwood in a south-south-west wind, Geo o' Busta in a south-easterly. Heswills Geo is the best driftwood site along the eastern coastline, while Hyukni Geo is the most productive in the west of the island. Krogi Geo, he notes, is never any good for driftwood. I've come to know which beaches to search for driftwood, though I have little use for it when I find it and perhaps it is better left on the shore as a habitat for invertebrates.

There are still a few livelihoods and pensions supplemented by beachcombing in Shetland. Sea glass is collected and made into jewellery, and creel marker buoys, boat fenders and mussel rope floats are salvaged to sell on. But for most of us, beachcombing is just a pleasurable hobby. In recent years, social media has once more conferred status to the act of beachcombing. It is good to make these digital connections, to see what might be found elsewhere. Beachcombers from very different shores can compare finds – those affluent enough to access technology, at least. I like to follow a beachcomber in Japan and beachcombers closer to home. As with so many things, beachcombing can be reduced to little more than lifestyle content, but it is still possible to find rawer forms of beachcombing joy within the strandlines of the Internet.

The thin strandline of the Texel beach is both familiar and full of new possibilities. To my annoyance, Maarten is considerably better than I am at finding things. He finds the first eggcase and I am disappointed to see that it is the familiar form of a small-spotted catshark's tendrilled capsule. Blonde ray eggcases, gloriously spiky and large, can be found on this stretch of shoreline, and I have yet to find one anywhere. I take a moment to check my greed and churlishness. This beach owes me nothing; I do not tend to it. And even on a beach that I do tend to, it never pays to be presumptuous.

Maarten hands me a thick ribbon that seems to be made from jelly and sand – the egg 'collar', he explains, of a necklace shell. My son finds the eggcase of a thornback ray buried in the dunes. I offer my husband a soggy bouquet of roses, no doubt spurned a few days before, on Valentine's Day. My daughter finds a pine cone which is tightly closed.

This pine cone would be a dream find in Shetland, an archipelago of few trees.

We find a two-pronged light bulb, and then another and then more, until ten or so fill a pannier. Maarten speculates that they may have spilt from a cargo ship container lost at sea. He has seen some strange scenes on Texel's North Sea beaches after container spills. Once there was a strandline full of bananas; another time, television sets littered the sand.

As he strides along the beach pushing his now-laden bicycle, Maarten anticipates that he will soon start to find the spoils of storms Ciara and Dennis – things that were washed into English rivers and then spat out into the Channel. My thoughts turn to what will drift across the ocean to Shetland when cities like New York flood catastrophically. Sometimes, it seems feasible that beachcombing will one day become a necessity again. I picture people rising early to be first at the beach to take their pick of the plastic containers. Our last find on the beach in Texel is a sachet of emergency drinking water.

Back in the shelter of the car, Maarten takes us on a short tour. We sit squashed up next to a length of driftwood that stretches from the front passenger seat all the way to the door of the boot. My children are unperturbed. They are used to sharing car space with all sorts of beach finds, some smellier than others. Maarten drives across the island towards the Wadden Sea shore, where he parks in a layby under a tall levee. We climb over a low fence and clamber up its steep grassy banks. After the undulating dunes of the North Sea shore, it is disorientating to meet the hard lines of this engineered coastline.

From the top there is a view to Den Helder and the strange sight of the Afsluitdijk, the Enclosure Dyke. This 32-kilometre-long dam runs through the Zuiderzee to protect inland areas from flooding. On the landward side of the dam, salt water has turned to fresh water; a lake has been made from the sea. A motorway runs the length of the dam's top. It is to be heightened soon.

On the seaward side of the levee, a new beach has been created from richly coloured sand extracted from elsewhere. A coastal defence of a soft-engineering kind. Maarten is sceptical; he is more concerned that the dunes on the island's North Sea coast will be breached in another catastrophic storm surge. We stand in silence and watch a snow bunting forage among rock armour.

The day before we arrived in the Netherlands, I read an article in the *Guardian* newspaper. It quoted a Dutch oceanographer called Sjoerd Groeskamp, who described his plan to protect 25 million Europeans from sea level rise. His idea was to dam the North Sea. Two giant barriers would be constructed, one stretching between Scotland and Norway, and the other between France and England. Over time, the enclosed sea would transform into a body of fresh water. Groeskamp claims that this is technically and financially viable, but he also admits that he is trying to shock people into addressing the reality of the climate emergency.

Meanwhile, climate scientists have established that the Gulf Stream is slowing and that the world's vast and interconnected relay loop of ocean currents, known as the Atlantic Meridional Overturning Circulation, is destabilising. The AMOC distributes heat and energy around the globe. It is this circulation that underpins the climate that has been so conducive to life as we know it. If the Gulf Stream crosses a tipping point by slowing too much, the consequences will be catastrophic. Recent analyses indicate that the Gulf Stream is now 'close to shutting down'. An event not predicted to happen in the twenty-first century could now happen within decades. There is panic in the tone of some of the scientists reporting on these findings. I don't know what such a collapse would mean for Shetland or for Texel. An eventual evacuation perhaps, but with few places to go.

We scramble down the levee and Maarten drives us through the beautiful coastal settlement of Oudeschild, with its traditional windmill. Great crested grebes ornament the tranquil water of the harbour with their long necks and grace. This stretch of the Wadden Sea is where the ships of the Dutch East India Company would lie at anchor, waiting for fair weather before sailing the north route, via Shetland, to colonised lands. *De Liefde* and the *Kennemerland* would have taken Texel's fresh water on board for the long voyage, and a few days later this fresh water would have spilt into the salt water that encircles the Out Skerries.

Beachcombing, and searching for a sea bean, has made me consider the connectivity of the oceans, but these wrecks have made me understand this connectivity more fully – meaning in social and political terms too. I think of the Caribbean often because this is where I picture sea beans growing. The wealth that colonisation generated fuelled the industrialisation that has caused this climate emergency. The Caribbean is already experiencing increasingly violent climatic events. In a just world, the UK and the

Netherlands – and all European colonial nations – would pay financial reparations, and do so before the climate emergency grows any worse.

Maarten leaves the coastline and drives inland and back towards De Waal. We pass many egrets standing tall on the banks of the waterways that edge the farmed land. They are newcomers, brought here by the warming climate. Maarten skated on these waterways as a child. His own children have never had the chance – ice is now too rare.

I regret that we didn't cast a message in a bottle into the southern North Sea; the wind blew onshore for the duration of our stay. I wish that it had been possible. It might have drifted through the time of the pandemic. It might have found a stranger on the shore of the Netherlands, Germany or Denmark, and given them a rare moment of delight. Sometimes now, when I cast bottles adrift from Shetland, I picture them floating into the future, ten years or more perhaps. Sent from a time when there was still a chance to slow the warming of the climate.

Neesick

Harbour Porpoise

Before we leave the island of Texel, we visit Ecomare, a seal sanctuary and nature museum. The sun shines but a cold wind is still blowing in from the North Sea, and there are small waves on the surface of the seal pools. We head inside and make for the whale hall to see the display of cetacean skeletons. I pose next to the upright penis of a sperm whale and my husband takes my photo. I am twenty centimetres shorter than the shrivelled specimen. But size is not everything, and it is the small skeleton of a female harbour porpoise that holds my attention the longest. With flesh, she would match my length almost exactly. The tiny skeleton of a porpoise calf flanks her, its rib bones as thin as wires.

Next we visit a series of interactive displays that illustrate the various impacts of humans on the marine world, where we meet a cardboard cut-out of Jan Andries van Franeker and a mock-up of his laboratory, complete with a taxidermied fulmar lying on a metal tray between a scalpel and a set of callipers. A Petri dish of plastic has been placed by its side. But we don't study these displays for long, because there is a window into the depths of an outdoor pool and it beckons us forward. The water of the pool is clear and sunlight ripples across white walls. It looks as enticing as a blue swimming pool on a hot summer's day.

The moment a porpoise swims into view, the pool immediately transforms into a tank. When the second porpoise swims in, we match each to their picture on a nearby information panel. Michael has a sharper division between the dark grey of his back and the pale of his belly, like a distinct sea-sky horizon on a clear day. Dennis has more diffuse colouration, the grey of his back bleeding into the pale of his belly like a grey cloud gently spilling rain. He swims close to the window and turns his head, as if to watch us, as he passes by.

Michael circles the tank, just under the water's surface. His fluke powers up and down and forms a large following wave. The water seems passive to the wind but comes alive in the presence of the two porpoises. My mind places my body in the tank and I shudder. The power is all mine as I watch through the window. In the tank, it would be all theirs.

In Dutch, porpoise is *bruinvis*, meaning 'brown fish'. In Shetland they are *neesicks*, a word formed from the Old Norse *hnísa*, 'to sneeze or snort', for the sound of their exhalations. Every now and then, as they circle their tanks, Michael and Dennis raise their heads above the water to breathe. It is very different from watching wild porpoises roll through the surface of the sea with tightly curved spines. Dennis sometimes nods his head repetitively.

There are faint scars on Dennis's skin. He was found stranded on a Dutch beach at just a few months old, with wounds that suggested he had been entangled in a fishing net. Michael was also found stranded on a beach when he was a calf. At such a young age, both porpoises would still have been dependent on their mother's milk. A decision was made by their rescuers to keep them alive, even though this would mean a life spent in captivity.

The language that scientists use to describe the threats to harbour porpoises is usually neutral. Humans are reduced to passive actors, and porpoises become regrettable if inevitable collateral damage. In 'fisheries conflicts', porpoises are 'bycatch' or 'incidental catch'. The level of porpoise 'bycatch' is 'unsustainable'. In less oblique terms, we are drowning porpoises in fishing nets faster than they can reproduce.

Gill nets drown more porpoises than any other kind of net. I sometimes find these nets washed ashore, heaps of fine mesh made from nylon monofilament – single strands of thin plastic, sharp enough to cut through skin if pulled. Weighted at their base and attached to floats at their surface, they hang in the ocean in vertical walls. When a fish swims into a gill net, its head passes through the mesh but its gill covers become ensnared.

A review of harbour porpoise bycatch in UK waters in 2019 identified the area north-west of Shetland as one of three high-risk sites for porpoise entanglement in gill nets. A lack of monitoring makes this hard to prove, but when gill nets are set in areas where porpoises swim, porpoises are killed. These nets kill many seabirds and seals too.

I know too little about the impacts of industrial fishing, of all kinds, in the seas that surround Shetland, but fragments of information come my way in the pages of the local newspapers or in conversations. No Shetland fishing boat uses gill nets. The boats that set gill nets near these islands are mostly Spanish-owned and fish for monkfish and angler fish. In one local newspaper article, a representative of the Shetland Fisherman's Association explains that a single gill-netting vessel can cover up to three hundred square miles of seabed. A screenshot of a digital map shows the track of a gill-netting boat off the north-west coast of Shetland. It sails back and forth in long and parallel lines and the nets cover a vast area. The ocean itself looks trapped. Rumours abound that these Spanish boats throw damaged gill nets overboard, along with the rest of the refuse that accumulates on a fishing trip. My beachcombing experience tells me that these rumours are probably true.

There is a passage in Rachel Carson's *Under the Sea Wind* that considers the fate of a fish in a gill net. A shad struggles to free herself, but the net only cuts deeper into her gill filaments. Carson uses the words 'burning' and 'choking'. In accounts of near-drownings, some people describe a burning sensation when water floods into their lungs. Could this be how porpoises experience drowning too?

We kill porpoises in other, more subtle ways. In *The Peregrine*, J. A. Baker writes, 'Foul poison burned within them like a burrowing fuse.' He was alluding to DDT, an organochlorine pesticide which accumulated in the bodies of these avian predators in the 1950s and 1960s and thinned their eggshells. However gently a peregrine would incubate its eggs, the shells would break.

DDT has also accumulated in the blubber of harbour porpoises, and when I begin to read about this, I chance upon a research paper on neurotoxins in juvenile harbour porpoises in the UK. This study focuses on PCBs, poly-chlorinated biphenyls. Both DDT and PCBs persist in the environment and they bioaccumulate – they concentrate in the cells of humans and non-humans. As predators at the top of the food chain, porpoises carry a high toxic load of PCBs even though these chemicals were banned in the UK for most uses in 1981 and then completely in 2000. Some of the PCBs that still persist in the environment come from early versions of flame retardants. Our increased dependency on synthetic materials has increased the flammability of the places in which we live and work. We used PCBs to keep our human bodies safe from burning, and in doing so we lit a toxic fuse that is still alight today.

A second research paper informs me that the accumulation of PCBs in female porpoises can result in 'reproductive impairment', which in plain language means that their foetuses die, or their bodies abort their foetuses, or their calves die when they are born. The immune systems of surviving calves can be compromised. Certain organochlorines can pass from the mother porpoise to her foetus via her placenta. And, after birth, more pollutants pass from the mother to her calf through her milk. In this way, mother porpoises offload some of their own toxic burden in their milk. Firstborn calves receive the highest dose of pollutants.

I breastfed both my children – not for very long because I mostly did not enjoy it. It was painful and exhausting and I also wondered what they were drinking in, along with all the water, carbohydrates, lipids and proteins. Years later, I read a newspaper article that confirmed my fears. British

women have some of the highest concentrations of flame
retardants in their breast milk in the world, in the form of
mostly banned and legacy PBDEs, polybrominated di-
phenyl ethers.

In the Faroe Islands, women are much more aware of
how their bodies can accumulate toxins. In 1998, Faroese
girls and women were advised not to eat whale blubber, to
protect their future children from the harmful effects of
PCBs. Pregnant and breastfeeding women were also advised
to abstain from eating the mercury-laden whale meat, liver
and kidneys. In November 2008, the Faroese government
updated their guidance to recommend that pilot whale meat
should no longer be consumed at all, by anyone.

At Ecomare we head outside to watch Michael and Dennis being fed. Their tank is surrounded by a dense crowd
of people. Herring gulls flock in, and white shit falls on a
man's jacket with an audible splat. Michael and Dennis circle faster and faster, pulling a fury of waves behind them.
One, I'm not sure which, comes to an abrupt halt and spy-
hops close to the edge of the tank. A teenage girl bends low
over the rail and says *hallo* in a voice thick with adoration.

Two keepers enter the enclosed area, each carrying a
zinc bucket containing small fish. Dennis and Michael halt
their circling and then hang motionless in the water with
their heads above the surface, while one of the keepers talks
about the ecology of porpoises. When both keepers kneel
down and raise a single hand, Michael and Dennis open their
mouths and let their teeth be inspected. They roll onto their
backs too, and hang upside down at the surface. After each

trick, they are rewarded with a fish. A keeper explains that they have been trained to follow commands so that their bodies can be inspected for signs of ill health. Michael and Dennis will never run short of fish but overfishing means that wild porpoises can face starvation, and the noise of marine traffic can run them out of their hunting grounds.

Ecomare seems an ethical place. But it is still uncomfortable to watch Michael and Dennis circling their tank, caught as they are, between our pity and our awe. When I watch the wild porpoises in our home *voe*, I know that their bodies probably contain legacy pollutants and that some will be caught in gill nets. I circle round the question of what I would have done had I found Michael and Dennis on the shore. If the decision had been mine, would I have kept them alive, knowing that they would only ever live in captivity, or would I have chosen to euthanise them on the spot?

In the summer of 2019, I see notice of a marine mammal medic course in Shetland. I sign up to learn what I can do if I find a porpoise live-stranded on the shore. I worry that I will not be physically strong enough. But on a chilly August day, I find that the strength of my body is enough when I add it to the strength of others.

The course is hosted by Jan and Pete Bevington, who run the Hillswick Wildlife Sanctuary. A team of people from British Divers Marine Life Rescue have travelled to Shetland to teach us the basics. We spend the morning inside listening to lectures on the biology, ecology, rescue and treatment of cetaceans and seals. Perhaps it is the room itself, with its stone walls and open peat fire, fairy lights and wildlife art, but it seems less like a training course and more like a gathering for the purpose of worship.

Jan and Pete's commitment to their work is undoubtedly a form of reverence. Jan is in her mid-seventies and started to care for wild creatures in 1987, when she found a common seal pup in trouble on the beach at Hillswick. Her reputation for nursing seals back to health grew, and soon she was taking in otter cubs too. In 1993, she cared for the seals and otters that were oiled when the *Braer* oil tanker wrecked on the cliffs of the South Mainland. All the seals and otters that she and Pete care for at the sanctuary are released back into the wild.

It strikes me that Jan has a deep spiritual connection to the otters and seals in her care – that she sees these creatures as something like kin. I've only ever seen her with a calm smile on her face, her wavy hair kept from the wind by a colourful woollen headband. She exudes the same kind of peace that envelops me when I watch porpoises on days of calm weather. Pete is similarly dignified, a tall man with a grey beard who looks, with his spectacles, wise and gently quizzical. They inspire me with their dedication.

After lunch, we head outside and into the toilet block to put on our wetsuits – or, in my case, an old survival suit that I have borrowed from my husband. On the shingle beach we are split into two groups, and I find myself alongside a plastic long-finned pilot whale that has been filled with water and inflated further by compressed air. It is lifelike, metres long, black in colour and blunt-headed. We lean into the whale's flank to keep it upright and find that it is incredibly heavy. I feel mildly heroic until I remember that a live-stranded long-finned pilot whale might writhe and thrash its fluke, or exhale explosively from its blowhole.

Dan, one of the BDMLR trainers, teaches us how to slide a large rectangular sling under the whale's belly, by gently rocking it from side to side. It is hard work and my body complains, but soon it is in place. Four of us stay and prop up the whale while others fetch two huge inflatable pontoons and manoeuvre them either side of the whale's body. The pontoons are bright yellow and marked with the green Helios logo of BP. My cynicism at the sight of this oil company's logo is short-lived. I am, after all, wearing an oil- and gas-industry survival suit. The yellow pontoons are clipped in careful sequence to the sling. The plastic whale rests snug and upright in this contraption. I begin to believe that we will re-float this stranded whale.

We use the pull of each retreating wave to coax the whale down the beach. It works, and the sea slowly takes its weight. It is peaceful to stand waist-deep in the water, warm and dry in the survival suit. The others, in their wetsuits, begin to look cold, except for Dan the trainer who looks completely at ease, as if he lives much of his life in salt water. Pale-pink moon jellyfish pulse between the gap of my braced legs. A retreating wave finally frees the whale from the land, and when it lurches forward I lose my footing and bob alongside its shiny bulk. And even though the whale is plastic and has been rescued many times, we all grin with elation.

After the successful rescue of the plastic long-finned pilot whale, we move on to saving a plastic porpoise, or perhaps it is supposed to be a small dolphin. I relax; it won't be as hard as shifting the whale. First, we cover the porpoise in wet seaweed to prevent it from overheating, and then we pour water over its skin. Cat the instructor watches closely to make sure that we do not pour water down the blowhole and drown the plastic porpoise on dry land. Then we place a towel under its belly and carry it down to the water's edge and into the sea.

Not all cetaceans that live-strand are in a healthy enough state to be re-floated, and euthanasia is not always straight-forward. The smaller of the cetaceans can be shot with a powerful rifle. Otherwise, barbiturates can be injected intra-muscularly. A large whale may require a needle long enough to reach through the blubber and into the muscle. Stood on the beach at Hillswick, Pete recalls the chemical euthanasia of a long-finned pilot whale and how blood began pouring from its orifices. It seemed more brutal, he tells us, than the natural death of another long-finned pilot whale that he and Jan had attended. They both stayed with the stricken whale until the end, talking to it in low voices and pouring water over its back to keep it cool. Whales know how to die, Jan adds calmly, and it is better to support them through a nat-ural death.

Two months after we return to Shetland from Texel, a friend sends a message to say that his children have found a dead porpoise on the shore not far from our house. I wait until the light of morning to go and see it. I set out in my car, disobeying lockdown rules. It is less than three miles away. I would walk there if I could, but all four of us are conva-lescing from a respiratory virus that we suspect is Covid.

My joints are painful; palindromic rheumatism flares more intensely than it has done in years. The inflammation mostly settles in the joints of my ribs. I can't walk the distance to the porpoise.

I sense the eyes of the community on me as I drive along the empty road, just as I have started to watch each and every rare car too. I park in a layby and walk slowly down through a sheep's field to the shore. The air is cold and increases my discomfort; my lungs sting. I find the body quickly enough, hauled above the reach of the tide and lying on a grass ledge under a low bank of dark peat. A great black-backed gull circles high overhead and calls an objection to my intrusion. Its wings are as wide as my outstretched arms.

The porpoise's body has been pecked by scavenging birds. Sharp beaks have left neat v-shaped cuts all over the tough skin. The flesh between the anus and genital slit has been excavated away. The porpoise's eye sockets are empty; the blowhole has been widened. Tiny teeth grin through a ragged window made in the skin and muscle of the jaw. One pectoral fin hangs limply by a thread of bloody sinew. Only the fluke remains untouched.

It looks small. The family who found the body took meas-urements and sent photos to the Scottish Marine Mammal Stranding Scheme. The reply confirms that it is a calf, born the summer before, and that it looks malnourished. A por-poise in good condition would be nicely convex in shape either side of the dorsal fin. This one looks too flat and lean. In the months before, we watched a young porpoise flank its mother's side. It might not be the same one, but I touch the dead calf lightly on its back.

In winter, on *days atween wadders*, I watch for the porpoises. If I find them, surfacing to breathe, I breathe more deeply too, in a body that is not braced to counter the weight of the wind. Sometimes, several will rest at the surface of the *voe*, spines straight and blunt noses clear of the water, like a raft of tiny submarines. On days of wind, they are harder to see because the waves hide their small dorsal fins. I can't imagine their bodies in the riot of a storm, but perhaps they map their watery world by shelter too.

I read on the Ecomare website that workers on a North Sea oil production platform have watched a porpoise teaching her calf to catch fish. She would leave the calf and then return to the surface with a live fish clasped in her mouth. Sometimes the calf would catch the fish; other times the fish escaped. The young porpoise lying dead on the shore was probably not long weaned. It seems strange that porpoise calves are weaned between February and April, when the sea is at its coldest, but perhaps if they suckled for longer, the energetic cost of lactation would be too great and more female porpoises would die. Maybe this young porpoise struggled to catch enough fish. Porpoises lose condition quickly if they cannot feed. Their high surface area, relative to their body's volume, makes them susceptible to hypothermia.

I could return home and fetch a knife. If I cut the porpoise open, I might see what, if anything, is held in its main stomach. I might find fish remains or I might find it empty. But I am not trained to do this and I am not sure that it would be legal. The bodies of cetaceans are protected by legislation in life and in death. It is illegal, even, to take a single cetacean bone from a beach. This is a rule set to prevent a trade in cetacean body parts, for which they might be intentionally killed. It is hard to leave a sea-cleaned cetacean bone in the strandline. Their vertebrae are sculptural. I would like one for my shelf. It is possible to apply for a licence to possess cetacean bones, but these are granted strictly for educational or scientific reasons. Tender amazement is not reason enough.

I haul the porpoise into the sea to stop any local dogs eating its newly putrefying flesh. The gull that is still circling overhead scolds me even more. The sea pours in through the pecked cavities of the porpoise's body, as if reclaiming it, and it sinks down through a dark mass of seaweed. Bubbles of oil rise up from the hidden body, and burst at the surface in bright rainbows of iridescence. The wind blows the oil away from the shore and it forms a neat path of smooth water that cuts through the waves. I think of Jan and Pete and wish that they were here with me, because it is easy to imagine that the spirit of the young porpoise is being led back out to sea. Overhead, the gull circles and keens into the cold east wind.

A month later, I receive my first-ever callout as a volunteer marine mammal medic. But when the phone rings, I am already watching the whale from the kitchen window. It is circling very close to the shore in the shallow water at the head of the *voe* – which is, from the whale's perspective, a dead end. I take my grab bag, packed with my husband's old survival suit, a buoyancy aid, masks, gloves, a wire cutter in case of entanglements, and an assessment sheet with a guided checklist. I take my BDMLR membership card too, just in case the police question why I am breaking lockdown rules. I'm anxious as I drive to the head of the *voe*. If this large whale strands, it will be very difficult to re-float. I hope that it will not need to be euthanised.

At the shore, I'm relieved to see that marine biologist and wildlife film-maker and photographer Richard Shucksmith is using a drone to assess whether the whale is in any difficulty. Jan and Pete from Hillswick arrive and join us. Hitched to the back of their car is a trailer carrying the yellow rescue pontoon, but we will not need it. Richard confirms that the whale is fine. It is not entangled in any fishing gear and looks in good health. It is busy feeding on plankton.

The whale lunge-feeds, sometimes so close to the shore that it swims over kelp. Its huge jaws distend to an impossibly wide angle and then bulge to a close. Further out in the *voe*, it dives with a spine that seems hinged at the point of its small dorsal fin. Occasionally, it rolls onto its back and arcs a long white pectoral fin into the air, and then slaps it back down onto the surface of the sea. We all want to see its fluke. In 2016, a Shetland naturalist and wildlife photographer, Brydon Thomason, captured a photograph of a humpback fluke that was matched to a whale that swam off the shores of the island of Guadeloupe in the Caribbean. But this humpback is too busy feeding in the shallow water, and its fluke remains hidden.

Richard voices the thought that the whale may have been lured in by a windrow of lipid-rich plankton. He points to a narrow strip of smooth water on the surface of the sea that leads down the centre of the *voe*. The wind is of the right strength and direction to form this path of plankton, on a day when a humpback whale just happened to be passing.

The humpback feeds all day long, and many people in the community gather at the shore and marvel at its presence. My husband drives our children down and we all watch the whale together. A police car comes by, and we tense in case the two officers suggest that we should disperse and head back home, but they stay and marvel at the whale too before driving away again. Children stand at the edge of the sea and shriek with joy as the whale surfaces just metres away and blasts its breath high into the sky. Everyone watching the whale is momentarily free from the weight of the pandemic.

The whale leaves at sunset, following the same windrow of plankton back out to the open ocean. The clouds of spray it exhales glow in the light of the low sun. A small crowd watches as it swims its way out through Swarbacks Minn, the narrow sound named after the great black-backed gull. It raises its fluke just once, as if in farewell. Moments later, a single porpoise surfaces for air.

Sea Glass

There are so many outside lights nowadays that one can
at times feel blinded and confused by the glare. Yet I can't
help trying to recall how it actually was years ago – before
electricity came along.

Chrissie Sandison

To some people, the hills and moors have souls as well –
they do not want them desecrated.

James Mackenzie

The beach where my family and I search for sea glass is
small and not particularly 'productive' compared to others
in Shetland, but it is special to us because it is only a short
walk from our home. All four of us like to search for sea
glass, small pieces of glass that have been smoothed by the
action of waves and made cloudy by the alkalinity of salt
water. We shuffle along the beach, heads bowed and lost in
our thoughts. When it is time to go, we unfurl our hands
and compare our best pieces. Rarer colours – lavender, teal
and cobalt blue – we display in glass jars. The more common
colours – white, green and brown – we leave by the front

door, where a small beach of shells and sea glass always welcomes us home.

I'm rarely more 'in the present' than when I am looking for sea glass. My mind clears of worries, stress falls away from my body. When my attention is held so completely, mild pain can be ignored. Sometimes, my attention is held too completely. I once glanced up from the beach to see an otter staring at me from within a wave. Another time, I did not see the orcas until they had passed right by.

It can take decades for sea glass to become sea-worn. The smoothest of pieces make me wonder how old they are and what Shetland was like then. But if the glass is still sharp and clear, I find myself thinking of the future. What it will be like to live in this island place, decades from now.

The sea glass beach that my family and I visit lies below the house in which the late Chrissie Sandison lived. In her later years, Chrissie wrote a memoir, *Slyde in the Right Direction*, in which she describes, in vivid detail, her childhood and early adulthood in this settlement during the 1920s and 1930s. Chrissie's memoir has deepened my understanding of Shetland in a way that no amount of beachcombing or watching birds ever will. When I read her words, I feel less of an incomer. Gathering sea glass on the beach below Chrissie's childhood home has become an act of connection to the place in which I live.

Chrissie's paternal grandparents came to live in this settlement because they were evicted from their croft in the Kergord Valley. As the raven flies, Kergord is not so far from here, but to reach it on foot requires crossing high ground. There is a pass at a place called the Muckle Scord – a notch in the ridgeline below Scallafield, the highest hill in this part of Shetland. This high hill ground is *scattald*, common land where crofters' sheep graze, a place of blanket bog, heather and sphagnum or bog moss. These hills hide many freshwater lochs where *rain geese*, red-throated divers, nest. The sight of Scallafield is a constant and steadying presence in my day.

Nearly two hundred people were cleared from Kergord and nearby Weisdale during the nineteenth century, to make way for the farming of sheep. *Shadowed Valley*, a novel by John J. Graham, is an evocative fictional account of these evictions. Chrissie's memoir is more matter-of-fact, but the detail of the *flitting*, the move from one settlement to another, on foot over high and boggy ground, is enough to imagine the distress that her grandparents must have felt.

In 1869, the laird, David Dakers Black, gave the young married couple and their extended household only twenty-eight days' notice to leave their home. It was winter and Chrissie's grandmother, Mergat, was pregnant. It took Mergat and her husband, Robbie, several trips on foot – back and forth, up a steep slope and over the hill ground – to move their livestock, the livestock's fodder and all their possessions. Nine of them moved: Mergat and Robbie; their two children aged six and four years; Robbie's mother, Johanna; and her four other children.

I remember too well how my body felt in pregnancy, and perhaps Mergat was fit and well but, even so, carrying the weight of her unborn child and the weight of their belongings over such terrain must have been uncomfortable, painful even. In her exhaustion, did she worry that she would lose her baby as well as her home?

Mergat's pregnancy did endure; a boy named Thomas, Chrissie's father, was born in a run-down croft by the shore that had previously been the home of a widow and her teenage daughters. A year later, Mergat and her extended family moved a short distance to the croft at Slyde, where my family and I search for sea glass. Chrissie remembered her grandmother sat by the stove at Slyde, with a footstool made from wood that *'cam wi da sea'*, and there she would rest and knit, sometimes singing while rocking a cradle with her foot. Mergat died aged eighty-three, after catching a virulent strain of influenza.

There are Clearance stories from Shetland that do not end so well. Wendy Gear, a writer and retired teacher, tells one such story in her meticulous book on John Walker, a particularly notorious factor – he was a property manager in the north of the island of Yell. In the foreword of the book, the Shetland archivist Brian Smith quotes Walker: 'I saw that the commons were of no use to the people, and were doing them harm . . . I at once resolved to take the commons from them.' The *scattald* was vital to the survival of crofting communities, Smith explains. It was here that the cattle grazed in the summer months and where peat would be cut to provide fuel.

The first chapter of Wendy Gear's book begins: 'Jane Mary Spence died, aged six weeks, on the first day of December, 1868. Her mother always said the baby caught cold on "the journey".' The mother is Wendy's great-grandmother, Margaret, and 'the journey' is the eviction from Bigsetter in Yell. It was a cold November day, and to reach their new home, Margaret and her husband, William, had to cross

Basta Voe in a small open boat in rough weather with little baby Jane Mary, just a few weeks old and 'cocooned in a leather bucket to protect her from the salt spray'. I think of Margaret trying to find her bearings in a new home, the weight of grief she must have felt, the way her body, still tender from the birth and from nursing her newborn, would have intensified her loss.

Chrissie Sandison's grandfather, Robbie, was in his twenties when he and Mergat were evicted. He had already spent several seasons as a fisherman, working on boats that travelled to the Faroes and as far as Greenland at times. Robbie's mother, Johanna, was a *howdie*, a midwife with no formal training. There is no mention of sea beans or of any other charms. We do not learn how Chrissie's forebears grounded their fears, whether her grandfather kept a drift-seed about his person when he was off fishing, or whether her great-grandmother used a drift-seed to comfort women in labour.

In Chrissie's memoir, I learn that two women died in child-birth in the house below ours. I think of them often. When a woman died in childbirth in a neighbouring settlement, Chrissie's grandmother walked miles over boggy ground to visit the widower. She returned home carrying the new-born, a little girl named Baabie, who she cared for from that moment on. There was no wet nurse available and so 'a piece of quill from a duck's wing served as an instrument to transfer the milk from bottle to baby'. Cloth was wrapped around the quill so that it did not hurt the baby's mouth. Infants 'soon learned to drink from a cup or saucer'. Absorbent bog moss and soft cotton grass lined cloth nappies.

Chrissie's own mother, Ann, had ten babies, two of whom were stillborn. When Chrissie herself was a baby of just nine months, Ann died of Bright's disease, an autoimmune disease of the kidneys. Two of her brothers drowned during a routine boat trip when she was eleven years old. They had been taking a parcel of hosiery, made by the women of the household, to the shop to trade for goods. There were few roads at this time and many journeys were made by boat. The body of one of her brothers was found. Her father walked the shore all summer, searching for the body of the other, but the sea did not return it. The parcel of hosiery floated ashore not far from their house at Slyde.

I would like to retrace the route that Chrissie's grandmother took when she and her family were evicted from Kergord, but it is a daunting walk for an unreliable body. The blanket bog can seem like an endless maze, an obstacle course of many deep gullies and bog pools. And now there is a further obstacle: an energy company, Scottish and Southern Electricity, is constructing a wind farm over a vast area of the central Mainland. Each of the 103 turbines will be 155 metres tall. The turbines will be connected by more than 70 kilometres of newly bulldozed tracks. Each turbine base will require 700 cubic metres of concrete. Rock, blasted from nine new quarries, will surface these tracks. In the autumn of 2020, those wanting to walk in the hill ground were met with signs that read: 'We're sorry but due to ongoing construction work, normal rights of access to the area marked within the red boundary on the attached plan layout are currently suspended. Land Reform (Scotland)

Act 2003. Section 6.' This removal of access rights breached a planning condition and, following a public outcry, access was restored.

I do not know the hill ground like I know the shore, because my body does not grant me the same access to both places. But I have walked there enough to have collected many vivid memories. When I think of the hill ground, I think of sounds. The cascading notes of a whimbrel's trill song, or the sharp notes of a merlin's rapid-fire alarm call. It is a place where golden plovers hide in a summer plumage that matches the colours of the boglands: a belly of peat under a quartz-trimmed cloak of green-gold sphagnum. If it were not for the piped notes of their alarm call, I would not see them. There are softer sounds too – the low conversational murmur between two *rain geese* that rest on the surface of a loch, heads tucked under wings. All this held in a silence so deep that it becomes something more than silence.

One warm summer's day, I walked up to Lamba Water and sat for a while next to a mound of ruby-red sphagnum. I became a giant looking down on a citadel. Ants and spiders contoured the slopes as if in a hurry to get somewhere, disappearing now and then into tangled thickets of pale reindeer moss. The sticky leaves of tiny sundews poked above the sphagnum's surface, glistening and speckled with the corpses of minute flies. The surface of the mound was warm to the touch.

Without thinking why, I slipped my fingers through its surface. It was wet inside, as if my fingers had passed through skin and slipped into the moist heat of a body. The sphagnum seemed vulnerable in the same way that a body can seem vulnerable. When I withdrew my fingers, they left a gaping hole that did not close. A memory of shame surfaced, of treading on a frozen mound of sphagnum and seeing it split right open, as neatly as a knife-cut wound.

Sphagnum was gathered in great quantities during the First World War, to be used in wound dressings. It wicks blood away. It can hold twenty times its dry weight in water, and presumably urine too, but perhaps this absorbency is lower for viscous blood and pus. I'm tempted to gather and dry a little, to see how well it absorbs my menstrual blood.

Sphagnum is vital for the health of our human bodies, and the bodies of myriad other creatures. It is both alive and dead. The tips of the plant grow upwards and the lower part dies and forms the peat that is the basis of all bogland habitats, including the blanket bog that cloaks much of Shetland. In this process of simultaneously growing and dying, carbon is stored. So much so that peatlands are the most important carbon sinks in the terrestrial environment. When the body of a bog is damaged, it dries and carbon dioxide is released back into the atmosphere. Water quality decreases and the risk of flooding increases. When we harm the bogs of this world, we harm our own bodies too.

The Viking wind farm is being constructed on areas of deep peat, formed over millennia, and patches of peat that are still actively forming. There are also places where sheep numbers have been too high in the past and peat lies bare to the elements, eroding and releasing carbon back into the atmosphere. But this grazing pressure has reduced in recent years. Meanwhile, there are areas in Shetland where eroded peatlands have been successfully restored.

Scottish and Southern Electricity claims that the damage caused by the wind farm's construction will be offset by peatland restoration. But by the time the construction begins in 2020, SSE have failed to agree the financial bond that will pay for this restoration and for the wind farm's decommissioning. Two years into construction, and still no bond is in place. Even if a bond is agreed, I'm sceptical that the peatlands can be restored after such extensive damage. I question whether Viking will save any carbon emissions at all. SSE estimate that they will excavate 2.3 million cubic metres of peat.

The environmental credentials of Viking are in doubt, but so too are the financial benefits to the Shetland community. On the Viking Energy website, the wind farm is described as 'a joint venture between the Shetland community and the energy company SSE'. It is important to clarify what the word 'community' means in this statement. Though this necessitates wading through a mire of sorry detail.

At the outset of the wind farm's genesis, the Shetland Islands Council joined with SSE and Shetland Aerogenerators, who own the five-turbine Burradale wind farm near Lerwick, to form the Viking Energy Partnership. It isn't surprising that the Council made this decision. In the 1970s, its shrewd negotiations with oil companies, during the early years of North Sea oil discovery and extraction, resulted in considerable oil wealth flowing into Shetland. The Shetland Charitable Trust was established to receive these

'disturbance' payments, and has since distributed more than
£320 million to local charities, organisations and individuals. This oil income has also built rural care homes, leisure
centres and the Shetland Museum and Archives.

The last disturbance payment was made in 2000, and the
Trust now relies on investment income. Shetland has no
shortage of wind, and it is only natural that the Council
sought to benefit from the shift to renewable energy production. Initially, the Shetland Charitable Trust expected to
receive a projected annual profit of £23 million from the
Viking wind farm.

In 2007, the Council sold its stake in Viking to the Shetland Charitable Trust for £1. The Trust then invested
£10 million in the wind farm's development. It is important
to note that twenty-two of the Trust's twenty-four trustees were also councillors. In terms of decision-making, the
Council and the Trust were effectively one and the same.
The Office of the Scottish Charity Regulator would later
insist, in 2012, that the Trust reform and the majority of its
trustees remain independent of the Council.

In the years that followed, onshore wind farm subsidies
changed, making the development less financially viable. In
May 2019, and in continued uncertainty, the Shetland Charitable Trust withdrew from the Viking Energy Partnership.
The Viking wind farm, which has been developed with the
inclusion of £10 million of public money, is now almost
entirely owned by a multinational energy company.

The investment of this public money in the Viking wind
farm suggests a governance structure in which elected
councillors act on behalf of the community that they

serve. The reality, in this instance, is somewhat different. The planning department of the Shetland Islands Council recommended that the councillors object to the Viking wind farm because it would have an 'unacceptable environmental impact'. In 2010, councillors voted against their own planning department's recommendation. Nine councillors voted for the development, three against, and a further nine did not attend the vote for reasons of conflict of interest. The Trust was already, by this point, the wind farm's co-developer.

In 2008, opponents of the Viking wind farm formed a protest group called Sustainable Shetland. This group proposed alternative models for power generation – localised and more genuinely community-based. Sustainable Shetland's objection to Viking was shared by the Council's own planning department and by two statutory bodies, Scottish Natural Heritage and the Scottish Environment Protection Agency. The Shetland Amenity Trust and the Shetland Bird Club also objected, as did the Royal Society for the Protection of Birds, the John Muir Trust and the Mountaineering Council of Scotland.

In the early stages of the wind farm's development, the Scottish government's Energy Consents Unit received 2,772 individual objections and 1,109 letters of support. The Viking Energy Partnership hosted four public consultation meetings in various locations in Shetland. On average, 75 per cent of those attending those four meetings objected to a wind farm of this scale being developed in Shetland.

The Trust, with its majority councillor trustees, ploughed on regardless. The Scottish government was not obliged to hold a public local inquiry because the Shetland Islands Council councillors had voted not to object to the Viking wind farm and granted the development planning permission.

It is striking that people in Shetland raised more than £200,000 to fund the costs of challenging the wind farm's consent at the level of a judicial review. Many of the donations came from crofting tenants, who could benefit financially should the wind farm go ahead. The judicial review found in favour of Sustainable Shetland but was then overturned, on appeal, by Scottish ministers. The Supreme Court supported the decision in favour of Scottish ministers, and the planning permission for the wind farm was cleared in 2015. Sustainable Shetland's challenge was ultimately unsuccessful, but it remains on the record as an act of protest and resistance.

An equal right of appeal would have allowed a public local inquiry. At present, only planning applicants have the right to appeal planning decisions. An equal right of appeal might also have allowed greater advocacy for the non-humans in our community, whether the nesting *rain geese* or a microscopic creature in the water held within a sphagnum leaf.

The wind turbines of island communities can often be seen as symbols of self-determination, from the Dancing Ladies of Gigha in the Hebrides, the first community-owned and grid-connected wind farm in Scotland, to the community turbine in the island of Westray, Orkney. In Shetland, the five turbines of the Garth wind farm stand in tribute to the tenacity and hard work of the community of North Yell. At Garth, each turbine is named after a local boat lost, with all lives, in the great storm of 1881. At this time, crofting tenants in Shetland were still subject to the brutality of the lairds. The naming of the Garth turbines is a powerful symbol of the dignity of autonomy.

To my mind, the Viking turbines will come to symbolise the disempowerment of a community. They will also symbolise the impossibility of defending peatland commons when corporate power colludes with disempowering structures of local and national governance. This wind that we have so much of here in Shetland will be harnessed to line the pockets of the shareholders of a private multinational energy company. Our peatlands and all that they mean are being damaged for a capitalist, extractivist development that has always had the pursuit of profit at its core. No amount of greenwashing, or claiming that the wind farm is a community project, can hide this sorry fact. It is difficult to quantify the impacts of such sustained disempowerment on a person or a community, but qualitatively we can say that they include depression and a form of collective grief.

The wind farm was given the final go-ahead in July 2020, when Ofgem approved the £600 million interconnector cable that will export the energy generated by the Viking wind farm to the Scottish mainland. On the day of this decision, I heard deep sorrow in the voices of people who live here. I feel this grief too, though I know the hill less intimately than those who have grown up here. It isn't surprising when people refer to the Clearances in connection to the Viking wind farm. The rigs of the last croft to be cleared in Kergord have now been bulldozed to clear the way for Viking's electricity converter station.

Work begins on the wind farm in the summer of 2020. I want to walk in the hill ground of Scallafield before the bulldozers arrive, but I haven't been able to walk far since the spring. One bright April day, the full moon caused an ebb tide that drained the firth more fully than I had ever seen before. It was a shock to glance out of the window and find so much of the seabed exposed. Waders displayed in the air above our house, as if responding to the new warmth in the sun. A curlew rose and fell in an undulating flight path, the shape of inhalation and exhalation. We spotted a snipe circling overhead and opened a window to listen to the dream-thrum of its tail feathers winnowing the air.

Inside, my son lay shivering on the sofa in the grip of a fever. In the days before, he had complained of a tightness in his chest. Covid was sweeping through Shetland, and though there were no tests available, I suspected that we had caught it too. I had packed a small bag with a washbag and a change of clothes, just in case. There is no intensive care unit in Shetland. The distance to the mainland of Scotland felt as acute as it did on the day I gave birth to my daughter. I watched my son through the night and his fever eased. On the day that our quarantine ended, we all chose to walk to the sea glass beach.

My husband and daughter recovered quickly from this illness. My son took two months to shake off a heavy lethargy. My body responded with an acute flare of palindromic rheumatism. I had to recalibrate my bodymind to the return of the disease after almost a year in near-remission. Spending time on the sea glass beach softened this blow. The beach was kind and I found a rare piece of lavender sea glass. On the summer solstice, I cast a message in a bottle into the sea. The message that I wrote was more heartfelt than usual.

By late December, the construction of the wind farm is well under way, and driving back from Lerwick one day I see that it will only be a matter of weeks before all the heavy machinery reaches the high ground of Scallafield. My body is still tender with palindromic rheumatism. A lengthy walk over uneven terrain is unappealing, but it is now or never. On a cold morning in early January, I lace up my walking boots and leave the house. The sun is yet to rise over the snow-clad ridgeline of Scallafield. Ice lips the shoreline and encircles the island broch. The ebb tide pulls sheets of ice down the firth and towards the open sea. Mergansers scurry across the free surface of the water. I am happy to be out walking on such a morning, but it is also like walking towards someone whom I love and will never see again.

The path begins by the narrow road-bridge over the Burn of Lunklet. The water of the burn is dark with peat and flows under broken sheets of ice and down towards the sea. I turn my back to the sea and start the walk up the path. A red grouse flies a low circle over my head, belly thrust out, calling 'go back, go back'. I carry on, up past the waterfall at Ramnahol, the Hill of the Ravens. Water plunges through an embrace of ice.

The quartz boundary stones that mark the ruin of an ancient dwelling lie hidden under the snow. I voice a greeting as I pass. It was built at a time, around 3,000 years ago, when the climate in Shetland became cooler and wetter, causing blanket bog to spread down from the hilltops and out from wet hollows. A stone lamp, roughly hewn and heavy to hold, was found in this ruin. The Viking wind farm has a projected lifespan of twenty-five years, and when I think of this short duration, I think of this stone lamp. That it may have cast light for many hundreds of years. Peat forms at a rate of one millimetre a year; a metre's depth of peat equates to a thousand years. A mechanical digger can excavate millennia's worth of carbon-storing peat in a matter of minutes.

The author and singer-songwriter Malachy Tallack teases out the meaning of hill ground to Shetlanders in his book *Sixty Degrees North*. He describes how we live with its 'constant presence' and how, in turn, its presence inhabits us. It is there when I need it, even if only viewed through a window. Sometimes, the sea is too much or not enough, and then I can find what I need in the hill ground. It is a transcendental place, free mostly from the distractions of human clutter, movement and noise. As Tallack writes, in the hill ground 'time seems to gather itself, to coil and unravel simultaneously. Here the past is closer.' I voice a greeting to the remains of the Neolithic dwelling because it would be wrong not to. As wrong as passing a neighbour without saying hello.

The surface of the Loch of Lunklet looks like a skating rink. Mountain hare tracks cross the ice in places. Some stop halfway across and then return to the shore, as if the hares had lost their nerve. I lose my nerve at times too. The snow makes the ground more even but hides holes, streams and wet flushes.

I stop for a rest at the Butter Stane, a *scattald* boundary marker, a large outcrop of coarse schist veined with smooth quartz. There is a strange sound, almost like the drumming of a displaying snipe. It is too early in the year, though. I listen more intently; it is not a snipe. It sounds more like the echo of a song. Spooked, I look about for its source and find none. In a *trow* story from this side of Scallafield, a fiddler called Magnie o' Lunklet is spirited away by the hillfolk on Yule morning. His captors force him to play his fiddle for a whole week of dancing before they let him return home. He is lucky; some are kept for years and others are never returned.

A woman before and during childbirth was said to be particularly at risk of being taken by the *trows*. The attending *howdie*, or the woman's family, would perform a saining and protect her with charms. A Bible and a knife would be placed in her bed. A black cockerel might be borrowed from a neighbour because they sense the *vaam*, the maleficent magic of *trows*. It is said by some in the Faroe Islands that the *Huldufólk* became extinct in the 1950s, when electricity arrived and, in the island of Nólsoy, storm petrels stopped nesting in the stone walls of houses.

I leave the Butter Stane and its strange song, eager to reach the Muckle Scord – the pass that Chrissie's grandmother and family crossed when they were cleared from their land in Kergord. The sound of metal clanging against rock grows louder, but even with this warning the view from the Scord is a shock. The clean ridgelines to the east are broken by the presence of many diggers; orange arms angle into the ground and cab windows glint in the sun. The narrow crest of the Mid Kames is marked by high walls of peat, all bulldozed aside for a new track that ploughs straight through the nesting territories of curlew, dunlin and golden plover. The noise of all the machinery is constant. An area marked by posts, close to where I stand, will soon be cleared of peat and the rock will be blasted away.

The notion of solastalgia falls short, I think, in this instance. There is a deeper level of trauma when the land that you are emotionally attached to is a carbon-storing peatland that is being destroyed for profit, under the guise of reducing carbon emissions. And yet I hold within me a pocket of doubt. A sort of nagging sense or a vague consideration of all the ways in which I consume, and sometimes waste, electricity. I see, with admiration, the work that others are doing to move towards living off-grid. But this is not something that I could physically endure, unless faced with no choice. My protest does come from a place of comfort and relative affluence afforded by my husband's work as a helicopter pilot in the oil and gas industry. But the fact remains that this wind farm will do nothing to help the households in Shetland that experience fuel poverty. In 2021, this is one in three households, and it is only set to get worse. A Viking Energy community fund will trickle money into Shetland in the form of new computers for schools or equipment for sports clubs, but this is scant compensation.

Below where I stand, I can see two houses that sit side by side. I could walk to them in minutes. The Scottish government recommends, but does not enforce, that high turbines should be sited no closer than two kilometres from houses. In England this distance would be three kilometres. Seventy of Viking's turbines will be built within two kilometres of homes. I would like to know why our homes here in Shetland matter less. I would like to know how our bodyminds will be impacted by the low-frequency sounds of more than a hundred giant turbines.

The hills that the turbines will sit on are not high. Scallafield rises to 281 metres. Each turbine tower will be 155 metres tall. I begin to imagine the hills as pinned moths in a lepidopterist's collection. When people in Shetland, including the Shetland Islands Council's own planning department, say that the Viking wind farm is out of scale, this is also what they mean. It is both vast in its expanse and disproportionately immense in the vertical space that it will occupy.

Wind farm marker posts lead up a gentle slope to the height of Scallafield. I flush a mountain hare from its cover and it bounds away at speed, leaving widely spaced prints in the snow. By the time I reach the trig point at the top of Scallafield, my body is distractingly sore but it is worth this discomfort. Far out in the Atlantic, a snow-clad Foula has become an iceberg, a small piece of the Arctic adrift. A snow shower falls on the grey surface of the Atlantic and swallows the Vee Skerries whole. To the east, the North Sea is cloud-free and bewilderingly expansive. An oil and gas supply vessel heads out to the oilfields that lie beyond the horizon.

To the south, an oil platform, the Ninian Northern, pokes out from behind a hill. It sits in a decommissioning yard in Dales Voe. We went to see it one day, all four of us, and my husband pointed to the door that he would enter if he needed to use the toilet. It has sat in the North Sea since 1978 and looks rusted and spent. A solitary wind turbine, all shining and new, looks down on the Ninian Northern from the low height of a hill called Luggie's Knowe. A little further to the south, and hidden by a hill, is the power station in Lerwick. This power station generates electricity by burning diesel and was due to be decommissioned soon, but the wind farm means that it will now need to be retained.

The Viking wind farm will export the electricity it generates through a newly laid interconnector cable. Shetland will import its electricity from the Scottish mainland through this same cable. When the cable that connects the Western Isles to mainland Scotland was recently broken, perhaps cut by a trawler, it left 18,000 homes temporarily without power. The diesel power station in Lerwick will be retained in case of such an interconnector failure, and so the Viking wind farm has prolonged the lifespan of this polluting power station. The more that I contemplate all the ins and outs of the Viking wind farm, the more I believe it to be a mistake, from multiple perspectives – the environment, the community and the security of our energy supply. I view the relationship between the energy company and Shetland as more parasitical than symbiotic. It is not, I would argue, mutually beneficial.

A snow cloud sweeps in over Scallafield and erases everything except the ground beneath my feet. The temperature falls away. I fumble in my rucksack for more clothes. The cloud passes through quickly enough but leaves me longing to be home and warm. I slide down the steep face of Scallafield on the seat of my waterproofs, and make my slow way back. By the time I reach the road, it is hard to walk and the tarmac jars my irritated joints further. The wind farm's many tracks will make walking in the hills easier, at least, for those of us who struggle on uneven ground.

During this first Covid winter, I switch my focus from searching for sea glass to looking for the pieces of earthenware pottery that is glazed a pale yellow on one side. Fragments of bowls or jars in which cream would be stored before being churned to make butter. The connection to the past in these fragments of earthenware feels stronger in my hand than it does with sea glass. They are a material link to the milking of the *coo* in the byre and to the summer herding of the *kye* on the *scattald* – to the work of women. I would like to know how old the fragments are. If they reach back to the time of the Clearances and to the days of Chrissie Sandison's grandmother Mergat.

Pieces of earthenware pile up on my desk and I am unsure what to do with them. And then I watch a short film by the Shetland poet Jen Hadfield. She generously shares a prompt for making a personal political manifesto, a small gesture of resistance, a way in which we can haul ourselves back to what is important. I have a go, self-conscious at first, but I soon lose myself in thought and my pen begins to move freely across a scrap of paper. When I am done, I take the pottery fragments and a pencil and write small phrases of intent on the yellow glaze. I take the pieces down to the sea glass beach at low tide and wade into the sea. When I lower my hands into the water, the waves lift the pieces away.

On New Year's Day, while seeking a small *hansel* or gift from the sea to bode well for the coming year, I find the first piece of earthenware that has been returned to the shore. It is still possible to read the faded pencil marks and they spell out the words 'in curiosity'. I search again, three days before a new moon, when the ebb tide has pulled out further than usual. I find a piece lying yellow-glaze down, next to a small rock where a deep-red anemone oozes and glistens and waits for the sea to return. I pick the piece up and flip it over in my hand. The word 'dissent' is faint but still legible.

Haaf Fish

Grey Seal

When my children return to school after the October half-term holiday in 2020, a wave of anxiety washes through me. I've spent the first six months of the pandemic just wanting to keep them close, and now I find that it is a little harder each time to let them go again.

I wait until the school bus pulls out of the drive, then gather my walking boots and packed rucksack and set off in my car to a stretch of coastline where grey seals haul out and give birth in the late autumn. Each year, NatureScot organises a grey seal pup census, and many of the people taking part are volunteers like me. I missed the beached bird surveys during lockdown. Not just the beaches – or the birds themselves, alive and dead – but the process of looking with the purpose of gathering data. It is good to be heading out again, though the walk to the seal geos will be taxing. My body is still tender from the Covid-triggered flare of palindromic rheumatism. But I am on my own and can walk at a slow pace.

There is no wind, and the water in the *voe* is flat-calm. I pull over in a layby to look for porpoises but see none. At the school, both my children are running around the busy playground with wide grins on their faces, and a little weight lifts from my shoulders. By the time I turn west at the junction, my spirit soars at the thought of a walk along the cliffs, though this excitement is tinged with fear. The cliffs are high. The seals haul out on beaches enclosed within the depths of geos, where they give birth among heaps of driftwood and much plastic litter.

When the cliffs come into view, I do a double take. Dense clouds of salt spray rise into the air like smoke. It is a calm and sunny day but the swell is immense and oily. The ocean seethes with power. The land cowers. There must have been a storm somewhere far out in the Atlantic. At the cliffs, fulmars sit on ledges with their heads tucked under their wings, as if trying to block out the thundering of the waves. The salt spray tightens my skin. Far out to the west, the island of Foula stays hidden behind low cloud, as if it does not want to see what will happen next.

The first of the two seal geos lies wide open to the Atlantic. The tide is midway through the ebb but white water covers the beach. There are no seals. The sun doesn't reach into the depths of the geo. It is a dark and lifeless place.

The second geo is smaller and more sheltered. Rocks guard the entrance and diffuse the power of the incoming waves. Much of the beach seems dry. I count three pregnant cows, their bellies huge. Four white-furred pups lie alongside the silvery-grey bulk of their mothers. Bright-pink umbilical cord stumps protrude from their bellies. They are newborns. Their skin is slack and wrinkled and their eyes are dark and huge. Unlike harbour seal pups, which can swim almost immediately, grey seal pups are born without blubber and cannot withstand the cold of the sea. They lose their white coats after two weeks or so, when they are fat and swollen from their mothers' milk. A mother seal will mostly stay ashore with her pup, in these first weeks, and will diminish in size as her pup swells.

All seems well. The waves fall short of the seals. I lie on my belly and they cannot see me. It is a pleasure to observe all the goings-on. Cows snooze, yawn and scratch. The pups are open-eyed and alert.

One of the cows suddenly lifts her head high. I can't hear anything but she can, and she begins to heft herself up the beach, towards higher ground. But too late, she cannot move fast enough and is engulfed by a large wave that roars into the geo. When the wave recedes, it pulls the pup from her side and drags it backwards down the beach and into the boil of white water. The front flippers of the pup splay wide as if it is trying to find purchase. It is all over in a matter of seconds. The cow is motionless, her neck stretched as she stares at the place where her pup disappeared. She is still staring when another large wave surges in and returns her pup to her side. She noses its sodden fur and it wails like a human baby.

For an eerie while there is a lull. Smaller waves wash in and the geo becomes quiet again. A rock pipit lands on the pebbles and forages between the bodies of the seals. A grey seal bull swims into the geo and lets the surf carry his heavy body onto the pebbles. He dwarfs the cows in length and bulk. His neck is creased and so thick that he looks an equal match to the power of the sea. The sodden pup continues to wail.

A movement at the edge of my field of view catches my

attention. A grey seal cow is in the surf beyond a spur of rock that hides a small pocket of the beach. She looks so human, with her head and shoulders held high above the mess of white water and her dark eyes so wide. Her breathing is hard and her nostrils are flared open. She turns her head in frantic movements, spins in a circle and then dives under the surface, only to reappear a little further along. A thick length of driftwood rides in on a wave like a battering ram and narrowly misses her head. She flinches in fright. I watch her dangerous search until I can stand it no more. Her pup is lost. I leave the cliffs and head for home.

The old names for seals in Shetland tell you where they are most likely to be found. The harbour seal was known by the name *tang fish*, and *tang* is seaweed of the *Fucus* genus – of the wrack kind, like the bladderwrack of the upper shore. The grey seal was known as the *haaf fish*, and *haaf* is the deep or open sea. Across the firth from where we live, there is a burn that flows down through the bog and a silage field to reach the shore. It is called Selkieburn, but only harbour seals haul out on the rocks there. To watch a grey seal, I need to follow the shore to the point where the firth turns outwards and joins the more open waters of the *voe*. It is almost as if grey seals cannot withstand being surrounded by land, and harbour seals need the shelter of relative enclosure.

Seals of both kinds, harbour and grey, are still called selkies in Shetland, and the retention of this name makes it easier to believe in the existence of the selkie folk, a supernatural race that shed their sealskins to take on a human form. I once shyly asked three Shetlanders if they knew of any selkies. Two said no so abruptly that I sensed their resentment at being asked such a ridiculous question. But the third person, without hesitation, said yes. There was a woman, a few generations back in her home island, she explained, who was thought to be descended from a selkie. And each time that I read a selkie story now, I think of this and take it just a little bit more seriously than I did before.

The most famous of Shetland's selkie stories takes place in the island of Papa Stour and the nearby and notorious Vee Skerries. Papa Stour is separated from the West Mainland by a dangerous tidal stream. It is inhabited by fewer than ten permanent residents. The Vee Skerries lie three and a half miles off the north-west coast of Papa Stour. These small and sea-scoured islets sit low in the water and have wrecked many ships. Submerged rocks make it dangerous for most boats to approach, and so they are seldom visited. Even if you can make it in, the swell can pick up suddenly, making it difficult to leave again. I look for the Vee Skerries from the hill track above my house. Or rather, I look for the white water that hides them from view on many days. It seems inconceivable to me but grey seals haul out on these skerries to give birth.

I've only ever visited Papa Stour in winter, to beachcomb. During one visit, on a bleak March day, I stood above the shelving pebble beach at Aisha and watched the waves, to gauge whether or not a beachcomb would be too dangerous. A gale had blown itself out the day before. The waves were roaring in but didn't seem to reach too far up the beach, and the strandline looked swollen and promising. A grey seal in the surf watched me clamber down the low bank.

I took an eggcase and left the torn skin of a lumpsucker fish, and I made the mistake of turning my back to the sea. I heard the wave when it was already too late. Water surged up and around my legs. The force of it nearly knocked me off my feet. There was a moment of slack water and then the retreat. I stayed upright but the sea carried me down the beach. I recognised the same slowing of time and calm acceptance that I remembered from falling off my road bike. The wave weakened its grip just before the shelf of pebbles fell away into deeper water. I scrambled to higher ground and sat on the grass to recover, still watched by the seal.

Subsequent visits have been without incident but I remain more wary of the sea here. The soft volcanic rock of the island is visibly storm-gouged. It becomes possible to imagine the land as a body, vulnerable and susceptible to injury. I envy the ease of the seals in the waves when I am walking the shores of Papa Stour.

In the 1940s, the writer and radio producer David Thomson travelled the Atlantic shores of Ireland and Scotland to gather selkie folklore. These journeys and their conversations form his book *The People of the Sea*. To read this book now is to be reminded of the wealth of selkie myths. I am tired of hearing the same old tale of a human man stealing the sealskin of a beautiful young selkie woman. He keeps her trapped in his home until the day she finds her skin and escapes back to the sea, leaving behind the children that she has borne him. The locus of shock in this story is not the entrapment or the rape, it is that the selkie chooses her freedom over her children.

The Shetland selkie myth that Thomson recorded so carefully in Papa Stour is a story of a seal hunt gone wrong, the mercy of a selkie and a seal hunter's redemption. There are several versions of this tale, and this is my retelling.

A long time ago, in the island of Papa Stour, there was a summer of poor weather. The men could not set sail for Vee Skerries to go sealing. When the first day of fair weather arrived, the older men warned that the sea would not stay placid for long. But the younger men had fallen behind on their rent, and a boatful of skins would mean that their wives could buy food for their bairns. They launched a boat and rowed out to the desolate haunt of seals.

The best skerry for cornering the seals is also the most difficult to set foot on, but they managed to manoeuvre the boat in and all the men made it ashore without mishap. They crossed the treacherous rocks in silence. Their stealth worked and they clubbed many seals. They worked quickly to cut the skins away from the flesh, before any of the seals regained their senses.

A sudden squall warned the men of the clouds gathering out over the Atlantic. The swell had picked up and the boat had started to buck wildly at its mooring. If it broke free, they would be left stranded. They gathered all the skins they could and hurried back across the jagged rocks to the boat. One of the men stumbled, and skins flew from his arms and scattered far and wide. The others shouted at him to leave the skins behind. But he ignored their commands, and by the time he had picked all the skins up, the rest of the men had made it to the boat and had already rowed away from the dangerous rocks. They tried three times to return to him, but each time the boat was nearly swamped by a wave. They left the man and rowed away home.

He sank to his knees, knowing only too well the fate of those who become stranded on these rocks in a storm. The waves would soon sweep him away. He wept at the thought of never seeing his wife and children again. But a strange sound roused him from his sorrowful state, a keening that carried over the crashing of the waves. He followed the sound to the gully and there he found a selkie crying at the sight of her son in human form, bruised and bloody, his skin red-raw and knife-cut in places.

The selkie fell silent at the sight of the man. They stared at one another and he feared that she might launch at him in rage, but she stayed quite still. Her eyes softened a little and then she said these words. 'I will carry you home to your family, if you fetch me my son's stolen skin. Without it, he is destined to live as a man upon the land and I will never see him again.' The man nodded. 'I will,' he told the selkie, 'but the waves will wash me from your back. Can I make cuts in your skin so that I may grip better?' The selkie dipped her head in agreement and did not flinch when the knife sliced right through her skin.

She swam through the raging ocean with the man upon her back, and they came ashore on the beach in the depths of Ekkers Geo. The man's hands were numb with cold and he struggled to climb up the steep rock wall, but the thought of seeing his wife and children again spurred him on. As promised, the selkie did not have to wait long before he reappeared at the top of the cliff. He flung her son's skin down to her. She swam away, back to the Vee Skerries, and the man never went sealing again.

David Thomson walked the cliffs of Papa Stour and found that the bleakness of Ekkers Geo came to haunt his dreams: 'I thought too of death in that place and once at night I dreamt that I was falling into Akers [sic] Geo.' I fear Ekkers Geo too. The land tilts you down towards the cliff edge, and even lying down, the pull of gravity seems stronger here. The savage feel of the place is intensified by the way that the geo's cliffs neatly frame a view of the Vee Skerries, a place that has long been associated with the loss of human life. Thomson wanted to visit the Vee Skerries during his stay in Papa Stour, but the weather was unfavourable. I never thought that I would ever visit this wild place, but one day, I did.

It is a fine August day in 2017, and my neighbour John Anderson calls to say that he is taking a small group of people out to the Vee Skerries in his boat and would I like to come along. I say yes, swallow down some sea sickness pills, and drive down to the marina where John already has the *Mary Ann*'s engines running. He helps me aboard the yellow-hulled boat and sets about readying her for the voyage. I am nervous, mostly about being sick in front of the others, but also because my joints are stiff. Climbing down the *Mary Ann*'s ladder and into the little metal skiff that we will row ashore in will be a challenge, and I don't want to be a liability. But I know I will be well looked after by John. He is an experienced sailor and takes people out sport-fishing or sightseeing along this stretch of coastline. He is tall and sturdy, and with his red hair he looks a little like a Viking.

John introduces me to Gibbie Fraser, who cuts a dignified figure in a checked flannel shirt, blue jeans and smart
yachtie wellies. He shakes my hand with considerable force
and a mischievous glint in his eye, perhaps detecting my
nervousness. Gibbie is a retired lobster fisherman who left
school at fifteen and went to work as a whaler in Antarctica,
arriving in South Georgia in November 1958. He left Shetland in the summer, when the skies were filled with Arctic
terns, and found them again in the summer of the Southern Ocean.

When he returned to Shetland there was little work available, and so he commissioned a boat and paid for it with
his earnings from the whaling, and from then on, Gibbie
fished for lobsters until he retired. He would sometimes set
creels near the Vee Skerries, or catch *piltocks* there – young
saithe for bait – when he struggled to find them elsewhere.
He knows the Vee Skerries better than anyone, and will
pilot us in.

In the wheelhouse with Gibbie and John are two men
from Lerwick, who chat about sailing and the islands,
inhabited and uninhabited, that they have visited. They
both look much older than me, not quite salty sea dogs but
still, both are at ease at sea. I sit outside, to avoid feeling
sick, next to Arthur, who lives across the *voe* from me. He
is also retired and has many years' experience of travelling
by boat in the seas around Shetland. He reassures me that
the swell is too gentle to make me feel sick. By the time we
pull away from the marina, I am more excited than fearful.
We leave the shelter of the *voe* under a blanket of cloud and
sail towards the sun. The surface of the sea is speckled with

tysties, black guillemots, and puffins. John slows the boat when a pod of porpoises crosses our path at speed, trailing fine spray from their dorsal fins.

Arthur and I talk about the Celtic monks who lived in Papa Stour and gave the island its name, 'the large island of the priests'. They sailed from Ireland in simple boats of oxhide stretched over wooden frames, and we both agree that neither of us would like to venture out in such a craft – but then Arthur tells me that he has rowed a small boat around the coastline of Shetland. I ask him what prompted him to take on such a challenge, and he explains that he completed the journey in memory of his wife who died of cancer. And then, for a while, we sit in silence.

From the sea, the cliffs of Papa Stour are grimly compelling. Caves gape wide and swallow great quantities of the ocean. Leera Skerry and Fugla Skerry, the skerries of the Manx shearwater and of the birds, stand sheer-sided and inaccessible. We catch sight of a sea stack in human form. In *The Coastal Place Names of Papa Stour*, George P. S. Peterson describes the Snolda stack as 'a robed monk, standing facing the distant Vee Skerries, head bowed as though praying for the souls of those poor sea-men lost there'. Further out, the sun shines on the white tower of the Vee Skerries lighthouse, and to the south-west Foula looms immense and imposing, seeming to watch the progress of our small boat with feigned disinterest.

The distance to the Vee Skerries closes and my fear returns. They sit so low in the ocean. The swell is very gentle but thoughts of rogue waves refuse to leave my mind. Gibbie guides John to a place where the *Mary Ann* can lie at anchor safely. My legs shake as I climb down the ladder and into the skiff. Two at a time, Gibbie rows us to Nort Skerry. Eider ducks slip off the rocks and into the water as we approach. There are many grey seals, some basking on the rocks and others swimming. They watch us but seem unconcerned by our arrival. I quickly count more than a hundred. The power of their collective gaze is unnerving.

Gibbie steadies the small skiff against a rock as we scramble ashore, and jokes a final cheerio as he rows back to the *Mary Ann*. When I find a place even enough to plant my feet and look up, I see barnacles at eye level. We have landed at low tide. At high tide, this part of Nort Skerry would be submerged. Sooth Skerry, also known as the Clubb, stands higher but not by much. The OS map gives a spot height of eight metres above mean sea level. But still, there are days when a storm-driven swell reaches higher than this. All of us are quiet and subdued. The rocks are very difficult to cross. I stay rooted to the spot and wait for Gibbie to return.

When Gibbie reappears, he is delighted to tell us that he and John have caught several fish. One is a large *waari* cod, its skin a rich orange in colour. These orange cod are common near the Vee Skerries. They prey on invertebrates rich in carotenoid pigments because they have been feeding on all the kelp that darkens the water around each of the rocky islets. When we arrive at Ormal, my heart sinks to see that the lighthouse and the small beach of pebbles is completely surrounded by a rim of broken and sharply angled rocks. I soon fall behind all the men, even the septuagenarian from Lerwick with his gammy knee, and this makes me seethe with frustration. I want to get to the beach first. There is a good chance that no one has visited the place since winter, and it might be laden with all kinds of interesting finds.

But the men make straight for the lighthouse, leaving me free to scour the beach of pale-grey pebbles in peace. The beach is circular and highest at its centre. It has three concentric strandlines. I stand in the middle of the smallest circle and imagine the tide rising up all around me but never quite reaching my feet. The smooth dome of a seal's skull lies among the desiccated seaweed. There are eight plastic drinks bottles, a single can of Asturiana whippy cream and a can of Spanish solvent. A v-shaped piece of metal, red with rust, lies wedged between two large pebbles.

When Arthur returns from the lighthouse, I show the metal to him. It is an air valve from a ship's engine, he explains, perhaps from the *Elinor Viking*, an Aberdeen trawler that wrecked on the Vee Skerries on a dark and wild night in 1977. The lifeboat was unable to reach the stricken vessel. The crew were winched to safety by an oil and gas helicopter just before the trawler broke into pieces. None of the helicopter crew were trained in this task, and the winchman had a narrow escape when the wind shoved him towards the ship's mast. The lighthouse on Ormal was built after this wrecking and to ensure the safe passage of oil tankers sailing into the newly built oil terminal at Sullom Voe.

All of the men join me on the beach and we scour the pebbles of Ormal for flint, ballast from centuries-old wrecks. It is easy to find and smells, to me, strongly of land. Before the days of ship-to-shore radios, the first sign of a wrecking on the Vee Skerries might be splintered wood, not yet saturated with salt water, washing up on Papa Stour. Or a cod caught with grain in its belly. But in 1930, islanders stood on the cliffs of Papa Stour and watched as the men lashed to the mast of the *Ben Doran*, a stricken steam trawler, fell into a sea so tumultuous that the rescue boats had to turn away.

Ormal in Shaetlan is usually used in the plural to mean 'fragments' or 'remnants', and in Old Norse, *ørmul* can mean 'ruins' too. It is an uneasy place to stand, among the flint from the ballast of wrecked ships and among fragments of stories true and mythological, on rocks that have been strewn with the bodies of clubbed seals and with the bodies of drowned men and perhaps some women too. These fragments of stories swirl round my head like the flocks of waders that wheel around the rocks, never settling for too long before taking flight again.

It is soon time to leave. The swell has picked up a little, and in the skiff on the way back to the *Mary Ann*, Gibbie is silent and serious-faced, the only sound the soft slap of the oars on the surface of the sea. But once we are all back on board, everyone relaxes with the delight of those who have been somewhere risky and returned to tell the tale. Gibbie takes the wheel for the journey home and John makes us all mugs of tea and passes round a packet of digestive biscuits.

For five anxious days, the weather keeps me from returning to the cliffs to see if any of the newborn grey seal pups have survived. Gales come thick and fast, and gusts of sixty miles per hour shake our house and keep us indoors. The first power cut of the winter has us searching for torches and fresh batteries. The storm comes from the west and coincides with a full moon. The tides are high, and the west-erlies will push the sea even further inland. I don't expect to find any pups alive.

On the sixth day, the wind eases. My children leave on the school bus and my husband and I drive to the outer coast. The sea is brimful and strandlines have been left high on the grass like an assertion of power. At the cliffs, Foula is distant. The sky is grey; sunlight falls through the gaps between clouds and dazzles patches of the dark sea. We walk in silence to the first seal geo. Flakes of freshly broken rock litter the back slope of the cliffs. Only one grey seal cow lies on the beach of the geo; she does not look preg-nant and there is no sign of any pup.

Before we reach the second and more sheltered geo, the voices of seals rise up through the din of the waves, and in response we quicken our pace and then slow again before the edge. The wind is steady and onshore, but the occasional gust makes us wary. We drop to our bellies and wriggle to the cliff edge with all the ungainliness of a seal on land.

A fat, white-coated pup lies in the waves, alive. It has sur-vived these last days, thrived even, but it is wet and struggling. Its mother lies seawards of its body and uses her own body to stop it from floating away. Waves come in and swamp them both. With each surge of water, the pup floats and the sea rolls it over and over like a barrel. When the waves retreat, it rights itself onto its belly and cries.

After a few minutes, the mother seal starts to move up the beach, slowly followed by the pup. And then we see what it is that stops her from reaching the safety of higher ground. Another seal blocks her path, guarding the high ground with bared teeth. She also has a pup. It is plump and its coat is shiny and dry.

The seal with the bared teeth begins to shuffle down the beach and lunges at the seal stuck in the surf. The wet pup is almost crushed between their bodies but then the dry pup crawls towards its mother and is caught by a wave. Mollified, she retreats to higher ground followed by her bedraggled pup. The seal and the pup stuck in the surf take advantage of this truce and move to higher ground too.

Drama over, we scan the rest of the geo, slowly edging round the cliff to get the whole view. There are seven white-coated pups in total. We are slow to notice the sinuous path of blood that coats the pebbles. It starts at the sea's reach and curves its way up to the dry ground at the base of the cliffs, where a seal lies on her side. Her hind flippers are drenched in fresh blood. A tiny, clean-furred pup is suckling, all skin and bone but looking vital and alive. The seal shifts and the pup unlatches; the fur around her teat is wet with a froth of milk. It makes me think of the grey seal who lost her pup to the waves, if her milk still seeps into the salt water of the sea.

Witch

One wild winter's night in 2017, storm waves left a young
orca high on the shore near Hamnavoe in Eshaness, in the
North Mainland of Shetland. The autopsy found bruis-
ing and lung damage consistent with a live stranding, but
otherwise the orca had been healthy and had fed recently;
refluxed seal claws were found in its oesophagus, seal fur in
its stomach. When I read of its death, I wondered if it was
the same young orca that I had seen the winter before, flank-
ing its mother's side below the high cliffs of West Burrafirth.

The day had been unusually cold but windless, and with
clear blue skies. Icicles hung from the banks of a stream, and
at the water's edge thick fingers of ice reached upwards, each
encasing a single strand of grass. Bulging sheets of ice covered
much of the boggy ground. Water trickled over the surface
and made them treacherous to cross. At first the novelty of
a frozen landscape was enchanting, but it soon became frus-
trating. I needed to check two survey points for the presence
of wintering shorebirds. They were some distance away, and

circumnavigating the ice would make the walk even longer. My body was sore with the flickering presence of inflammation. But I set out in high spirits. I hoped to see a small overwintering shorebird called a purple sandpiper.

If searching for storm petrels is a ritual of the Shetland summer, then searching for purple sandpipers is a compulsion of the Shetland winter. At first glance, a purple sandpiper is nothing much to look at. Not compared to the more charismatic of the overwintering birds, the great northern divers that sit on the sea's surface as solidly as a broad-hulled boat, or the long-tailed ducks with their dandyish plumage. Purple sandpipers are small and dumpy; the angle of their bill is downturned and, to me at least, they can look a little curmudgeonly. But they are extraordinary because they inhabit the hard edges of these islands in the worst of the winter weather, places of rock and white water. Places where it would seem impossible for a shorebird to eke out nourishment. I don't ever see them feeding on my home shore in among the curlews and redshanks, in the soft mud that is uncovered at low tide. To find purple sandpipers, I need to search sea-stripped places, bleak shorelines that meet the full force of the ocean.

Purple sandpipers may be intensifiers of winter but they also remind me that Shetland is south yet. It blows my mind to know that they also overwinter in Arctic Norway, where they must forage in darkness for two months. They make me question whether I would be able to withstand so much darkness, and how my bodymind might respond to the intensity of the cold in the far north. Would my boundaries dissolve, or would they harden?

The winter plumage of a purple sandpiper is dark grey and tinged mauve, a colouration that seems to capture the fading of light at dusk. When I saw the young orca with its mother, the sun had not long set. I had walked far and seen no purple sandpipers. I'd misjudged some ice and fallen into a boggy flush, up to my thighs. The wet skin of my legs burnt with cold. But it was a strange walk, irrespective of my disappointment and discomfort. There was something disquieting about the place. I had to keep checking over my shoulder.

On the way back to the car, I stopped one last time to look out over the ocean before leaving the height of the cliffs. The moon was almost full and dusk had settled into the land, but far out to the west, the ocean still glowed in the last of the light. All of a sudden, birds began to lift into flight from the sea's surface and they formed a chaotic and panicked flock. Most were shags, the smaller relative of the cormorant, and the rest were gulls. Some landed on needle-sharp skerries and, in the near-dark, the rocks bristled and came alive with the birds' presence. It took me a while to notice the fins. A small pod of orcas moving south at speed. One of the three females was flanked closely by a juvenile, and they surfaced and dived in perfect synchrony. Much further out, the towering fin of a bull orca looped a neat arc around a low-lying and sea-bound rock.

I did not know it then, but this rock has both a name and a story. It was my neighbour, John Anderson, who told me the story of the Black Stane first – the same neighbour who took me out to the Vee Skerries in his boat, the *Mary Ann*. John pointed to a tiny speck on the map. A woman, thought to have been a witch, was left on the Black Stane, he explained. If she survived the night, it would prove her guilt.

He moved his finger across the pale-blue ink of the map's ocean to the island of Vementry. This small beach, he said, is where her body is supposed to have come ashore.

I search for her story in the main texts on Shetland folklore but find nothing. Mark Smith, an archivist at the Shetland Museum and Archives, searches for me too, but he also finds no mention of the woman and the Black Stane. It is still possible that there is a grain of truth in the story, Mark tells me. Judgements did sometimes take place outside of the law in areas distant from administrative centres. He urges me to keep asking locally, and when I do, some have never heard of the story and others nod but tell a different version. In one, the story is of a straightforward murder: a woman was simply left on the rock to die. I hear too that the Black Stane is reputed to glow when there is a full moon, and wonder if I am being gently teased – but anyway, I don't have the courage to walk along the shores of West Burrafirth at night. It is an uncanny enough place during the day.

The story, remnant that it is, remains all-consuming. I experience two exceptionally vivid dreams. The first dream happens when I am away from home on my own and staying in the island of Papa Stour. The door of the house does not lock and I know that I will not sleep well. I dream of the room in which I sleep. A man stands over me, his hands tightly grip my neck and I know that he intends to strangle me. The intense fear I feel in this dream lingers on. The second dream seems as real as the first but it is strangely comforting. I watch myself sleep in my own bed. A woman stands behind me. I cannot see her face. She reaches down to touch my spine, slips her fingers through my skin, pulls apart the flesh of my back and climbs inside.

During a visit to the quiet sanctuary of the School of Scottish Studies Archives in Edinburgh, in 2017, I read through a file of notes made by the late Alan Bruford, who was once the school's senior archivist. In the mid-1970s, Dr Bruford travelled to Orkney and Shetland to gather the folklore of these islands. I have come to search his notes for records of the use of drift-seed charms. It still perplexes me that I have been unable to unearth any evidence that sea beans, or drift-seeds of any kind, were used as protective charms in Shetland. I visit the archives with the same sense of anticipation that comes before beachcombing after a storm. Outside, the city is bitterly cold. I'm glad to be inside in the warmth of the archives. The lights are on and it is pleasant to sit in a room insulated by so many books.

There is an imperceptible sense of something in these archives, not a hum or a vibration exactly, but a glow of a feeling that comes from being in a space dedicated to keeping the embers of stories alight. Louise and Fiona, the archivists, are welcoming. Louise is from Shetland and comes to my side to help me read Shaetlan. She is younger than me and wears a beautiful woollen cardigan that she has knitted herself. I feel instantly at ease in her presence. Fiona is a warm presence too; she listens to my talk of drift-seeds and nods. She is from the west coast of Scotland and is familiar with drift-seed lore, but soon she is busy assisting Maggie, who is researching the place names of her community in the island of Lewis. They converse in Gaelic. It is a convivial space where islanders need not explain themselves.

I make notes with a pencil but my fingers are resistant, stiff and painful, and my progress is slow. I copy out an Orcadian treatment for 'rheumatics' as told to Dr Bruford by James Henderson, from South Ronaldsay and Burray:

> rub goose grease kept in the stomach of a dogfish
>   on the affected area
> bathe joints in heated seawater containing *craa tang*.

I will search for this seaweed, *craa tang* or *crow tang*, on the shore below my house when I return home. It is said to be yellowish with clusters of branches on a single stalk; it should be possible to work out which one it is.

Almost fifty years have passed since Dr Bruford worked in Shetland and so much has changed. From the island of Yell, Liza Tulloch recalls that her mother would make starling soup. She would add two or three of these birds to the pot to get some meat into it. I feed the starlings in my garden birdseed that I buy from the agricultural supplies store in Lerwick. But when I read the treatments for arthritis, some of this distance closes. I would try the seaweed treatment and, if I had lived in a time before analgesics, I would have tried the dogfish goose-grease cure too.

The medication that I took in the morning before leaving for the archive isn't working, but it is making me ill. I am yet to meet the rheumatologist who will help me to manage my condition. My head swims and it is hard to focus. The pain in my fingers is distracting, and if it increases any more, I will have to stop making notes. I read Liza and Tom Tulloch's explanation of the word *snorr*, which describes the tide when you are unsure if it is ebbing or flooding. I read on and become so absorbed that I don't even notice when the pain begins to recede.

Throughout the notes there are snatches of tide traditions. I add them to the fragments of tide lore that already eddy around my head. *Dockens*, an arable weed, must be pulled on a flowing tide, and ploughing should not be done on an ebbing tide. The cream will churn better on the flood tide. If someone dies during an ebbing tide, this bodes ill for the household, but if the death should fall within the flowing tide, this means better fortune.

I think I understand that, in some way, it is possible to harness the power of the flood tide, or that a flood tide brings good energy, and that an ebb tide is draining, resistant. But even so, I am more at ease with the ebb than I am with the flood. In cold weather in winter, it is sometimes possible to watch the ebb as it flows down the firth and carries thin sheets of ice out into the open *voe*. The flood tide is more difficult to detect from a distance.

During spring flood tides, after a full or a new moon, the sea is sometimes no longer constrained by land. It creeps up over the low banks and begins to swallow the fields. On these days I find it hard to settle; there is no shore, just land and sea. I keep watch to make sure that the tide does turn. And when it does, the ebb tide can drain the firth so fully that it can be crossed by foot. Then it is possible to step carefully between the frayed structures of sand mason worms. Jets of water squirt upwards as *spoots*, razor clams,

bury themselves deeper into the silt in response to the odd-
ity of human footfall. It is both a gift to walk on the seabed
during these *spoot* ebbs, and something of a transgression.

In accounts of the folklore of Orkney and Shetland, the
ebb, the area that is uncovered by the ebb tide, is sometimes
described as belonging to the Devil. As such, the ebb is the
place to go to make a pact with the Devil – to offer one's
body in return for knowledge. There are ways of doing this
and they go something like this:

> go down to the ebb at midnight
> turn your body three times, *widdergaets*, against the
>   path of the sun
> lie down on the shore, between the high-water
>   mark and the low-water mark, on your back
>   with your head pointing south
> find seven stones, two must be flat
> place a stone by each outstretched hand and each
>   foot, by the head
> place the flat stones on the heart and on the chest
> shut your eyes and recite the incantation which
>   you have learnt by heart and which so begins
>   'O, Mester King o' a' that's ill . . .'
> offer yourself, all of yourself, to the Devil
> lie a while quietly
> rise on your left side and throw each stone, one by
>   one, into the sea while speaking maledictions.

This is my retelling of a ritual and incantation collected in
the 1800s by an Orcadian folklorist, Walter Traill Dennison.
It was told to him by an older woman from the island of

Sanday, whose grandmother was said to have been a witch of note. Ernest Marwick, an Orcadian folklorist who died in 1977, casts doubt over the authenticity of the wording of the incantation collected by Traill Dennison, and suggests that it might have been 'improved'. Marwick also describes a much shorter version from Shetland which, in its brevity, seems more believable:

> lie down in the ebb at night
> place a hand on your head, a hand on the soles of
> your feet
> three or nine times, utter these words, take all that
> is between my two hands.

I would never try this.

If the use of drift-seeds as charms throughout the Norse realm can be traced to pre-Christian times, then perhaps this ritual might also hint at a longer history of the ebb being used as a place in which to call upon supernatural powers. As Marwick points out, the Devil only appeared within accounts of ritual practice when people, mostly women, were tortured into confessing his presence.

When the Faroese linguist Jakob Jakobsen came to Shetland at the very end of the nineteenth century, he noted that fishermen in Lunnasting asked *de Midder o' de Sea*, the Mother of the Sea, to keep them safe from the Devil. Marwick describes the tumultuous relationship between the Mither of the Sea and Teran. The Mither of the Sea ruled the summer months and, under her dominion, the sea would be calm and fish would be plentiful; but come the autumn, Teran would challenge her reign and their fights raised wild storms.

Teran would always defeat the Mither of the Sea in these autumn battles because she would be exhausted from her summer sovereignty. Winter under Teran's reign would be monstrous and wild. In the spring the Mither of the Sea would return renewed to regain control, and this explains the storms of the vernal equinox. All summer, Teran would lie bound by ropes on the ocean floor. Now, when the storms of the autumn equinox are slow to arrive, or don't come at all, I imagine searching for Teran and untying him. There are times too, some winters, when I wish to bind him again.

Sat in the warmth of the School of Scottish Studies Archives, I read fragments of interviews in which women are described as witches. I scan the notes quickly for a sign of the use of charms but find none. Mrs Stickle from Unst recalls how her uncle's *sixareen*, a wooden boat built to a Norse design and used for deep-sea fishing, was kept from coming ashore for a day and a night by a 'contrary wind'. It was thought by some that this contrary wind had been raised by a 'notorious local witch'.

Mrs Lizzie Priest and Mrs Jaikie Mouat, two sisters also from Unst, tell of how their father had known a skipper of a *sixareen* who claimed that a neighbour's wife 'had come off to witch him so that on a moderate day he fell in with bad weather, when no other boat had it'. The skipper saw the woman around the masthead. One of his crew affirmed that the weather had been bad but that he had only seen a kittiwake at the mast.

By the time the archives close for the day, I have found no trace of sea bean lore in Orkney or Shetland. But before I leave, I tell Louise about the story of the woman who was left on the Black Stane to die. She suggests that I search the online database of Scottish witchcraft trials. I diligently make a note but, in my haste to reach the airport, forget all about it. After the quiet of the archives, it is disorientating to step out into all the noise and movement of the city.

Months later, on a warm June day, while waiting in my car for the ferry to the island of Whalsay, I find myself thinking about the Black Stane, and for some reason I remember Louise's suggestion. I switch on my tablet and connect to the Council's free Wi-Fi to call up the online database of Scottish witchcraft trials. I can see the ferry approaching but it is still a way off. There are several Shetland records. I am scrolling through the list of women who were executed when the ferry approaches the pier. As the vehicles and foot passengers disembark, I find an entry for a woman called Katherine Jonesdochter. She was executed in 1616. In the evidence used against her, I read the term *sey nutte*. It takes a moment to realise that this must mean a drift-seed of some kind. The deckhand signals for the first car in the queue to drive onto the ferry. I start the car's engine and drive on board, and when the ferry departs I lose all signal. I spend the day walking cliffs under a blue summer sky but can think of little else but Katherine Jonesdochter and her sea nut.

I borrow a copy of the *Court Book of Shetland, 1615–1629* from the library, a recent transcription in a legible typeface. Katherine was tried in October 1616 in Scalloway Castle. Two other women were also tried for witchcraft on the same day, Jonet Dynneis and Barbara Thomasdochter (who was also known as Barbara Scord).

The clerk, or scribe, of the court recorded that Katherine had first lain with the Devil as a young lass, forty years or more ago. At the time of her trial, she was not much older than me, but if she had children they are not mentioned. The clerk asserts that she would meet the Devil each year and especially at *Hallowevin* and on *Holy Crosday*:

> and that the last time he lay with hir, he gave hir ane mark
> on the privie memberis and left with hir ane sey nutte and
> ane cleik quhairby she sould be hable to do ony thing she
> desyrit . . .

A *cleik* is a strong hook, of the kind that a large cauldron would hang from over a fire.

The text of the trial reads like a confession but it is unclear as to how this confession was reached – if torture was used. Did she confess to having sex with the Devil, and to the mark on her genitalia, or was she stripped and was her body searched by the witch-hunting men of the Shetland presbytery? Either way, this assault and her humiliation is documented and there for us to read and repeat, more than four hundred years later.

The court documents describe the specific powers of Katherine's *cleik* and the drift-seed:

> that the cleik is guid gif the kyne want the proffeit of thair
> milk to milk thame throw the ring of the cleik and that the
> nutte being keipt upoun ane is guid to keep thame frome
> danger . . .

In the lore of stealing the profit of a cow's milk, a charm or ritual is used to make the milk of a neighbour's cow dry up. The milk of the cow in the home byre then flows more freely. Katherine is not accused of stealing the profit of the milk. She is said to have cast the illness of her husband onto another man, who subsequently died. The drift-seed and the hook seem incidental to this specific accusation but her possession of both is reason enough for her accusers to prove a licentious pact with the Devil. She was sentenced to death. She was strangled and then her body was burnt.

Word would have spread. Women would have felt for the drift-seeds in their pockets and wondered whether they should hide them away or dispose of them entirely. The charms that had kept them safe in childbirth, their mothers too, now endangered them. Perhaps there were men who tossed their drift-seeds over the sides of their boats, watched them float away, more fearful now of being accused of witchcraft than of drowning at sea. I think of Katherine's drift-seed. Did she find it on the shore, and if so, where? Was it a sea bean or some other kind? Was it burnt along with her body?

In the court records I read that Katherine was married to Thomas Kirknes of Stenhous, a place that is now called Stenness. I beachcomb at Stenness often; it is a darkly charismatic beach on the Eshaness peninsula, Atlantic-facing and not so far from where the young orca was pushed onto land by hurricane-force winds. Eshaness is a breathtakingly bleak peninsula that ends in cliffs formed from layers of lava and pyroclastic rock. The windows of the lighthouse, which stands on these high cliffs, are cracked from sea-thrown rocks; and a little further north, at the Grind of the Navir, storm waves have gouged out slabs of rock and floated them inland to form a storm beach that defies belief. The first time that I visited these cliffs of black rock, I recognised them from the recurring dreams that plagued me in the weeks before we moved to Shetland. I still find Eshaness to be a disconcerting place.

In common with the cliffs of West Burrafirth, where I watched the bull orca swim past the Black Stane, stories can be sensed in Stenness before they are known. The experience of beachcombing in Stenness is intensified by the way the sea has stripped much of the soil from the black volcanic rock. When storms pile in from the Atlantic, waves explode over the offshore islands and holms, and the wind carries salt spray high into the air in writhing, wraith-like forms. Entire headlands drown in spindrift. It is a place in which to imagine the end of the world. I go there in winter to watch purple sandpipers feed within the reach of the waves, taking flight a fraction of a second before white water engulfs their small bodies. My focus is always sharper in Eshaness; a sense of vulnerability heightens my perceptions and I remember more clearly what I find. I only beachcomb there when I am feeling strong.

In the summer, when purple sandpipers are at their nests in the tundra of the Arctic and when Teran lies bound on the ocean floor, the beaches of Stenness soften, but only a little. Ringed plovers lure intruders away from their nests, by trailing a wing that looks broken across a storm beach of shattered rock. Circles of pale limpet shells surround the shallow scrapes of oystercatcher nests. Bones and driftwood lie among boulders, and bleach in the sun. I can picture Katherine here in the summer, pausing to look at the white bells of sea campion shuddering in the breeze. I imagine her in winter too, the wind pulling at her hair as she bends down to gather *neverspel* and driftwood with hands red and raw from the cold.

In the court documents, Katherine is said to have 'confessed' to:

> . . . seing the trowis ryse out of the kirkyeard of Hildiswick and Holiecross Kirk of Eschenes and that she saw thame on the hill callit Grienfaill at monie sindrie tymes and that they come to ony hous quhair thair wes feasting or great mirrines, and speciallie at Yule . . .

The Holy Cross Kirk in Eshaness lies not far from Stenness and was razed by a zealous minister called Hercules Sinclair in the year 1660, in an attempt to stamp out superstitious practice.

It was, and maybe still is, one of four known *aamos* kirks in Shetland. Offerings would be placed in the crevices of *aamos* kirk walls, to keep someone safe from harm or to cure an illness or to heal an injury. These offerings were revealed when the Holy Cross Kirk of Eshaness was pulled down. There were silver objects in the shape of a head or a limb, and a single bronze horse figurine, a fourteenth-century weight from Norway. This beautiful bow-headed horse makes me wish to know what was asked of the *aamos* kirk when it was placed in its walls. A safe crossing to Norway, perhaps, in the depths of winter. It makes me think of the wooden beads that I strung around the gearstick of my car in the days when I would drive to work on busy roads. I would rub the beads in the hope of staying safe.

In Shetland there is still such a thing as 'laying on an *aamos*'. Jenny Murray, a curator at the Shetland Museum, has written about this practice. Her writing is rich in detail, not least because she herself still lays on an *aamos* now and then. It works like this. A friend, let's call her Inga, applies for a job that she really wants. I am rooting for her and so I lay an *aamos* on another friend, Magnus. If Inga gets the job, I must then give Magnus a present. But I must take care not to tell either of them, or anyone else for that matter, that I have laid an *aamos* on Magnus. If I do not follow through with my part of the bargain, and I fail to give Magnus a present, it will be pointless to try to lay on an *aamos* again.

No amount of luck would have helped Katherine Jonesdochter in her trial. In the Shetland Archives, I delve into a book called *Witches of the North: Scotland and Finnmark*, written by the historian Liv Helene Willumsen. When I read Dr Willumsen's analysis of the witchcraft trial of another Shetland woman, Marion Pardoun, I begin to understand more clearly what Katherine would have faced.

Marion Pardoun lived in Hillswick, where Katherine is said to have seen *trows* dance in the kirkyard. Hillswick is the place, with its beach of fine shingle, where I learnt how to re-float live stranded porpoises and pilot whales. Marion was accused of transforming into a porpoise in order to drown men. At the time of her trial, in 1644, she was thirty-nine, married and had 'a reputation of knowing sorcery and healing'. She would have been a girl when Katherine Jonesdochter was executed in 1616. They lived in the same part of Shetland and perhaps they even knew of one another. The terror of the 1616 executions must have permeated through her girlhood.

On 15 March 1644, the moderator and the other brethren of the Shetland presbytery signed an indictment against Marion that listed fifteen accusations of spell-casting to cause illness to people and illness and death to livestock. She was not, at this point, accused of causing death to any human. But then she was tortured, deprived of sleep, until she was, as Dr Willumsen explains, 'clearly out of her mind'.

Marion, the scribe wrote, clothed her spirit with the porpoise. And so transformed, she capsized a boat and four men drowned. The boat is reported to have been close to shore, away from any hazards, and the weather had been fair. Whatever the actual cause, cetacean or not, the boat's tragedy became Marion's and she was executed. She too was strangled and then her body was burnt. Dr Willumsen's analysis of Marion's trial is compelling:

> The voice of the scribe is heard particularly through the text's repetitive demonological phrases. An understanding of Marion Pardoun's sorcery activity in relation to the Devil, thus leaving her God and Christian faith, is superimposed on her by male questioners, and this becomes distinct in the document. The whole rhetorical apparatus of condemning a fallen woman because she is an enemy of God and has given herself to the Devil is used repeatedly, almost like an exorcism. The arguments for condemning her come from the witch-hunters. They interpret her deeds in the same way as if she had confessed to a demonic

pact – and judge accordingly. This demonic aspect of the text is taken good care of by the scribe, hammering and hammering on the same expressions, an indication that the text itself reveals important ideological attitudes on the part of the interrogators.

It is clear that Marion, like Katherine, never stood a chance.

Dr Willumsen lists all the people, all women, for whom there is a record of execution for witchcraft in Shetland:

Jonet Dynneis (1616)
Barbara Scord (1616)
Katherine Jonesdochter (1616)
Juenit Fraser (1644)
Marion Pardoun (1644)
Helen Stewart (1675)

It makes me question how many women were killed without record. The story of the Black Stane seems all the more plausible after reading through Dr Willumsen's text. In Shetland, most of the accused in witchcraft trials were women. This is also true of Finnmark in Arctic Norway, where many more people were executed, although Dr Willumsen notes that Sámi men were accused more often than Sámi women, because Christian missionaries, as men, had less access to the women of the Sámi community.

Dr Willumsen was instrumental in the creation of the Steilneset Memorial which can be found in the small island of Vardø, where most of the executions in Finnmark took place. She describes the memorial's art installation, designed by Louise Bourgeois, as expressing 'sorrow and feelings in a strong and wild way'. Vardø is noted, in *Birding Varanger*, as a good place to see purple sandpipers. I would like to visit the memorial one day, maybe in winter, and perhaps these birds will be resting on the shore at high tide, motionless and dark against the white of ice.

A mild winter's day in November 2020. I park my car under the tall sycamores of Hillside Road in Scalloway and climb over the stile that bridges the boundary of the town and the slopes of Berry Hill, the gallows hill where Katherine would have been strangled and burnt. My progress up the steep slope is very slow, more pauses than movement, and must look strange to anyone watching. My body is still in the throes of a Covid-triggered flare and there are no rheumatology clinics. Accepting the return of daily pain and fatigue has been hard. I walk up the hill with difficulty, carrying a weight of stress from the year that has passed. The pandemic has brought to the fore the fatal consequences of deeply ingrained structural racism. Levels of domestic and sexual violence against women skyrocket. Children, already severely impacted by austerity policies, suffer even more. Ableism reaches a sickening fever pitch.

But despite everything, there are small pockets of hope. In June, more than 2,000 people in Shetland took part in a Black Lives Matter protest organised by a group of women. Blackface was finally banned by the organisers of all the winter fire festivals – thanks, in large part, to the outspokenness of one young woman, Ellie Ratter. In August, a young activist working with Shetland Rape Crisis, Rhea Isbister, organised a powerful social media campaign, #wistoo, to break the silence surrounding the issue of sexual violence in these islands. There is talk of organising the first-ever Shetland Pride. I see a report in the paper that describes how the maternity department in the local hospital is working towards putting procedures of care in place for people who miscarry. Shetland is changing for the better.

I'm proud to have played a small part in this. In 2018, I began working with others to end the exclusion of girls and women from Shetland's largest fire festival, the Lerwick Up Helly Aa. It was stressful work but, ultimately, our sustained and collective effort was successful and in June 2022, the organisers of the festival removed the ban on women and girls taking part.

To speak up about a feminist issue in an island community is to make yourself more visible. There is a social pressure not to rock the boat, and when conflicts do inevitably arise, it is not always easy to leave an island place for a change of scene. If I had to define what being an islander truly means, it is the ability to withstand a social environment that can be highly pressurised at times. It is the determination to keep working to effect change when there is a strong social pressure to do nothing. It is the importance of building a community of care in a tightly bound and sometimes stifling community of place. It is hard work, but it can be done.

Through this feminist activism, I begin to get to know the many women who support survivors of domestic abuse and sexual violence in these islands. I learn that sea beans have been presented to survivors of domestic abuse as a symbol of their strength, and in recognition of the journey they have taken in escaping an abusive relationship.

It is emotional to hear this. Drift-seeds have at last been reclaimed by the women of Shetland, four hundred years after Katherine Jonesdochter was executed. Drift-seeds have become, in these islands, a symbol of resilience in the face of patriarchal harm. My desire to find a sea bean of my own grows even stronger.

A thin layer of high cloud veils the sun, and the light is soft and gentle. Beyond the rooftops, a silvery sea comes into view. A boat leaves the harbour. Another returns. To the west, the small islands of Oxna and Papa lie encircled by a thin rim of white water. To the south, bridges tether the islands of Trondra and Burra to one another and to the Mainland. The ruin of Scalloway Castle, where Katherine was sentenced to death, towers over the eastern part of the town. It all looks so normal, but the streets of Scalloway are pandemic-quiet.

At the top of the hill there is a telecommunications mast that stands over the town like a mad metal monster. A hooded crow lifts from the ground and lands on the mast as if perched on the monster's raised wrist. Three curlews take flight and rasp winter-hoarse calls. A ragged flock of redwings disappears over the brow of the hill. There are plans for a simple stone memorial to be placed somewhere up here, to commemorate the witch trial victims. Of the same kind that was inaugurated in 2019, at Gallow Ha in Kirkwall, Orkney. On this Orcadian memorial, the words *they were cheust folk* – they were just folk – are carved into its stone.

I search the ground, near the metal mast, for the place where rabbits have burrowed into soil that is said to be blackened from the burning site. But I don't expect to find it. This ground was ploughed and reseeded some time ago. Bonfires have been lit here more recently, and that might be the reason for blackened soil – not the burning of women's bodies. I walk back and forth but find no charred soil, and I am glad of this. I meant to bring a small token to leave here. Deep in the corner of my jacket pocket I find a tiny piece of clear sea glass shaped like a teardrop, taken from the beach nearest to the deep and dark geos where grey seal cows haul out and give birth. I place it on the ground. I still hope to find a sea bean of my own, and now, if I find a second, I will take it to Stenness and slip it somewhere safe in memory of Katherine Jonesdochter – a rock crevice of the kind that a storm petrel might nest in.

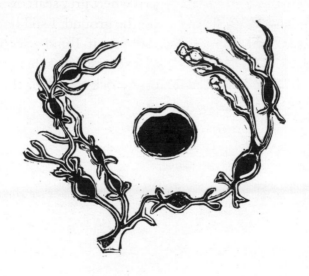

Epilogue

A few weeks after visiting Berry Hill, a virus – a common cold – causes an autoimmune flare to intensify, and when the pain subsides fatigue sets in and leaves me unable to walk to the sea glass beach near my house. There have been no rheumatology clinics since the beginning of the pandemic. Our GP leaves for pastures new and the steady stream of locums are no replacement for the consistency of his dedicated and compassionate care. My husband sees my spirits fall and offers to drive me to a beach called Sand where it is possible to park right next to the shore. We wait for our children to leave on the school bus and then we set out too. The sun has not yet risen above the hills but the sky is growing light. A gentle wind ruffles the sea.

At Sand, we park below the house of a laird that was built, in part, with stones taken from Scalloway Castle. It is a tall and mean-windowed building and it glowers over the beach. The information panel notes that seventy or so long-finned pilot whales were slaughtered here in 1899. Now, the panel's text explains, this bay is one of the best places in Shetland to watch porpoises.

There are no signs of their small fins out in the *voe*, though the wind is light and the waves are small. A flock of long-tailed ducks sit on the surface of the sea, close to the shore; and further out, there is a single great northern diver. The sun has nearly breached the low-rising peninsula of Foraness. Ravens sit, one apiece, on fence posts above the beach. They watch over the body of a ewe that lies on the kelp. A length of bank has been washed away in a recent storm, toppling a section of the fence, and it lies in a mess of wire and fresh soil.

A new moon has pulled the tide in high. It is beginning to ebb. The strandline is still wet and sits elevated on a slope of pebbles. It looks promisingly thick, with egg wrack dripping with goose barnacles and many pieces of plastic, and within minutes I find a red lobster trap tag from Maine. A stream flows over the pebbles and down to the sea. We trace its course upstream and find soil banks plastered in fragments of plastic. My husband spots a tiny blue plastic flower, and then I trump his find with a toy gherkin. In the marsh behind the beach, an otter swims along a channel and past a loose raft of empty engine-oil containers.

Back on the pebbles of the beach, I leave the vertebra of a small cetacean but take the shining eggcase of a spotted ray and a few pieces of smooth sea glass in shades of cornflower and cobalt blue. I'm pleased enough with these finds. The sun rises over Foraness and we stand and watch. This is enough – the sun and the smell of the sea, the company of my husband and my hand warmed by his hand. My melancholy begins to ease in the same way that the sun can be felt when the haar begins to lift.

It is cold and so we turn back towards the car. Out of habit, I look down at the strandline and there it is, a sea bean lying between pebbles, still wet and shining gold in the low light of the morning sun. My hands shake a little as I bend down to pick it up. I hold it high above my head and face the sea. I thank the beach and I thank the sea. My husband does a celebratory jig and I laugh at the sight of him.

On the drive home, I keep the sea bean in my hand, and it warms with the heat of my blood. I show my children when they return from school and we take it in turns to shake it and to hear the rattle that means it is no longer viable. It would not grow even if we tended to it well and kept it in a heated place.

I put my sea bean on a shelf with the scapula of a seal, the skull of a puffin, three cigarette lighters from Greenland, one from Iceland, and the eggcase of a thornback ray. It sits above a collection of large glass jars that once contained coffee granules and now contain beachcombed finds. A jar for Nólsoy, a jar for Sanday, a jar for Foula, a jar for the Out Skerries and a jar for the Vee Skerries. And most treasured of all, a jar for the best of the sea glass and earthenware that all four of us have gathered from the home beach.

On my bookshelf, I have a poetry collection by Lydia Harris. The poems within honour her home island of Westray in Orkney. It is called *Objects for Private Devotion*. When I look from my desk at my collection of beach-found treasures, some natural and some plastic, this phrase comes into my mind. I sometimes think that beachcombing itself can be seen as an act of devotion – to life and all that this can mean.

My sea bean still sits on this shelf and keeps its mysteries. I will never know where it grew or how long it took to reach Shetland. At first, I am a little disappointed that it does not immediately feel like a protective charm. Nothing discernible changes. I don't feel any trace of magical power when I hold my sea bean in my hand; there is no electro-static shock, no diffuse flow of warm energy through my skin. But from time to time I do reach for my sea bean and use it to ground my fears or to ask for courage when my nerve falters. I catch sight of it and think of the words of the late Amos Wood, who beachcombed the Pacific shores of the USA: 'Beachcombing is not what you find, it is what you hope you will find.'

I set out on each beachcomb with the hope of finding a sea bean. It was this hope that made me venture out in all weathers and on days when it was not so easy to walk. It took me many years of searching before I found a sea bean of my own, but in this time I did return to myself.

I make plans to go back to the mica-rich sand of the beach at West Sandwick in Yell, one sunny summer's day. There, I will join my family in the sea, and when I return to the shore, my wet limbs will be gilded with gold.

Acknowledgements

I had no connection to Shetland, or to any writing community, when I moved to these islands. I'm grateful for the multitudes of support that I have been given. This is a long acknowledgements section by necessity and it is, perhaps, still not long enough. Thank you to everyone who has helped me along the way. If any errors have crept into the text, they remain mine.

My sincere thanks to Brian Smith, Angus Johnson, Mark Ryan Smith, Jenny Murray and Ian Tait at the Shetland Museum and Archives. Mark Ryan Smith has read and encouraged my work from the outset and always agrees to read more. Thank you to Jenny Murray for reading through the Witch chapter and for all her wonderful writing on how to lay on an *aamos*. I'm very grateful to Ian Tait for his articles on scran and his kind permission to quote from them. Thank you also to Laurie Goodlad for enabling me to explore the various drift-seed collections in the museums of Shetland and for all the rich conversations on Shetland's history. Thank you to Charlotte Anderson for the opportunity to accompany her to the Out Skerries, as part of her maritime heritage work.

Thank you to Louise Scollay, at the School of Scottish Studies Archives, for guiding me through a wealth of material and for helping me find my way to the story of Katherine Jonesdochter. I am grateful to Ian Riches at the National Trust for Scotland, and Sian Loftus, Heritage Consultant, for their help in relation to the drift-seeds found at Woodwick. Heartfelt thanks to Liv Helene Willumsen, Professor Emerita of History at the University of Tromsø, for her generous permission to quote from *Witches of the North: Scotland and Finnmark*.

In Shetland, I would especially like to thank Mary Blance, who has supported my writing from its beginnings and who alerted me to the word *brimbortend*. I am also very grateful to Sheila Gear in Foula, for kind permission to include extracts from *Foula: Island West of the Sun* and for the treasured discussions on the seabirds of this astonishing island. Hazel Tindall has thoughtfully guided me through the text of *Slyde in the Right Direction* by her late mother, Chrissie Sandison, and this book, more than any other, has made me feel at home in Shetland. My thanks to Hazel for her encouragement to quote from this book and for all the many warm conversations and cold walks. I had the pleasure of talking about the writing process with Wendy Gear and I am very appreciative of her encouragement and generous permission to quote from *John Walker's Shetland*. Thank you to Andy Gear too, for kindly sharing his most curious beachcombing finds with me. I am grateful to Alice Arthur, Anna Henderson of Houll and Chris Harris for their help and good company in the magical Out Skerries. Thank you to Jen Hadfield for all the joyful beachcombs and for willingly wading through an early and dense draft of *Sea Bean* and emerging the other side with words of fortifying enthusiasm.

I am grateful to the Shetland Museum and Archives for allowing me to quote from the poem 'Bound is the Boatless Man' by Vagaland, T. A. Robertson. The late George P. S. Peterson was kind in his permission to include a line from my much-treasured copy of *The Coastal Place Names of Papa Stour*. Thank you to Helen Budge, Shetland Islands Council, for permission to quote from

Nordern Lichts, Beryl Graham for permission to quote from the late John Graham's *Shadowed Valley* and Charlotte Black at the *Shetland Times* for permission to quote from *Out Skerries: An Island Community* by Joan Dey. I am indebted to all at Birlinn for license to quote from their beautiful 2001 edition of *Night Falls on Ard-namurchan* by Alasdair Maclean.

When I moved to Shetland, I knew very little about seabirds. Thank you to Martin Heubeck for his patient encouragement. I would especially like to thank Will Miles who has also been incredibly generous in answering my many seabird queries. Will has also read through early drafts, provided me with research papers that I would otherwise not be able to access and gave me the opportunity to attend a workshop on fulmar dissection. Thank you to Jenny Sturgeon for reading a draft of the manuscript. A brief conversation with Jenny, while she and Will monitored the guillemot cliffs of Sumburgh Head, one day many years ago now, helped me to commit more fully to writing; and her beautiful music has sustained me through the drafting of *Sea Bean*.

Thank you to Jan Andries and Yvonne Franeker for the training in fulmar dissection and especially to Jan and Susanne Kuehn for reading through and commenting on the Maalie chapter. I would like to thank Jenni Kakkonen for the good company and transport in Orkney. Jens-Kjeld Jenson and Sjúrður Hammer very kindly shared their in-depth knowledge of the natural history of the Faroe Islands. I am also grateful for the warm hospitality of my hosts in Nólsoy. In Texel, I would like to thank Maarten and Belinda Brugge-Laan at the wonderful Hotel de Waal for their insights into beachcombing along the southern shores of the North Sea.

Closer to home, my sincere thanks to Oliver Cheyne for so generously sharing his knowledge of the hill and the shore, and for guiding me through the blanket bog. Thank you to John Anderson for the opportunity to visit both the Vee Skerries and Papa Little and for telling me the story of the Black Stane. I beachcomb on John (Tex) Tait's patch and appreciate his welcome and gifts of 'Russian' floats. When I mentioned the idea of casting this book adrift in a St Kilda mailboat, Alan Moncrieff made me *Sea Bean*, the small model boat. I am very grateful to him for the opportunity to launch my book in the most meaningful way. Heartfelt thanks to Lynn Ritch-Bullough and Luke Bullough for sheltering us that first stormy Christmas and for helping us find a place to call home. Thank you to Louise Polson Farquhar and Peter Farquhar for the loan of a beautiful edition of Shetland folklore and for all the discussions about Shetland's past, present and future.

Warmest of thanks to Chloe Garrick-Tallack for the invaluable conversations on bodyminds and living in island places. And to Sarah Laurenson, who has greatly helped me to think through what being an islander, and island writing, can mean. Thank you to Malachy Tallack and Jordon Ogg for publishing my work in the *Island Review* and for all the encouragement since.

Thank you to Lydia Harris in Orkney, who has deepened my knowledge of many things, including writing and island life, both past and present, and who has been a constant source of encouragement. In Shetland, I deeply appreciate conversations with Shona Main, whose approach to life and creative practice continue to both inspire and ground me. I would also very much like to thank Roxani Krystalli, for the many enriching discussions on writing, feminism and the joy of gardening. Thank you to both Roxani and Shona for their guidance in relation to the Netukulimk chapter.

ACKNOWLEDGEMENTS

I would like to thank Jaqueline Whitaker, Chief Midwife at NHS Shetland, for taking the time to tell me about the improvements to miscarriage and bereavement care in the maternity unit, and for giving me an overview of abortion procedures in Shetland. Thank you to Clare Archibald for reading through, and commenting on, Eggcase. A warm thank you to Karen McKelvie for explaining the symbolism of sea beans in relation to trauma therapy.

I am grateful to Jane Matthews at Shetland Arts for the opportunity to create a strandline in the gym hall of the old Anderson High School in support of the Artangel Natural Selection exhibition. I learnt much from the school students who came and beachcombed this strandline. Thank you to Rachel Laurenson and Shona Anderson for the treasured beachcombing and beach cleaning company. Kristi Tait's warm encouragement of my printmaking has been a gentle nudge to keep going. Sincere thanks to all the incredible folk at GAADA, Amy Gear, Vivian Ross-Smith and Daniel Clark, who sustained me during a bleak winter of Covid, through the means of a visual art workshop bursary.

I would not have been able to write the Neesick chapter without the incredible work that Jan and Pete Bevington do at the Hillswick Wildlife Sanctuary. James Mackenzie and Frank Hay guided me through the many troubling complexities of the Viking wind farm.

Many people have helped me to understand the natural history of Shetland. Thank you to Jill Slee Blackadder of the Shetland Field Studies Group, especially for the conversations on Loki's candles, many moons ago. Thank you to Paul Harvey and Rory Tallack at the Shetland Biological Records Centre for answering my many queries with generosity. Thank you to Cat Gordon at the Shark Trust, Jane Dodds at Natural Scotland and Dan Wise at the Orkney Skate Trust for information on eggcases and flapper skates. Thank you to Howard Towll for showing me the seal survey ropes and for the print-making tips. Rachel and Richard Shucksmith are always happy to share their extensive knowledge on the marine environment and have been integral in opening my eyes to another world. A special thank you to Lucy Gilbert for the opportunity to travel to Foula to gather bonxie pellets and for vivid and sustaining discussions about Shetland and its ecology. Stephen Rutt does not live in Shetland but I often still send him natural history queries and he is ever-generous with his knowledge. Thank you to both Steve and to Miranda Cichy for reading through an early draft of the first two chapters and for all the writing encouragement.

The late Davy Cooper, a much-respected storyteller, told me the tale of 'Death and the Eggcase', and encouraged me to tell it in my own words. Thank you to Roseanne Watt for reading through the Witch chapter, and for the inspiration of her words, especially *Lukkie Minnie's Foy* (published by GAADA in *We Axe For What We Want*). I am indebted to Tim Martin for his help in understanding the Mi'kmaq harvesting concept of *netukulimk*. Jim Muise, retired lobster fisherman, kindly gave me an insight into lobster fishing on the other side of the Atlantic. Tony Soper generously shared his best beachcombing finds with me. Dr Charles Nelson permitted me to quote from his remarkable book, *Sea Beans and Nickar Nuts*. It is this book that set me on my quest to find a sea bean of my own.

I first wrote about beachcombing for *EarthLines* magazine and am grateful to Sharon Blackie and David Knowles for giving me such a vital start. My *EarthLines* essay on driftwood was informed by conversations with Martin Gray in Orkney, a know-ledgeable beachcomber who determined the origin of *neverspel*, long-drifted birch bark.

Thank you to Andrew McNeillie at Clutag Press, who included an earlier version of the Witch chapter in *Archipelago 12*, and to Nicholas Allen and Fiona Stafford for including this early version, in the form of an essay called 'Black Stane', in *Archipelago – a Reader*.

I am a recipient of a Scottish Book Trust New Writers Award and this assistance made it possible to start writing *Sea Bean*. Thank you to the SBT team for all the work that you do and especially to Lynsey Rogers. It was a joy to be mentored by Sara Maitland as part of this award, whose deft feedback would make me both laugh and pull my socks up. Thank you to Jane Outram who gave me an invaluable opportunity to spend time away from home to write, when my children were young.

Thank you to my brilliant editors, Charlotte Cray and Helen Conford, for patiently guiding me through the process of writing my first book and to everyone at Hutchinson Heinemann – Rose Waddilove, Linda Mohamed, Marie-Louise Patton and Sam Rees-Williams – for your great care with *Sea Bean*. Thank you to Ceara Elliot for going above and beyond to design such a beautiful and meaningful cover. I am also very grateful for the expertise and work of the copy-editor, proofreader and typesetter.

Heartfelt thank you to my agent, James Macdonald Lockhart, for gently keeping me on course at all times and for the many sustaining conversations about birds.

To my daughter, son and husband, thank you for all your love, encouragement and practical support. This book is for you, with all of my love.

Glossary

I am not a Shaetlan speaker, although after ten years of living here, sometimes a Shaetlan word or sentence structure comes naturally. If you are not a Shaetlan speaker either, I urge you to seek out these three beautiful poetry collections:

De Luca, Christine, *Parallel Worlds, Poems in Shetlandic and English* (Luath Press, 2005)

Jamieson, Robert Alan, *Nort Atlantik Drift* (Luath Press, 2007), in which Shaetlan poems are accompanied by translations and commentary in English

Watt, Roseanne, *Moder Dy / Mother Wave* (Polygon, 2019), poems in both Shaetlan and English.

Some of the words listed below, like *hekla*, are *tabu* (taboo) words used by the *haaf* or deep-sea fishermen of Shetland. Most *tabu* words are Norn in origin – the language that was spoken in these islands before it was replaced by Scots. In the introduction to a section on *tabu* words in *Shetland Words: A Dictionary of the Shetland Dialect*, A. & A. Christie-Johnston describe how they stem from superstitious practices originated in pagan times. They were a means of placating, among other things, sea gods. Land words were *tabu* at sea, and so, for example, a skate became a *hekla*, which in Old Norse means 'cloak'.

Dictionaries

Graham, John J., *The Shetland Dictionary* (The Shetland Times Publishing, 2004)

Jakobsen, Jakob, *An Etymological Dictionary of the Norn Language in Shetland* (David Nutt, 1928)

Christie-Johnston, A. & A., and Neil Anderson (contributing ed.), *Shetland Words: A Dictionary of the Shetland Dialect* (The Shetland Times Publishing, 2014)

Scott, John W., *Orkney and Shetland Weather Words: A Comparative Dictionary* (The Shetland Times Publishing, 2017)

See Shetland ForWirds for more information and an online dictionary: www.shetlanddialect.org.uk/

Glossary

aamos	gift promised in the hope that a wish will be granted to the donor
alamootie	storm petrel, *Hydrobates pelagicus*
atween	between
böd	fisherman's bothy or hut
bonxie	great skua, *Stercorarius skua*
brimbortend	this word can mean different things depending on context, but in this text it means a fishing ground quite stripped of fish
bruck	rubbish
caa	drive of sheep, cattle or whales
calloo	long-tailed duck, *Clangula hyemalis*

coo	cow
craa	hooded crow, *Corvus corone cornix*
craws-siller	crows' silver; mica
daggri	dawn
dagalien	dusk; decline of day; beginning of twilight
dockens	dock, *Rumex spp.*
eela	rod or handline fishing from a small boat; the inshore fishing competitions that take place each summer
flan	sudden squall or downdraught of wind
geo	cleft in a rock; cliff ravine
globeren	glaring staring one, *tabu* name for the moon
haaf	deep sea, beyond coastal waters
haaf fish	grey seal, *Halichoerus grypus*
haar	cold sea fog, a term used in the east of Scotland and north-east England
hansel	gift to commemorate an occasion
hekla	*tabu* name for skate
howdie	midwife
kye	cattle
laeverek	skylark, *Alauda arvensis*
leerie	Manx shearwater, *Puffinus puffinus*
lightsome	uplifting; cheerful
lintie	twite, *Carduelis flavirostris*
lukki lines	sea lace or dead man's rope seaweed, *Chorda filum*
maalie	northern fulmar, *Fulmarus glacialis*
mareel	phosphorescence in the sea in autumn
mön	moon
mootie	very small; term of endearment

neesick	harbour porpoise, *Phocoena phocoena*
neverspel	one of many names for the fragments of birch bark found in the strandline
noost	hollow at the height of a beach for boats
ormal	remnants; particle; a scrap
piltock	coalfish, 2–4 years old; saithe, *Pollachius virens*
planticrub	small circular drystone enclosure for growing cabbage seedling in
pund	pound, as in enclosure for livestock
rain goose	red-throated diver, *Gavia stellata*
scooty alan	Arctic skua, *Stercorarius parasiticus*
scran	useful beachcombed items
selkie (or *sylkie*)	seal
shalder	oystercatcher, *Haematopus ostralegus*
shoormal	hide-tide mark; the turning point of the waves on the beach
sillock	coalfish in its first year; saithe, *Pollachius virens*
simmer dim	twilight in midsummer, between dusk and dawn when it is never quite dark
sistie moose	Shetland wren, *Troglodytes troglodytes zetlandicus* (*T.t. fridariensis* in Fair Isle)
sixareen	six-oared clinker-built boat of Norwegian design
skjogg	rudimentary drystone shelter from which to scan the sea for driftwood
snorr	tide when you are unsure if it is ebbing or flooding
spoot	razor clam, *Ensis magnus*
spoot ebb	the lowest of spring tides
sten-shakker	northern wheatear, *Oenanthe oenanthe*

sungaets	turning with the sun
tang	seaweed of the *Fucus* kind
tang fish	harbour seal, *Phoca vitulina*
tirrick	mostly applies to Arctic tern, *Sterna paradisaea*, but sometimes used for common terns too
trow	troll
truss	trash; useless odds and ends
tystie	black guillemot, *Cepphus grylle*
vaam	spell; magical influence
voar	spring
voe	sea loch; narrow sea inlet
waari	kelp-covered; kelp is seaweed of the *Laminariales* kind
wadder	weather
whaup	curlew, *Numenius arquata*
widdergaets	turning against the path of the sun

Further Reading

Beachcombing

Allardyce, Keith, *Found: Beachcombing in Orkney* (The Orcadian, 2012)

——, *Found Vol. II: Beachcombing in Orkney* (The Orcadian, 2015)

Soper, Tony, *The Shell Book of Beachcombing* (David and Charles, 1972)

Sprackland, Jean, *Strands: A Year of Discoveries on the Beach* (Vintage, 2013)

Trewhella, Steve, and Julie Hatcher, *The Essential Guide to Beachcombing and the Strandline* (Wild Nature Press, 2015)

Williams, Tracey, *Adrift: The Curious Tale of Lego Lost at Sea* (Unicorn, 2021)

Woollett, Lisa, *Rag and Bone: A Family History of What We've Thrown Away* (John Murray, 2020)

Shetland

Dalby, Kery, and Claire Dalby, *Shetland Lichens* (Shetland Amenity Trust, 2005)

Gear, Sheila, *Flora of Foula* (Foula Heritage, 2008)

Harvey, Paul, and Rebecca Nason, *Discover Shetland's Birds* (Shetland Heritage Publications, 2015)

Nature in Shetland, including Shetland Bird Club: www.nature-shetland.co.uk

Pennington, Mike, et al., *The Birds of Shetland* (Christopher Helm, 2004)

Promote Shetland: www.shetland.org

Scott, Walter, et al., *Rare Plants of Shetland* (Shetland Amenity Trust, 2002)

Scott, Walter, and Richard Palmer, *The Flowering Plants and Ferns of the Shetland Islands* (The Shetland Times Publishing, 1987)

Shetland Museum and Archives: www.shetlandmuseumand archives.org.uk

Smith, Mark Ryan, *The Literature of Shetland* (The Shetland Times Publishing, 2014)

Sumburgh Head: www.sumburghhead.com

Sea Bean

Alm, Torbjørn, 'Exotic drift seeds in Norway: Vernacular names, beliefs and uses', *Journal of Ethnobiology*, vol. 23, no. 2 (2003), pp. 227–61

Drymon, J. M., et al., 'Tiger sharks eat songbirds: Scavenging a windfall of nutrients from the sky', *Ecology*, vol. 100, no. 9 (2019), p. xi

Graham, John J., and T. A. Robertson, *Nordern Lichts: An Anthology of Shetland Verse and Poetry* (The Education Committee of Shetland County Council, 1964)

Lönnrot, Elias, *Kalevala*, trans. John Martin Crawford (Vintage, 2017)

National Trust for Scotland Collections: T.UNS.474, 2 lucky beans: 2 sea beans or 'drift seeds', possible early twentieth century – note reads 'Found amongst "mother's" sewing things', belonged to Ida Sandison, mother of the donor

Nelson, E. C., *Sea Beans and Nickar Nuts*, BSBI Handbook No. 10 (Botanical Society of the British Isles, 2000)

Nelson, E. C., and W. Scott, 'Pods of the flamboyant tree on Shetland coasts', *The Shetland Naturalist*, vol. 3, no. 2 (2014), p. 49–52

Perry E. L., and J. V. Dennis, *Sea-Beans from the Tropics* (Krieger Publishing Company, 2003)

Robertson, Thomas A., *The Collected Poems of Vagaland*, ed. Martha Robertson (The Shetland Times Publishing, 1975)

Tait, Ian, 'Buoyant Earnings', *The New Shetlander*, no. 278 (2016)

Alamootie

Armstrong, Edward A., *The Folklore of Birds* (Collins, 1958)

Bolton, Mark, 'GPS tracking reveals highly consistent use of restricted foraging areas by European storm-petrels *Hydrobates pelagicus* breeding at the largest UK colony: implications for conservation management', *Bird Conservation International*, vol. 31, no 1 (2020), pp. 35–52

Jensen, Jens-Kjeld, *Puffin Fowling: A Fouling Day on Nólsoy* (Jens-Kjeld Jensen, 2010)

——, *Mallemukken på Færøerne: The Fulmar on the Faroe Islands* (Jens-Kjeld Jensen, 2012)

——, and Jógvan Thomsen, *The Faroe Islands' European Storm Petrel* (Forlagið í Støplum, 2022)

Low, George, *Fauna Orcadensis; or, The Natural History of the Quadrupeds, Birds, Reptiles and Fishes of Orkney and Shetland* (G. Ramsey, 1813)

Manson, T. M. Y., *Drifting alone to Norway* (The Shetland Times Publishing, 2020; first published 1986)

Näsström, Britt-Mari, *The Great Goddess of the North, Freya* (Clock and Rose Press, 2003)

Soper, Tony, *The Shell Book of Beachcombing* (David and Charles, 1972)

Williamson, K., *The Atlantic Islands* (Routledge and Keegan Paul Books, 1970)

Message in a Bottle

Brown, Paul, *Messages from the Sea* (Superelastic, 2016)

Dey, Joan, *Out Skerries: An Island Community* (The Shetland Times Publishing, 1991)

Ebbesmeyer, Curtis, and Eric Scigliano, *Flotsametrics and the Floating World* (Collins, 2009)

'Foula Message in a Bottle and Message on a Puffin', *Shetland News*, 6 February 1892, Shetland Museum and Archives: D1/134/v2

'Landowner Briggs could offer tentative optimism in Skerries: A new hope?', *Shetland Times*, 28 September 2018

'Skerries under siege', *Shetland News*, 8 November 2012

Slater, Charlotte, *From Myths to Meids: Maritime Heritage of Fair Isle, Papa Stour and Skerries* (NAFC Marine Centre, 2019)

Slave Voyages Database: www.slavevoyages.org

Tait, Ian, *Shetland Vernacular Buildings 1600–1900* (The Shetland Times Publishing, 2012)

Eggcase

Briggs, Billy, 'Suspicious scallop dredging reported in the Sound of Mull', *The Ferret*, 26 February 2019, theferret.scot/scallop-dredging-sound-mull/

Orkney Skate Trust: www.orkneyskatetrust.co.uk

Sharklab-Malta: www.sharklab-malta.org

Shark Trust: www.sharktrust.org

Skatespotter: skatespotter.sams.ac.uk

Comb Jelly

Barbellion, W. N. P., *The Journal of a Disappointed Man & a Last Diary* (Chatto and Windus, 1920)

Gordon, G., 'Phronima sedentaria and its beroe', *The Scottish Naturalist*, vol. 6 (1881), pp. 56–9

Hejnol, Andreas, 'Ladders, Trees, Complexity and Other Metaphors in Evolutionary Thinking' in Anna Lowenhaupt Tsing, Heather Anne Swanson, Elaine Gan and Nils Bubandt (eds), *Arts of Living on a Damaged Planet* (University of Minnesota Press, 2017)

Porter, Joanne, *Guide to Bryozoans and Hydroids of Britain and Ireland* (Marine Conservation Society, 2021)

Quigley, Declan et al., 'The Pram shrimp Phronima sedentaria (Forsskål, 1775) (Crustacea: Amphipoda: Hyperiidea:

Phronimidae) in Irish waters and a review of its association with gelatinous zooplankton', *Irish Naturalists' Journal*, vol. 34, no. 1 (2015), pp. 1–7

Williamson, I., 'The amphipod Phronima sedentaria (Forsskål) in Shetland, with notes on its distribution, morphology and life strategies', *The Shetland Naturalist*, vol. 2, no. 4 (2007), pp. 121–8

Foula

The word *brimbortend* can be found in 'Löd a Langer', a poem by the late Rhoda Bulter, *Hairst is Coosed: The Rhoda Bulter Collection*, 2014

Gear, Sheila, *Flora of Foula* (Foula Heritage, 2008)

——, *Foula: Island West of the Sun* (Robert Hale, 1983)

Hammer, S., et al., 'Plastic debris in great skua (*Stercorarius skua*) pellets corresponds to seabird prey species', *Marine Pollution Bulletin*, vol. 103, no. 1–2 (2016), pp. 206–10

Hourston, John, 'Where have all the sandeels gone', Blue Planet Society [website], June 2009, www.blueplanetsociety.org/where-have-all-the-sandeels-gone/

Jakobsen, Jakob, *An Etymological Dictionary of the Norn Language in Shetland* (David Nutt, 1928)

Johnston, J. L., *A Naturalist's Shetland* (Poyser Natural History, 1999)

Low, George, *A Tour Through the Islands of Orkney and Shetland: Containing Hints Relative to Their Ancient, Modern, and Natural History, Collected in 1774* (W. Peace, 1879)

Tulloch, Bobby, *Migrations: Travels of a Naturalist* (Kyle Cathie Limited, 1991)

Venables, L. S. V., and U. M. Venables, *Birds and Mammals of Shetland* (Oliver and Boyd, 1955)

Votier, S. C., et al., 'Changes in fisheries discards rate and seabird communities', *Nature*, vol. 427 (2004), pp. 727–30

Maalie

For information on fulmars and plastics research, please see: www.wur.eu/plastics-fulmars

Dell'Ariccia, G., et al., 'Comment on "Marine plastic debris emits a keystone infochemical for olfactory foraging seabirds" by Savoca *et al*.', *Science Advances*, vol. 3, no. 6 (2017)

OSPAR, 'Plastic articles in fulmar stomachs in the North Sea', oap.ospar.org/en/ospar-assessments/intermediate-assessment-2017/pressures-human-activities/marine-litter/plastic-particles-fulmar-stomachs-north-sea/

OSPAR Commission, *The OSPAR System of Ecological Quality Objectives for the North Sea, a contribution to OSPAR's Quality Status Report 2010*, www.ospar.org/documents?v=7169

Savoca, M. S., et al., 'Marine plastic debris emits a keystone infochemical for olfactory foraging seabirds', *Science Advances*, vol. 2, no. 11 (2016)

Shetland Oil Terminal Environmental Advisory Group: www.soteag.org.uk/

van Franeker, J. A., 'Fulmar wreck in the southern North Sea: preliminary findings', *British Birds*, vol. 97 (2004), pp. 247–50

Netukulimk

Edwards, Rob, 'Fish farm pesticides have polluted 45 lochs', *The Ferret*, 28 February 2017, theferret.scot/45-lochs-polluted-fish-farm-pesticides/

Morin, Brandi, 'Indigenous women are preyed on at horrifying rates. I was one of them', *Guardian*, 7 September 2020, www.theguardian.com/commentisfree/2020/sep/07/canada-indigenous-women-and-girls-missing

Native Council of Nova Scotia et al., *Mi'kmaq Fisheries, Netukulimk: Towards a Better Understanding* (Native Council of Nova Scotia, 2013)

Native Land Digital: native-land.ca/

Quinn, Mark, 'Beothuk remains returned', CBC, 12 March 2020, www.cbc.ca/news/canada/newfoundland-labrador/beothuk-remains-returned-nl-1.5494373

Ryan, Haley, 'The lobster trap', *Star Halifax*, 10 June 2019, projects.thestar.com/climate-change-canada/nova-scotia/

'Sea lice rampant on salmon farm', Salmon and Trout Conservation Scotland [website], November 2020, salmon-trout.org/2020/11/02/sea-lice-rampant-on-salmon-farms/

Talaga, Tanya, *All Our Relations* (Scribe, 2020)

The Mi'kmaq Treaty Handbook (Native Communications Society of Nova Scotia, 1987)

Strandjutter

Brú, Heðin, *The Old Man and his Sons*, trans. Paul Eriksson (Telegram, 2011)

Carrington, Damian, 'Climate Crisis: Scientists spot warning signs of Gulf Stream collapse', *Guardian*, 5 August 2021, www.theguardian.com/environment/2021/aug/05/climate-crisis-scientists-spot-warning-signs-of-gulf-stream-collapse

Eunson, J., *The Coastal Names of Fair Isle* (Pensord Press, 2007)

Henley, John, and Alan Evans, 'Giant dams could protect millions from rising North Sea', *Guardian*, 12 February 2020, www.theguardian.com/environment/2020/feb/12/giant-dams-could-protect-millions-from-rising-north-sea

Mackay Brown, George, *Greenvoe* (Hogarth Press, 1972)

Maclean, Alasdair, *Night Falls on Ardnamurchan: The Twilight of a Crofting Family* (Victor Gollancz, 1984)

Shetland Amenity Trust, 'Da Voar Redd Up', www.shetland-amenity.org/da-voar-redd-up

Tait, I., 'Declaring wir scran in World War Wan', *The New Shetlander*, no. 274 (2015), pp. 25–31

'Texel' [topographic map], en-gb.topographic-map.com/maps/dlg1/Texel/

VVV Texel: www.texel.net

Williams, Tracey, *Adrift: The Curious Tale of Lego Lost at Sea* (Unicorn, 2021)

Neesick

Breast Cancer UK, *BCUK Background Briefing: Flame Retardants*, Version 1, 31 July 2017

British Divers Marine Life Rescue: bdmlr.org.uk/

Calderan, Susannah, and Russell Leaper, *Review of harbour porpoise bycatch in UK Waters and recommendations for management*

(WWF 2019), www.wwf.org.uk/sites/default/files/2019-04/Review_of_harbour_porpoise_in_UK_waters_2019.pdf

Ecomare: www.ecomare.nl/en/

Hillswick Wildlife Sanctuary: www.hillswickwildlifesanctuary.org/

IJsseldijk, Lonneke L. et al., 'Spatiotemporal mortality and demographic trends in a small cetacean: Strandings to inform conservation management', *Biological Conservation*, vol. 249 (2020)

Joensen, Jóan Pauli, *Pilot Whaling in the Faroe Islands* (Faroe University Press, 2009)

Low, George, *Fauna Orcadensis*

Murphy, S., et al., 'Reproductive Failure in UK Harbour Porpoises Phocoena phocoena: Legacy of Pollutant Exposure?', PLoS ONE 10 (7) 2015

Williams, R. S., et al., 'Juvenile harbour porpoises in the UK are exposed to a more neurotoxic mixture of polychlorinated biphenyls than adults', *Science of the Total Environment*, vol. 708 (2020), pp. 1–10

www.independent.co.uk/news/health/toxic-chemicals-flame-retardant-food-packaging-plastics-cancer-mps-environment-government-a9005931.html

Sea Glass

Burradale Wind Farm: www.burradale.co.uk/

Gear, Wendy, *John Walker's Shetland* (The Shetland Times Publishing, 2005)

Graham, John J., *Shadowed Valley* (Lerwick Publishing Company, 1987)

Hingley, Marjorie, *Microscopic Life in Sphagnum*, Naturalists' Handbook 20 (Richmond Publishing Co., 1993)

Irvine, J. W., *Footprints: Aspects of Shetland Life over the Last 100 Years* (Shetland Islands Council Education Committee, 1980)

Lindsay, Richard, and Scottish Natural Heritage, *Bogs: The Ecology, Classification and Conservation of Ombrotrophic Mites*, (Scottish Natural Heritage, 1995)

Local Energy Scotland, 'Case Study: Garth Wind Project, North Yell Development Council, Scotland', YouTube, 1 February 2019, www.youtube.com/watch?v=PEr7mmttsnE

Mackenzie, J., 'A refutation of nimbyism', 2013, Full Moon Press (now defunct)

Marter, Hans J., 'Access restrictions for Viking Under Review', *Shetland News*, 22 September 2020, www.shetnews.co.uk/2020/09/22/access-restriction-for-viking-site-under-review/

Planning Democracy, 'What is the equal right of appeal?', www.planningdemocracy.org.uk/what-is-equal-rights-appeal-campaign/

Riddell, Neil, 'Councillors reject planning recommendation and vote strongly in favour of wind farm', *Shetland Times*, 14 December 2010, www.shetlandtimes.co.uk/2010/12/14/councillors-reject-planning-recommendation-and-vote-strongly-in-favour-of-windfarm

Robertson, John, 'Scale of erosion on hilltops clear but expert fails to endorse Viking', *Shetland Times*, 19 November 2010, www.shetlandtimes.co.uk/2010/11/19/scale-of-erosion-on-hilltops-clear-but-expert-fails-to-endorse-viking-figure

RSPB, 'Strathy South', www.rspb.org.uk/our-work/our-positions-and-casework/casework/cases/strathy-south/

Sandison, Chrissie B. J., *Slyde in the Right Direction* (The Shetland
    Times Publishing, 2008)
Shetland Charitable Trust: www.shetlandcharitabletrust.co.uk/
Stout, Jen, 'Climate pollution from wind farms on peatlands
    "underestimated"', *The Ferret*, 29 October 2021, theferret.
    scot/wind-farms-peat-climate-pollution/
Tallack, Malachy, *60 Degrees North* (Polygon, 2015)
Viking Energy: www.vikingenergy.co.uk/

Haaf Fish

Fraser, Gibbie A., *Shetland Whalers Remember* (Nevisprint,
    2001)
Maclean, Alasdair, *Night Falls on Ardnamurchan: The Twilight of a
    Crofting Family* (Victor Gollancz, 1984)
Peterson, G. P. S., *The Coastal Place Names of Papa Stour* (Nelson
    Smith, 1993)
Smith. B., 'Waithing and Waith in Shetland (with a note on waifs)',
    in *Shetland Folk Book*, vol. IX, ed. John J. Graham and Brian
    Smith, pp. 102–8
Thomson, David, *The People of the Sea* (Canongate, 2011)

Witch

Armundsen, Tormod, (ed.) *Birding Varangar : The biotope guide to
    the best bird sites in Arctic Norway*, Biotope (2015)
Brownlow, Andrew, Nick Davison and Mariel Ten Doeschate,
    Scottish Marine Mammal Strandings Scheme Annual Report 2017, 2020

Black, G. F., and Northcote W. Thomas (eds), *County Folklore Vol. III: Orkney and Shetland Islands* (David Nutt / Folklore Society, 1903)

Bruford, Alan J., 'Orkney Notes 1970–1975', SSSA MSS 56, School of Scottish Studies Archives, University of Edinburgh

——, 'Shetland Notes 1973–76', SSSA MSS 60, School of Scottish Studies Archives, University of Edinburgh

Cope, Chris, '"Ignorance does not make this acceptable" – pressure grows on blackface to be banned in Up Helly Aa squads', *Shetland News*, 9 June 2020, www.shetnews.co.uk/2020/06/09/ignorance-does-not-make-this-acceptable-pressure-grows-on-blackface-to-bc-banned-in-up-helly-aa-squads/

——, 'New report featuring first-hand accounts aims to raise awareness of sexual harassment and violence in isles', *Shetland News*, 3 August 2020, www.shetnews.co.uk/2020/08/03/new-report-featuring-first-hand-accounts-aims-to-raise-awareness-of-sexual-harassment-and-violence-in-isles/

Donaldson, Gordon (ed.), *Court Book of Shetland, 1615–1629* (Shetland Library, 1991)

Goodare, Julian, et al., 'The Survey of Scottish Witchcraft, 1563–1736', January 2003, www.shca.ed.ac.uk/Research/witches/

Huband, S., 'Northern Raven', in Kathleen Jamie (ed.), *Antlers of Water* (Canongate, 2020)

Marwick, Ernest W., *The Folklore of Orkney and Shetland* (Birlinn, 2011)

Murray, J., 'Lay du on an aamos', *The New Shetlander*, vol. 263 (2013)

Watt, Roseanne, *Luckie Minnie's Føy: We Axe For What We Want* (Gaada, 2021)

Willumsen, L. H., 'Memorials to the Victims of the Witchcraft Trials: Orkney and Finnmark, Norway', in *Commemorating the*

Victims of the Orkney Witchcraft Trials, *New Orkney Antiquarian Journal*, vol. 9, pp. 19–30

——, 'Witches of the North: Scotland and Finnmark', *Studies in Medieval and Reformation Traditions*, vol. 170 (2013)

Wood, Amos L., *Beachcombing for Japanese Glass Floats* (Binfords and Mort, 1967)

Quotation Permissions

Epigraph on p. 27 from 'Bound is the Boatless Man' by Vagaland, used with the permission of Shetland Museum and Archives.

Second epigraph on p. 27 from *Nordern Lichts*, used with the permission of Shetland Islands Council.

Extract on p. 39 from *Sea Beans and Nickar Nuts* by E. Charles Nelson, used with the permission of the author.

Extract on p. 43 from the notes of Joy Sandison, used with the permission of the National Trust for Scotland.

Extracts on pp. 145, 146 and 149 from *Flora of Foula* and *Foula: Island West of the Sun* by Sheila Gear, used with the permission of the author.

Extracts on pp. 192 and 197 from *Mi'kmaq Fisheries, Netukulimk: Towards a Better Understanding*, used with the permission of Tim Martin of the Netukulimkewe'l Commission.

Extracts on pp. 201 and 208 from *Night Falls on Ardnamurchan*, reproduced with the permission of the licensor, Birlinn Limited, through PLSclear.

Extracts on pp. 206 and 207 from an article in the *New Shetlander* by Ian Tait, used with the permission of the author.

Epigraph on p. 239 and extracts on p. 243 from *Slyde in the Right Direction* by Chrissie Sanderson, used with the permission of Hazel Tindall.

Second epigraph on p. 239 by James Mackenzie, used with the permission of the author.

Extracts on pp. 242 and 243 from *John Walker's Shetland* by Wendy Gear, used with the permission of the author.

Extract on p. 273 from *The Coastal Place Names of Papa Stour* by George P. S. Peterson, used with the permission of the author.

Extracts on pp. 296 and 297–8 from *Witches of the North: Scotland and Finnmark* by Liv Helene Willumsen, used with the permission of the author.